GOD'S WIDER
PRESENCE

GOD'S WIDER
PRESENCE

RECONSIDERING
GENERAL REVELATION

ROBERT K. JOHNSTON

Baker Academic
a division of Baker Publishing Group
Grand Rapids, Michigan

© 2014 by Robert K. Johnston

Published by Baker Academic
a division of Baker Publishing Group
P.O. Box 6287, Grand Rapids, MI 49516-6287
www.bakeracademic.com

Printed in the United States of America

Library of Congress Cataloging-in-Publication Data
Johnston, Robert K., 1945– author.
    God's wider presence : reconsidering general revelation / Robert K. Johnston.
        pages cm
    Includes bibliographical references and index.
    ISBN 978-0-8010-4945-3 (pbk.)
    1. Revelation—Christianity. I. Title.
BT127.3.J64 2014
231.7′4—dc23   2014032343

14   15   16   17   18   19   20   7   6   5   4   3   2   1

For Eleanor, Jayne, Anna,
James Harris, and Thomas Robert

May God's wider Presence
surprise you often

One of the best gifts for the critical mind and for a living tradition is the gift of a new question.

Mary Collins

For man [and woman] does not see God by his own powers; but when He pleases He is seen by men, By whom He wills, and when He wills, and as He wills.

Irenaeus

Ring the bells that still can be rung
Forget your perfect offering
There is a crack in everything
That's how the light gets in.

Leonard Cohen

Contents

Acknowledgments

As with all theological projects, there are many to thank. Theology is always collaborative. Particular thanks go to Michael Gilligan, president of the Henry Luce Foundation, and Lynn Szwaja, its program director for theology, for their generous grant that funded my time away from Fuller Seminary so that I could deepen my initial research. Their commitment to furthering conversation between the world's major faiths continues to bring the world closer together. Thanks go as well to colleagues in the Brehm Center for Worship, Theology, and the Arts at Fuller Theological Seminary. Their encouragement and engagement has allowed me to deepen my thought and explore new arenas of interest. Bill Dyrness, my colleague as professor of theology and culture and my longtime dialogue partner should be particularly recognized. He has given me new ideas and has provided a sounding board for much that I have developed. One other fellow professor at Fuller also deserves mention—Bob Meye. Retired from active teaching, he has nonetheless shared ideas, bibliography, and helpful critique during the whole length of the project.

In my research of over a decade or more, I have had a dozen or more research assistants at Fuller Theological Seminary, where I teach. They have done much to deepen my thinking and broaden my range. I am deeply in their debt. Of particular significance have been several graduate students who have done research for me, some even writing insightful papers that have pushed me deeper—Kutter Callaway, Craig Detweiler, Nelleke Bosshardt, Anthony Mills, Chad Lunsford, Patrick Oden, Tim Basselin, Steve Wiebe, Brian Pounds, Jennifer Bashaw, David Hunsicker, David Johnson, Lincoln Moore, Kris Chong, and Richard Goodwin. I am appreciative of their reflections, encouragement, and bibliographic help.

There are also others who have read the manuscript in draft form and have generously offered their insights—Kutter Callaway, Alexey Vlasikhin, Richard Peace, Erik Kuiper, Alexis Abernethy, and Joe Gallagher. I am similarly in debt to students in two doctoral seminars, one on general revelation and the other on aesthetic theology, that I cotaught with Bill Dyrness. Here ideas were explored, conversation sustained, and my manuscript vetted. Of particular help were Meredith Ainley, Nick Barrett, Karyn Chen, Bob Covolo, Kevin Nye, Chuck Slocum, and Matt Tinken, who gave me helpful, written feedback on a draft of this book.

But having said this, my deepest thanks extend to Catherine Barsotti, my partner in life and in work. We have been teaching classes together both in theology and in theology and film for over a decade. Cathy's own research has pushed me both deeper and wider, and her feedback has kept me honest and centered. Of particular note are the classes we have cotaught over the last decade for close to two thousand staff members of Young Life, a student ministry to nonchurched high schoolers. To explore the value of God's wider revelation with these who are daily in dialogue with youth who have little interest in traditional Christianity has given my research an urgency and focus for which I am grateful.

Preface

What are we as Christians to make of those occasional encounters with God in our everyday lives that seem more real than everyday reality, more fundamental than everything else? Whether observing a sunset that serendipitously becomes the occasion for something More, being overcome by the Gift and the Giver at the birth of one's child, feeling awe as we have joined others and the Other in communal acts of justice, or being ushered into the divine Presence by a work of art, music, or literature, such experiences are deeply cherished and remembered in their unpredictability. They are more than mere deductions based on the footprint of God's act of creation. They are more than mere echoes or traces of his handiwork, though that is sometimes how they are described by Christian theologians. Those who experience the Numinous speak instead of a transformative moment, something illumining, even if precritical and hard to adequately name. While not having to do with one's salvation in any direct way, and occurring outside the church and without direct reference to Scripture or to Jesus Christ, such encounters, for that is what they are experienced to be, are seen, heard, and read as foundational to life. This book attempts to think constructively—both critically and imaginatively—about such experiences. What is the inherent value of God's wider revelation, of experiences of God's Presence not directly tied to our salvation? And how are they to be understood theologically?

The impetus for writing this book comes from at least three sources. The first is a personal experience.[1] On my nineteenth birthday I went with my sister to see the movie *Becket*. In my book *Reel Spirituality* (2006), I described the event.

---

1. Interestingly, this is often the case for those writing on general revelation. Kutter Callaway notes (private correspondence, July 15, 2009) that Tim Gorringe (*Discerning Spirit: A Theology of Revelation*) wrote his book about the movement of the Holy Spirit outside religious and

Nominated for twelve Academy Awards and starring Richard Burton and Peter O'Toole [1964], the film *Becket* tells the story of Henry II, the Norman king of England, and his drinking buddy, Thomas à Becket. King Henry wanted free rein to live and act as he chose, to whore and wage war and tax the citizenry as he saw fit. His one obstacle to complete license was the archbishop of Canterbury, who had his own independent authority as the leader of the Church of England. The archbishop often frustrated Henry's designs. In order to solve his problem, King Henry ingeniously decided to appoint his companion in "wine, women, and song," Thomas, as the next archbishop. Brilliant, except for one problem: Thomas decided to take his new vocation—his calling to be God's servant—seriously and to serve God rather than the king. King Henry tried to persuade him to compromise and accommodate to his old friend's (and king's) wishes. But Thomas remained steadfast. As a result of his faithfulness, Thomas was martyred in Canterbury Cathedral on the altar steps.

When I first saw this film as a freshman in college, I did not much identify with Thomas's martyrdom (or subsequent sainthood!). But I did hear God calling me to the Christian ministry. My struggle with accepting the call to become a minister was with my image of the pastor as needing *first* to be a holy person. My Young Life leader, who ministered to me during high school, was such a person, as was my church counselor. I knew I was no saint. In the film, however, I heard God saying to me through his Spirit, "You need not be holy. Thomas was not. You only have to be obedient to my call." And I responded like Thomas and said, "God, I will be loyal to you with all my being."[2]

Interestingly, when I once told my story at a conference, one of the other speakers, Father Gregory Elmer, a Benedictine monk who often uses film in the spiritual retreats he leads, commented that he too had heard God speak to him while watching *Becket* for the first time. He, too, had had an experience of God's wider revelatory Presence. It was a different scene that had triggered his numinous encounter, and his call had been into the monastic life. But what is noteworthy in this "coincidence" is that while watching the same movie the two of us heard God's call to service in unique ways. I heard God's call to active service in the world, and I became a professor of theology and culture; Father Elmer heard a call to purity of heart and single-minded devotion, and

---

institutional boundaries after having such an experience. Avery Dulles (*Models of Revelation* and *A Testimonial to Grace*) writes on revelation in light of his experience of God's general revelatory Presence in nature. Bruce Demarest's interest in the topic (*General Revelation*) arose from questions posed in his missionary experiences. G. C. Berkouwer wrote his book (*General Revelation*) in reaction to the German church's misuse of general revelation to baptize Hitler's assent to power.

2. Robert K. Johnston, *Reel Spirituality: Theology and Film in Dialogue*, 2nd ed. (Grand Rapids: Baker Academic, 2006), 37–38.

he became a Catholic monk and mystic. Others went home and ate ice cream! The revelatory Presence of God's Spirit spoke (or didn't speak) into the differences of our lives in unique ways, but it was the same cultural artifact—the movie *Becket*—that was the catalyst for these experiences.

It is not just human culture that occasions such experience. It happened to me as well when I was sitting alone under the stars at night beneath towering pine trees in the mountains near Lake Arrowhead in Southern California, as well as when, as a boy, I heard the account of Jim McReynolds, who after coming down with polio was reduced to life in an "iron lung." I can recall vividly "hearing" God's call to pray for him daily, which I did for the next several years. How was it fair (I doubt I would at that age have said "ethical") that Jim would never move again? Culture, creation, conscience—our experiences as humans in each of these three arenas become in God's good pleasure the occasions for the in-breaking of God's revelatory Presence.

Many describe similar experiences, as we will note in the pages that follow. But there has been next to no constructive theological reflection on how we are to understand these experiences—experiences that happen to Christians and non-Christians alike. What sense can we make theologically as Christians of these moments of Transcendence? Others in the movie theater that evening saw *Becket* and experienced nothing remotely spiritual. It was simply an epic drama. Were they insensitive? Others knew of Jim McReynolds's tragedy and felt no inner, divine compulsion to pray. Were they too callous? Surely not. But part of the mystery of divine Presence is that at particular moments in time, God revealed himself to me. And though these experiences are singular to me, they are by no means unique as a category of experience. Most of us can name such experiences out of our past.

When, for example, I ask students to speak or write about movies that have been significant to them spiritually, for I teach courses in theology and film, perhaps a third of my students also speak of meeting God at the Cineplex (but more of that in chapter 3). And when I share with friends or when speaking about my encounter with the Creator (as when I once rounded the corner while driving only to confront a huge full moon barely above the horizon and filling my whole environment with its Light), I inevitably hear similar creation-based stories concerning walking on the beach or seeing a sunset or perhaps a rainbow. And though my childhood conscience was divinely pricked by the total paralysis of a friend, for others they experienced God's Presence while in a crowd singing "We Shall Overcome" during protests against the Vietnam War, or while in a group crying out for justice for one wrongly accused. My experience, though singular, is also common; though particular, it is also universal. You, as readers, have no doubt already plugged in your own experiences. What are we to make of our experiences and those of our neighbors? It is this question that has motivated my research over the last decade and has led to this book.

Besides the need to make sense theologically of those experiences of God's wider revelation that are common to most of us, however infrequent, a second motivation for writing this book in constructive theology is the growing disconnect between how the church has traditionally spoken of God's self-revelation outside the church and how those who are not Christians speak of that same reality. Christians, on the one hand, have typically downplayed the importance, the significance, of God's self-revelation through creation, conscience, and culture, finding in such experiences at best a mere echo of the divine Presence. This trace of divine reality is thought insufficient to provide any real insight—in many cases, only enough, given our sinful condition, to condemn humankind for not responding to God's light. Certainly, it is claimed, these experiences are insufficient to compel obedience or devotion. Typically, such general revelation has been defined as what can be known of God by all people at all times and in all places, if they would but look and listen. This knowledge (and it is knowledge, not divine encounter) is based on what can be inferred about God based on his creation and/or what can be intuited about God based on his creation of humankind in the *imago Dei* (image of God).

Those outside the church, on the other hand, have responded to such numinous encounters by describing them as foundational and even transformative in their lives. Take, for example, this description by Janet Soskice, a philosopher: "In my case . . . faith came from a dramatic religious experience. . . . I was in the shower, on an ordinary day, and found myself to be surrounded by a presence of love, a love so real and personal that I could not doubt it. . . . Above all, I felt myself to have been addressed, not with any words or for any particular reason, and certainly not from any merit—it was in that sense gratuitous—but by one to whom I could speak."[3]

While the church has feared idolatry and self-deception, those outside the church have often described their responses in terms of humility and awe. Such disparity, though long-standing, has simply multiplied as we have entered what many have labeled "postmodernity," where spirituality is once again considered a public virtue. It has also been heightened by our engagement with those of other faiths who in our global village are now figuratively, or literally, our neighbors. The disconnect between church and world is growing, though it has gone largely unnoticed by too many in the church. Is it any wonder that

3. Janet Martin Soskice, "Love and Reason," in *Philosophers and God*, ed. Michael McGhee and John Cornell (New York: Continuum, 2009), 77–86.

in such circumstances, a growing number of people in the West are finding the church irrelevant, if not judgmental? Is it any wonder that we have become a largely "post-Christian" culture in the West? Rather than affirming with our brothers and sisters God's Presence throughout God's world, Christians have too often been pouring cold water on that spark. The unfortunate result has been twofold: on the one side, there has been for those of us in the church a loss of opportunity for dialogue and witness. If Christians are uninterested in our neighbors' spirituality, why should they be interested in ours? And on the other side, turning from what might be labeled "evangelism" to that which is often termed "discipleship," if God has indeed revealed himself to others through creation, conscience, and culture, then we ourselves are impoverishing ourselves in our relationship with and knowledge of God to the degree that we are insensitive to that divine Presence in others.

Last, my interest in writing this book has been triggered by wider changes that are going on in Western culture, particularly around the ordering given to what are often labeled life's transcendentals—truth, beauty, and goodness. In the 1960s, Christianity's theological orientation circled around notions of truth, and as a culture we would have ordered the transcendentals as truth, then goodness, and finally beauty. To give one example, at Fuller Seminary, where I teach, this was the decade where the seminary rewrote its statement of faith in order to be more accurate in setting forth the truth of the gospel. It was also the era when students sometimes removed the first "o" on the sign for Fuller Theological Seminary so that it read, "Fuller The logical Seminary." By the '70s and '80s, however, our Western culture, having lived through the Vietnam War and having seen the assassinations of John and Robert Kennedy and Martin Luther King Jr., had reordered these verities. We now began with the need for goodness, before moving on to truth, and finally to beauty. To again use Fuller Seminary as an example, this was the period in which the seminary wrote its "Mission beyond the Mission," which centered on a call to act responsibly in the world. It also was the time when the seminary aggressively recruited women as well as men for training for ministry, worked for empowerment of ethnic churches by setting up a series of institutes to train their leaders, and sponsored a major conference on peace. But as modernity came to an end and the millennium dawned, the sterility of the West's rationalism imploding in on itself, the ordering of the transcendentals again changed. As we are now comfortably into the new century, increasing numbers are saying that we should begin with beauty, and then move to goodness, before considering truth.

Such seismic shifts in the cultural plates of the West have had deep implications for theology. And one of these is surely an ever-increasing openness to a neo-Romanticism in our culture. Here is our growing openness as a society to spirituality, particularly as it is mediated through culture and the arts, even as that same culture increases its suspicions of institutionally defined religious truth. Again, to use Fuller Seminary as a case study, over 20 percent of the student population comes today to the school because of our recently opened Brehm Center for Theology, Worship, and the Arts. As Pope John Paul II said in a speech to artists at the turn of the century, it will be beauty that will prove to be the church's connection with its youth and with those outside the church. This surely is the experience of my seminary. Here is a third impetus for attempting a new constructive theology of general revelation. What are we to make of the increased importance given to beauty? How are we to understand those spiritual experiences often testified to with regard to the arts? How might a constructive theology of God's wider revelatory Presence be instructive?

Two brief comments triggered by theological colleagues might be helpful to readers as I close this introduction. In her book *She Who Is*, Elizabeth Johnson quotes Mary Collins: "One of the best gifts for the critical mind and for a living tradition is the gift of a new question."[4] Here is what Johnson herself offers readers as her feminist glasses help deconstruct faulty theology from the past; glimpse new possibilities from Scripture, church tradition, and life; and reconstruct theology in a new key. Johnson's stated goal is to change the discourse about God's revelation. As a white male Protestant, my purview is obviously different from Johnson's, but our goal is the same: to change the discourse about revelation. By wearing a new set of spectacles, one focused on God's wider revelation, I hope to allow a new set of questions to emerge.

In seeking to address this question, I have found a word picture provided by another good friend and theological colleague, Cecilia Gonzalez-Andrieu, to be of help. She speaks of the interdisciplinary, theological task central to constructive theology as an *interlacing* of various disciplines or approaches.[5] One needs to look at theology's subject matter from a variety of vantage points, she argues, letting each inform the other. Here is what I will attempt in this book. My intention is not to look only at the intersections, or convergences, that might be present, but instead to interlace insights from experience and our contemporary culture both with reflections on authoritative biblical texts and with conversations with theologians of the church, past and present, mindful of the importance of the illumining Presence of the Holy Spirit

4. Mary Collins, "Naming God in Public Prayer," *Worship* 59 (1985): 291–304, quoted in Elizabeth A. Johnson, *She Who Is: The Mystery of God in Feminist Theological Discourse* (New York: Crossroad / Herder & Herder, 1992), 29–30.

5. Cecilia Gonzalez-Andrieu, *Bridge to Wonder: Art as a Gospel of Beauty* (Waco: Baylor University Press, 2012), 87–100.

if new insight is to emerge. My goal will be to construct a strong interwoven cable. (As the Preacher says, "A threefold cord is not quickly broken," Eccles. 4:12.) Loose ends are inevitable, but as with any cord, if the strands are woven together sufficiently, such loose ends do not compromise the integrity of the cord. Thank you, Cecilia, for naming the "obvious." "Interlacing" is in fact what the constructive theological task entails.

But enough by way of introduction.

1

God's Wider Revelation

George Steiner, in his wonderful book *Real Presences*, writes of the "triumph of the secondary" in our Western culture. What he bemoans is not, "as Ecclesiastes would have it, that 'of making many books there is no end.' It is that 'of making books on books on those books there is no end.'" Rather than concentrate on direct encounters with God's "real Presence" through art, music, and literature, we seek out talk about such talk—talk that is a diversion, "both in the sense of deflection and of entertainment." He writes, "We seek the immunities of indirection. In the agency of the critic, reviewer or mandarin commentator, we welcome those who can domesticate, who can secularize the mystery and summons of creation."[1] Steiner's comments remind me of the story Søren Kierkegaard once told. He said that in the vestibule of an auditorium there were two doors. Above the one door was a sign labeled "heaven." Above the other door was a sign labeled "lecture about heaven." And people flocked through the door labeled "lecture."

For many, Steiner's and Kierkegaard's critiques of Western civilization's Enlightenment project seem particularly apropos of theology. Book after book is written as a dialogue with other books on the same subject. Little attention is given to the Original source of their reflection. Everything seems second order. While there is much to be gained from the wisdom of others, there is also much to be said for beginning from the beginning, with first-order

---

1. George Steiner, *Real Presences* (Chicago: University of Chicago Press, 1989), 39.

1

experience, particularly when the subject matter is God's revelation to us. Rather than understanding theology as "knowing God," what some today label "spirituality," we instead have defined theology over the last several centuries as "knowledge about God." Rather than reflecting on our personal experience with T/transcendence, we have too often settled for intellectual conviction based on detached philosophical argument.[2] It is such sterility that has led to a dead end in regard to the topic of general revelation that this book seeks to address. The time for an experientially rooted, biblically based theology of God's wider revelational Presence is surely at hand.

Some Initial Stories

As modernity comes to its end and we move ever more strongly into the post-modern era, the use of first-order testimony is increasingly important. The overreliance on detached argument has become suspect. Most of us now recognize that we think perspectivally. For this reason, we long for story, whether others' or our own. And theology is no different. Consider these two examples.

While many commentators on Paul Tillich's theology have referenced his method of correlation as key to understanding his thought, others have rightly noted an experience he had as a young adult that proved foundational to his thinking. Living through the horror of World War I as an army chaplain on the front lines, Tillich was granted a furlough. Traveling back to Berlin, he went to an art museum for respite. There he saw a painting by Botticelli titled *Madonna and Child with Singing Angels*. Tillich likened the event to a baptism. He said the experience was transformative of his spirit (he called it "almost a revelation"), opening him to an element of depth in human experience that provided him a "potent analogue" for talking about religious experience more generally. What happened to him, he said, was a "breakthrough."[3] Tillich labeled this early experience with Botticelli's painting "revelatory ecstasy." He wrote, "A level of reality opened to me which had been covered up to this moment, although I had some feeling before of its existence." Tillich had, he said, "an encounter with the power of being itself."[4] We will return to this experience in chapter 3. It is enough, here, to note that in Tillich's theological formulations, his primal experience of God's Presence, mediated through

2. See David Hay, *Something There: The Biology of the Human Spirit* (Philadelphia: Templeton Foundation Press, 2006), 128.

3. Paul Tillich, *On the Boundary: An Autobiographical Sketch* (New York: Charles Scribner's Sons, 1966), 27–28.

4. Paul Tillich, "Human Nature and Art," in Paul Tillich, *On Art and Architecture*, ed. John Dillenberger and Jane Dillenberger (New York: Crossroad, 1987), 12.

and within a painting, proved foundational for all his later theological reflection. Without rooting his thought in this revelatory event, readers of Tillich's theology risk reducing his thought to a system, in the process failing to grasp adequately its origin in mystery and wonder.[5]

In a similar way, one cannot understand the theology of C. S. Lewis without reading his autobiography, *Surprised by Joy*. In that book, Lewis describes a series of sporadic experiences that occurred during his youth—playing with the toy garden his brother made for him in the lid of a biscuit tin, listening to Beatrix Potter's *Squirrel Nutkin* read by his mother, smelling a currant bush, listening to Wagner, reading Norse mythology, and, while at university, encountering Euripides's *Hippolytus*. Most significant, he said, was his reading of George MacDonald's *Phantastes*. These experiences surprised him with "Joy." He reflected: "It was as though the voice which had called to me from the world's end were now speaking at my side. It was with me in the room, or in my body, or behind me. If it had eluded me by its distance, it now eluded me by its proximity—something too near to see, too close to be understood, on this side of knowledge."[6] Again, we will return to a fuller dialogue with Lewis later in the book. But what is to be noted here is that crucial to his understanding of theology were these foundational encounters with the Divine that occurred outside the church and without any explicit reference to Jesus Christ.

Tillich later labeled his experience of God's wider Presence a "feeling of ultimate concern." Lewis spoke of a "Bright Shadow," or simply "Joy." We will in the pages that follow consider Friedrich Schleiermacher, who wrote of "a feeling of absolute dependence," and Rudolf Otto, who described such experiences as a "*mysterium tremendum et fascinans*" (a mystery that is awe-filled and yet inviting). It is not just theologians, however, whether liberal or conservative, who reference such experiences as foundational or transformative to their life and thought. Such encounters are the repeated subject of artists, as well. For example, in her novel *All New People* (1989), Anne Lamott has Nanny Goodman, her quasi-autobiographical young heroine, say about her parents, "Now my father didn't believe in God, but he believed in the existence of the sacred, of the holy; it was pretty hard not to believe in anything in the face of Bach, or our mountain. . . . My mother believed that God lit the stars and spoke directly through family and friends, musicians and writers, madmen and children, and nature—and not, as she had been raised to believe, through

5. See Kenneth Hamilton, *The System and the Gospel* (New York: Macmillan, 1963).

6. C. S. Lewis, *Surprised by Joy* (New York: Harcourt, Brace & World / Harvest Books, 1955), 180–81.

a booming voice from the heavens."[7] Writing in a similar vein, John Updike has one of his characters, David Kern, speak of an experience he has had as "supernatural mail on foreign soil." His transcendent experience took place while on his way home from the hospital where his wife was giving birth to their daughter, as he helped a dying cat that had been hit by a car. The juxtaposition of death and life, life and death, came together for him as a moment in time, yet out of time. David concluded, "The incident had the signature, decisive but illegible."[8]

Two Reasons for the Importance of Our Investigation

One of the characters in Ingmar Bergman's film *Fanny and Alexander* (1982) speaks in similar terms of the arts as providing "supernatural shudders." This is seemingly also what happened to Albert Einstein when he went to a concert early in the career of the violinist Yehudi Menuhin. After the concert, Einstein said to the musician, "Thank you, Mr. Menuhin; you have again proved to me that there is a God in heaven."[9] In narrating the story, Richard Viladesau concludes, "Aesthetic experience seems to play a major role—at least for some people—in the exercise of the practical judgment for belief in God—perhaps a great deal more than the traditional 'proofs' of God's existence set forth in apologetic theology."[10] Confirming such a judgment, George Barna in a poll taken in 2000 found that 20 percent of Americans turned to "media, arts and culture" as their primary means of spiritual experience and expression, and the percentage was growing.[11]

If the reality of "media, arts and culture" as a primary locus of spiritual meaning for many in Western society is one stimulus for reconsidering our theology of God's revelatory Presence outside the church and without direct reference to Jesus Christ, our increasingly frequent encounters with adherents of other religions is a second. What are we to make of the faith-filled insights and numinous experiences of those we meet who are not Christians? The witness to God's wider revelatory Presence in life is the testimony of many, perhaps most, people.[12] David Hay and Kate Hunt report, for example, that

7. Anne Lamott, *All New People* (Washington, DC: Counterpoint, 1989), 29, 37.

8. John Updike, "Packed Dirt, Churchgoing, A Dying Cat, A Traded Car," in *Pigeon Feathers and Other Stories* (Greenwich, CT: Fawcett, Crest, 1962), 172.

9. Albert Einstein, quoted in Richard Viladesau, *Theological Aesthetics* (New York: Oxford University Press, 1999), 104.

10. Viladesau, *Theological Aesthetics*, 107.

11. George Barna, *Revolution* (Wheaton: Tyndale House, 2005), 48–49.

12. See A. W. Tozer in his classic devotional book *The Pursuit of God* (Harrisburg, PA: Christian Publications, 1948), 78–79: "Everyone of us has had experiences which we have not been able to explain: a sudden sense of loneliness, or a feeling of wonder or awe in the face of

in a national sample in England taken in 2000, while less than 10 percent of those polled went to church, 76 percent reported having a spiritual experience of some kind, and these 76 percent clearly went beyond those with a Christian background.[13] Hay and Hunt also observe that their findings are consistent with the evidence from comparative religion, where there are few, if any, limitations on where or when such moment(s) of religious awareness can take place: "There are records of such moments during childbirth, at the point of death, during sexual intercourse, at a meal, during fasting, in a cathedral, on a rubbish dump, on a mountaintop, in Islam, in association with a particular plant, stone, fish, mammals, bird and so on ad infinitum . . . though it is worth repeating that there seems to be no way of 'switching them on.'"[14] With this testimony and warning, Hay and Hunt echo what believers have recognized for centuries. As Irenaeus said in his *Against Heresies*: "For man does not see God by his own powers; but when He pleases He is seen by men, by whom He wills, and when He wills, and as He wills."[15]

The theologian Paul Metzger says he was converted to Christ in a Buddhist temple. For my student David Johnson, a significant encounter with God came while watching the movie *Grand Canyon* (d. Kasdan, 1991). For another student, Chris Min, it was while watching *Magnolia* (d. Anderson, 1999); for me, it was while watching *Becket* (d. Glenville, 1964); for Patrick Oden, it was while reading Milton. According to the vision statement of Sanctus 1, an emerging church in Manchester, England: "We believe that God is already active in our world." "We recognise God's indefinable presence in music, film, art and other key areas of contemporary culture." This church states that it wishes to affirm and enjoy all in our culture that gives voice to one of the many voices of God, while challenging those areas that deafen the call of God.[16]

---

the universal vastness. Or we have had a fleeting visitation of light like an illumination from some other sun, giving us in a quick flash an assurance that we are from another world, that our origins are divine. What we saw there, or felt, or heard, may have been contrary to all that we had been taught in the schools and at wide variance with all our former beliefs and opinions. We were forced to suspend our acquired doubts while, for a moment, the clouds were rolled back and we saw and heard for ourselves. Explain such things as we will, I think we have not been fair to the facts until we allow at least the possibility that such experiences may arise from the Presence of God in the world and His persistent effort to communicate with mankind. Let us not dismiss such an hypothesis too flippantly."

13. David Hay and Kate Hunt, "Understanding the Spirituality of People Who Don't Go to Church," Research Report, Centre for the Study of Human Relations, University of Nottingham, August 2000, www.facingthechallenge.org/nottingham.php.

14. Ibid.

15. Irenaeus, *Against Heresies* 4.20.5.

16. See Sanctus 1 Manchester, "What is Sanctus 1?," under "What do we believe?," www.sanctus1.co.uk/.

In my teaching in theology and the arts, it is a common experience for me to hear students relate stories of their own transcendent experiences that they have had while reading a book or viewing a movie. *March of the Penguins, Magnolia, Lars and the Real Girl, The Year of Living Dangerously, Field of Dreams, American Beauty, The Last Temptation of Christ, Departures, The Tree of Life*—the list of movies referenced by them includes secular and religious themes, documentaries and feature films, movies that are "G" rated and "R" rated, gritty and romantic, studio and art house. We will return to look at these testimonials more carefully in chapter 3. Others speak of such revelatory moments as occurring at the birth of their child, as with David Kern, or when on a mountaintop, or when listening to music, or when joining others in a march for justice. One cannot predict or produce on demand these revelatory moments that occur outside of the church; they come as moments of grace. But however infrequent and serendipitous, they are nonetheless the experience of most of us. The experiences do not come from the arts alone, nor are they only a response to encountering nature, or participating in the furtherance of goodness. Unable to be coerced, they come randomly, but persistently, through creation, conscience, and culture. We will need to consider these three loci of God's wider revelational Presence in some detail as the book unfolds. But here it is enough to note the phenomena.

The question I wish to deal with in this book is this: What are we to make theologically of these repeated descriptions of wider experiences in life that are understood by the participants as "revelatory" of God? How, that is, are we as Christians to understand such divine moments that seem not to be primarily directed toward our salvation and/or judgment (except, of course, in the larger sense that all God's activity is ultimately interconnected), but rather focus simply on grace and encounter. (Think Job, not John; Abimelech, not Joshua.) How are we to understand those theological experiences of God that find their trinitarian roots pneumatologically, not christologically? Such revelatory experiences seem not to be deducible by human reason as we observe God's footprints in creation, though some such deduction/imprint/vestige/trace (what Luther called "natural knowledge") might have its own very limited validity. Nor are they producible solely by human effort, though they can be invited and certain aspects of creation, conscience, and culture seem more conducive to their reception than others (e.g., a sunset rather than a concrete parking lot; music of Mozart rather than the sound of nails on a chalkboard). No, the experiences that many judge revelatory are more than the reception of an echo of God's past activity or human projection of that which is transcendent to ourselves. Rather, these encounters with God's wider revelatory Presence are always serendipitous, something that lies beyond all human wisdom or agenda, but that nevertheless has inherent and at times transformative value for those experiencing them. It is on such revelatory experiences that we will focus in this book.

Revelation outside the Walls of the Church: A Largely Neglected Topic

Revelation, said Karl Barth, "is what human beings cannot tell themselves."[17] It is, in Tim Gorringe's words, "the bridge between heaven and earth, human experience and the transcendent."[18] Yet Christians have largely ignored that bridge when it has occurred outside the Christian community and without direct reference to Jesus Christ. They have too often been leery and skeptical to talk about God's wider revelatory Presence. Perhaps this is because we are unsure how to sort out human projections from such revelation—"the making-known of what we truly *cannot* tell ourselves in and through the events we experience and in our language," to again quote Gorringe.[19] It appears to many, particularly among those Christians of a more conservative theological persuasion, that, to paraphrase Barth, those testifying of such transcendent experiences are simply speaking of God by shouting "man/woman."

But though some of us are quick to posit such judgments, we also live uneasily with our own sporadic experiences of the "More"—with those moments of Grace that seem to put all other moments into perspective. We are unsure what to say about those liminal occurrences that cross the threshold beyond human projection. As C. S. Lewis came to realize, the joy he experienced through art and nature was not of his making, but was his response to a "Joy" that he encountered from beyond. But how can we be sure? Again, the question intrudes: How are we to understand theologically such "sacred" encounters?

There have been in the last fifty years relatively few monographs written on "general revelation"—the term usually given to that communion with the divine that takes place outside the church and its Scripture, and without direct reference to Jesus Christ. (In the pages that follow, I will argue that the term is a misnomer, as these experiences are far from general, occurring not everywhere and to all people but sporadically to individuals in their everyday lives. But more on this below.) And there have been even fewer such books as of late. Perhaps here is one reason for the present disconnect between the

17. Karl Barth, quoted in T. J. Gorringe, *Discerning Spirit: A Theology of Revelation* (Philadelphia: Trinity Press International, 1990), 6.
18. Gorringe, *Discerning Spirit*, 6.
19. Ibid.

burgeoning literature on spirituality in our broader, post-secular culture and the specifically Christian literature on spirituality and church life that has simultaneously arisen, texts either turned inwardly to a focus on building up the body of Christ through worship and contemplation or outwardly in service, whether to humanity or the environment. What has been largely ignored is reflection on God's revelation through creation and creature, conscience and creativity, art and science, family and public life.

Among the few theological studies on general revelation, one thinks of H. Richard Niebuhr's *The Meaning of Revelation* (1941), G. C. Berkouwer's *General Revelation* (1955), Avery Dulles's *Revelation Theology* (1969), H. D. McDonald's *Theories of Revelation: An Historical Study, 1700–1960* (1979), Bruce Demarest's *General Revelation* (1982), T. J. Gorringe's *Discerning Spirit: A Theology of Revelation* (1990), and Jürgen Moltmann's *The Spirit of Life: A Universal Affirmation* (1992), though the purview of most of these studies is broader than general revelation per se. A more philosophical exploration has been made by Ingolf Dalferth in *Becoming Present: An Inquiry into the Christian Sense of the Presence of God* (2006). Interestingly, a majority of these studies of revelation outside the walls of the church have arisen because of a personal experience of God's wider Presence by the author. Without such compelling attraction, theologians have more typically been content to write historically referenced studies on correlative topics—common grace, prevenient grace, natural revelation, or natural theology—related subjects to be sure, but also distinct.

Explaining the Silence

Too Narrow a Definitional Focus

Why is there this dearth of theological and experiential reflection on God's revelatory Presence in the world, in the arts, and in the experience of non-Christians, particularly when the topic is increasingly a central concern for postmoderns? One reason, perhaps, is a sometimes faulty definition of general revelation itself. Rather than understand general revelation as any encounter with the Transcendent that occurs outside the believing community and that is not directly concerned with redemption, many have wrongly reduced it to a perceived "lowest common denominator" by limiting "general revelation" to those general truths that are communicated by God to all persons at all times and in all places. If revelation is revealed only to certain people, but not to others, then, as the logic goes, it is not "general," but some sort of "special" revelation. General revelation, so the argument has gone, is "information that is common knowledge to all."[20] Similarly, as it is argued, general revelation cannot be the result of human choice, nor can it prove transformative in the compelling power of its new affection. Rather, "it is divinely generated revelation imposed on the whole human race and impossible for mankind to avoid."[21] And what is that revelation that is conveyed? It is, argue some, information about God that humankind invariably rejects (Rom. 1:18) or twists to his or her own purposes—that God exists and is the Creator and Sustainer of the universe, that God is righteous and sovereign, self-sufficient and transcendent, and so on. Defined thusly, general revelation remains largely an abstraction—something that Deists might affirm, but far from the wonder that is at times generated in some by God through a sunset or in the transformative reality of a new birth.

A better description of "general" revelation would recognize that God reveals himself not only through Scripture and in the believing community but also through creation, conscience, and culture. Here is a more expansive locus for God's gracious, ongoing involvement in and through his Spirit. Some would use alternate descriptors—nature, conscience, and human creativity; or cosmos, conscience, and the human spirit. Others would say general revelation occurs through nature, history, and the inner being of the human person. The scope of general revelation is hard to pin down, as God's interaction with humanity extends across both history and creation. What one can say, however, is that the content of such revelation is much more than mere knowledge. Rather than simply conveying new information that is then ignored, general revelation instead involves a numinous encounter, one that is often transformational.

Traditionally, theology's definition of general revelation derived from reflection on Romans 1 and 2. For this reason, we will consider these texts in more detail in chapter 6 when we turn to insight from the Christian tradition. The church has often spoken of the outer (creation, see Rom. 1) and the inner (conscience, see Rom. 2) loci of general revelation. But such a delineation is unduly restrictive. For general revelation's inner locus involves not only an ethical but also an aesthetic aspect. (Conscience is not a sufficiently expansive term; the imagination is also a portal for divine encounter given God's ongoing mystery.) And the outer is accessed not only through creation but also through history. Without a description that matches human experience, one that makes room for wide-ranging, serendipitous encounters with the divine, a theology of general revelation will continue to fail in gaining traction. It will

20. Robert L. Thomas, "General Revelation and Biblical Hermeneutics," *The Masters Seminary Journal* 9, no. 1 (Spring 1998): 10. Cf. Bernard Ramm, *Special Revelation and the Word of God* (Grand Rapids: Eerdmans, 1961), 17; Millard Erickson, *Christian Theology* (Grand Rapids: Baker, 1986), 154; Charles Ryrie, *Basic Theology* (Chicago: Moody, 1986), 28.

21. Thomas, "General Revelation and Biblical Hermeneutics," 10.

fail despite a renaissance of interest in those who experience God through the arts, or despite the growing need to find avenues for authentic dialogue with adherents of other religious faiths. Those seeking answers or explanations for the revelatory events they or others experience will find Christianity wanting.

Too Narrow a Biblical Focus

If too narrow a definitional focus is one reason for the paucity of helpful theological reflection on God's revelatory Presence, a second part of the answer as to why most Christians have undervalued the topic has to do with the focus of Scripture itself. The Bible centers its power and meaning on God's mighty acts in history, culminating in the birth, life, death, and resurrection of Jesus Christ—that is, on saving grace. Special revelation's focus on salvation history has rightly defined theology's central conversation. But we must also ask if all of Scripture has truly been listened to. That is, have we come to the Bible in its entirety asking the right questions, wearing the right "spectacles"?[22] Or have we allowed past priorities and past questions to color present interpretation unduly, so that portions of Scripture have been overlooked and/or wrongly interpreted? What of the Bible's creation-centered texts, for example? Why has this portion of God's Word been largely ignored in discussions of revelation? Or, conversely, why is it that the biblical discussion of God's revelation outside the believing community has usually focused only on an interpretation of Romans 1 and 2, John 1, and perhaps Acts 17? (And why, despite no textual evidence to support the interpretation, have many marginalized the narrative in Acts 17 by considering it a failed effort on Paul's part, an example of what not to do in missional preaching?)

What of the recorded experiences in Scripture of men and women who were outside the covenant community and yet experienced God's revelation? Melchizedek? Abimelech? King Neco? King Lemuel? King Nebuchadnezzar? Balaam? The Pharaoh in Moses's day? Why are their stories largely ignored in discussion of God's revelatory Presence, giving priority by default in our theological inquiry regarding general revelation to the overarching, second-order reasoning of New Testament writers whose purposes were elsewhere, as they sought to spell out the logic of salvation? Theology's bias toward the redemptive over the creational, and toward the propositional over the narrative, is perhaps a second explanation for the relative paucity of theological thinking

22. In using the metaphor of "spectacles," I am of course playing with an image from John Calvin, but reversing its meaning. It is not Scripture that provides us "spectacles" by which to look at culture, but culture that can provide us a new set of questions and experiences (i.e., new "spectacles") by which to look at Scripture.

on general revelation. First-order, primary experience has been ignored, and thus biblical source material limited. As a result, general revelation is more typically judged to be a side issue, a necessary inference from a theology of redemption, but little more.

Too Pessimistic a View of Humankind

A third reason for the marginalization and subsequent sterility of much theological reflection on general revelation has been the theological judgment that sin has so clouded and warped human receptivity to divine revelation that general revelation, even though present, is of little if any value other than to confirm our sin—our "hardness of heart." What we believe to be revelatory, it is thought, is more often simply disguised humanism, or worse, idolatry. Here, in a nutshell, is the theological interpretation given by many to Romans 1 and 2, and John 1. While general revelation has been acknowledged, the effect of sin has been thought to be so devastating as to preclude any positive contribution from God's continuing Presence among us. Avery Dulles labels this typically "Reformed" approach to general revelation "Revelation as Doctrine," associating it with the biblically centered, more propositional theology of conservative evangelicals like B. B. Warfield, Carl Henry, and J. I. Packer.[23] More recently, one could add John Piper.

Perhaps most representative here is G. C. Berkouwer in his monograph *General Revelation* for his series Studies in Dogmatics.[24] Although Berkouwer takes pains to distance himself from those like Barth who would equate the exclusivity of salvation in Jesus Christ with the exclusivity of revelation in Jesus Christ, in practice this important distinction seems to matter little to him. In particular, although Berkouwer recognizes that there is a "natural" knowledge of God and his will that is outside of the revelation of Jesus Christ, he allows such general revelation to be overwhelmed by human depravity. Though revelation is present to us, we simply choose to remain ignorant of it as human beings. When Scripture seems to suggest otherwise, Berkouwer "finds" other explanations for what the text might mean. For example, Berkouwer believes that the nature psalms do not really suggest that a knowledge of God is possible for all in and through creation, though this is what they might seem to be saying. Rather, such knowledge is dependent on redemption categories. Those psalms that glory in creation (e.g., Pss. 8; 19; 29; 65; 104; 147) are, for Berkouwer, actually rooted in "faith knowledge," arising out of the community

23. See Avery Dulles, *Models of Revelation* (Maryknoll, NY: Orbis, 1994).
24. G. C. Berkouwer, *General Revelation*, Studies in Dogmatics (Grand Rapids: Eerdmans, 1955).

of Israel as a response to the saving acts of God. Creation alone is insufficient to mediate God's Presence to us regardless of what these psalms seem to say. Writes Berkouwer, "The Creator of heaven and earth is adored even as the Redeemer of Israel is praised: for Israel the two are identical. Hence it is impossible to appeal to the 'nature psalms' on behalf of a natural theology."[25]

At one level, Berkouwer is no doubt correct. The book of Psalms is Israel's hymnbook, her response to the saving acts of Yahweh. But can creation theology be so easily conflated with redemption theology and then dismissed? Surely the Wisdom literature of the Old Testament would resist such leveling, given its repeated borrowing of creation texts from other cultures and its choice rarely to appeal directly to God's mighty acts of redemption in Egypt for supporting authority. To bring the Wisdom texts under the rubric of "salvation history" was the mistake of a past generation of biblical scholars that has today largely been rejected as unhelpful in understanding these texts on their own terms. And Berkouwer is again correct to resist "natural theology," if it means something apart from the continuing illumination and activity of God through his Spirit. We do not whisper God by shouting "man," and creation on its own must be read "tooth and claw," but, again, things are somewhat more complex than Berkouwer suggests. For if "natural theology" is more to be equated with "natural revelation," with the Creator speaking in and through his creation, then the nature psalms and books like Job do give voice to God's revelatory Presence through nature.

Similarly, Berkouwer discusses Elijah's confrontation with the prophets of Baal on Mount Carmel, concluding that "Elijah shows, on the basis of the irrefutable facts of God's deeds, that there is no *revelation* in the Baal worship."[26] No power, yes. But does Elijah's confrontation with the priests of Baal irrefutably show that God cannot be seen in creation, even as he shines in all that's fair? Idolatry has wrongly been generalized outward to include all experiences with nature. Or again, Berkouwer's sense of human depravity is so far-reaching that when he comments on Paul speaking in Romans 1:25 about the gentiles "knowing" God, he must reinterpret Paul, saying that Paul was simply using "hyperbole." That is, for Berkouwer, because of our sin, no real knowledge of God is possible. Paul could not mean what he seems to have said. Although for Berkouwer, "knowledge and revelation are *not* identical,"[27] the fact of human blindness cancels out any value or possibility that general revelation might have. Thus, though

25. Ibid., 137.
26. Ibid., 124–25.
27. Ibid., 314.

Berkouwer tries to distinguish between "salvation as being only in Christ" and "revelation being also outside of Christ," in the end this is a formal distinction without substance, having no experiential consequence except to condemn humankind given our hardness of heart. There is no possibility for Tillich's "revelatory ecstasy," or David Kern's "supernatural mail on foreign soil," or Yehudi Menuhin's violin.

Reacting, in part and rightly, to the German church's misuse of general revelation to baptize Hitler's ascent to power, Berkouwer wrongly concluded that, though revelation has priority over knowledge, because of sin, general revelation is sufficient only to make known to humankind our guilt. Writes Berkouwer: "Contact with God in the community of life is broken and man, though continuing to take his place in created reality, accordingly no longer understands its purpose, the language or song of creation. God's greatness and glory are no longer observed by a lost humanity."[28]

But is this true? What are we to make of the repeated testimony to God's greatness and glory that those outside the church give to God, based in their experiences of creation, conscience, and culture? How are we to understand the repeated witness of humankind to revelatory experiences of a *mysterium* that is simultaneously *tremendum* and *fascinans*—that is, a mystery that is both awesome and compelling?[29] We will look at some of this testimony in chapters 2 and 3. How are we as Christians to reconcile our theology with the experiences of the numinous, or sacred, that Christians and non-Christians alike describe? If truth is one, should not our understanding of God through our experience of the numinous, not to mention the narratives of transcendence from others in our wider culture, match Scripture's and the Christian tradition's understanding of how God has in fact revealed himself? We are thrown back upon the question of theological hermeneutics. Who qualifies as God's messenger (Hermes)? How do we hear God's revelation to us? That culture/experience is theology's context and application is today little debated; but can culture/experience also be more than this, a means as well of hearing God's story?

The Question of Theological Hermeneutics

Jürgen Moltmann tells the story of Galileo, who "wanted to show his opponents Jupiter's satellites." But "they refused even to look through the telescope." They believed, as Berthold Brecht puts into their mouth in his *Life of*

28. Ibid., 312; cf. 305–14.
29. See Rudolf Otto, *The Idea of the Holy* (New York: Oxford University Press, 1923).

Galileo, "that no truth can be found in nature—only in the comparison of texts."[30] Rather, Moltmann argues,

> There are no words of God without human experiences of God's Spirit. So the words of proclamation spoken by the Bible and the church must also be related to the experiences of people today, so that they are not—as Karl Rahner said—merely "hearers of the Word," but become spokesmen of the Word, too.
>
> But this is only possible if Word and Spirit are seen as existing in a *mutual relationship*, not as a one-way street.[31]

Barth uses an even more basic metaphor when he speaks of the theologian having a Bible in one hand and the newspaper in the other.[32] That is, the theologian's task is a dialogical one. My colleague Bill Dyrness understands theological method in similar terms, believing that the theologian must bring together in reflective obedience the telling of our stories and the hearing of God's stories.[33]

One can add components to theology's basic methodological schematic, but theology's two-way dialogical task remains. The hearing of God's story is not only through Scripture but also through the church, past and present. And our stories reflect both our own experiences (sometimes of God) and those of the wider culture (including those of the Transcendent). My own understanding is that the theologian has five resources at his or her disposal through the work of the Spirit. All are interactive, even while the Bible's ultimate theological authority for faith and practice is recognized. Hearing God's story has three components—one's particular worshiping community, the whole of the Christian tradition, and Scripture—while telling our stories includes our own experiences as well as the insights and expressions of the wider culture. As theologians, we (1) read the authoritative biblical text (2) from out of a worshiping community (3) in light of centuries of Christian thought and practice (4) as people embedded in a particular culture (5) who have had a unique set of experiences. Such a process is not linear, as the description might suggest, but dialogical, multiperspectival, and ongoing. The aim is to

30. Berthold Brecht, preface to *The Life of Galileo*, trans. D. I. Vesey (London, 1967).

31. Jürgen Moltmann, *The Spirit of Life: A Universal Affirmation* (Philadelphia: Fortress, 1992), 3.

32. Karl Barth, quoted in "Barth in Retirement," *Time*, May 31, 1963. Barth made similar remarks in an early letter to his friend Eduard Thurneysen (November 11, 1918). See Karl Barth and Eduard Thurneysen, *Revolutionary Theology in the Making: The Barth-Thurneysen Correspondence, 1914–1925*, trans. James D. Smart (Richmond: John Knox, 1964).

33. William Dyrness, "How Does the Bible Function in the Christian Life?," in *The Use of the Bible in Theology: Evangelical Options*, ed. Robert K. Johnston (Atlanta: John Knox, 1985), 159–74.

be generous in our assessments, inclusive in our reach, and coherent in our conclusions. Here is the theological process, the interlacing of various resources as we think Christianly.

Rather than through a hermeneutic of suspicion, or even of caution, with regard to human experience and culture, I would understand the revelatory experiences of Lewis and Tillich, of David Kern and Nanny Goodman's mother, as inviting dialogue and even appropriation by theologians interested in understanding God's revelatory Presence outside the church and without direct reference to Jesus Christ. We need a hermeneutic that includes not only Scripture and the tradition of the church but also cultural receptivity and human experience. Scripture and the theological formulations of the church past and present cannot be ignored, but neither can the witness of our culture and our own personal experiences. A robust, two-way conversation is called for. Not only can Scripture provide an interpretive grid for our experiences (we might use Calvin's metaphor of "spectacles" for this), but experiences from out of our individual and collective lives can also become the "spectacles" through which we reread the Scriptures and church tradition, looking for insight from God's Word that might provide further interpretation and illumination, and vice versa.

The experiences of those individuals with whom I began this introduction, and scores like them, are not simply subjectivity in disguise, though that remains at times a possibility. For creation, human conscience, and culture to be revelatory, there needs to be God's in-breaking Presence. Berkouwer provides the helpful example of astrology to illustrate the truth that revelation is not to be thought of as being resident in creation or creature independent of God's illumining Spirit. Astrology is not to be confused with astronomy. Some Romantics made the mistake of confusing the artist with the divine muse, as if we could, like the astrologist, conjure up revelation by an act of the imagination. Rather, it is through creation, conscience, and culture that we can observe how God acts and hear him speak. Each retains the possibility of actually being an encounter with God's Spirit, as God chooses to be present. There is, in Jürgen Moltmann's words, an "immanent transcendence," paradoxical but not dialectic, unifying rather than competing.[34] Here, as we will explore in chapter 7, is the subject matter of general revelation, and it is to be seen as complementary to special revelation.

The nonoppositional nature of general and special revelation is perhaps best seen in Psalm 19. Here the psalmist relates, "The heavens are telling the glory of God. . . . There is no speech, nor are there words . . . yet their voice

34. Moltmann, *Spirit of Life*, 7, 17.

goes out through all the earth" (Ps. 19:1–6). Creation's "wordless speech" finds its analogy, perhaps, in C. S. Lewis's description of Joy's experience as a "bright shadow," something on this side of knowledge, too close to be seen or heard. Such is the "immanent transcendence" of our Creator God. It is worth noting that the divine encounter of this psalmist is referenced not to "Yahweh," Israel's covenanting God; it is with *elohim*, the generic name for the God of the universe. It is the experience of *elohim* within nature that elicits the songwriter's praise.

In Psalm 19, the songwriter follows his praise of God's glory in creation with parallel praise for God's revelation through his Word, the law (Ps. 19:7–10). The songwriter experiences Yahweh's commandments as vivifying, making wise, causing rejoicing and enlightenment, as being true, righteous, and enduring, as preeminently desirable, like fine gold or honey. Here the focus is on God who has revealed his name, *Yahweh*, to his people and covenanted with them, providing them further revelation as to how to live. Creation and the law, *elohim* and *Yahweh*, general revelation and special revelation—the paradox is united, but never confused, in the experience of the psalmist. God is to be praised, both as Creator and as Redeemer.

Our Path Forward: Adopting an Experiential Focus

It is experience that allows the psalmist in Psalm 19 to unite that which otherwise might remain distinct, whether in creation or redemption, whether in general or in special revelation. And it is this same experiential focus that offers the best potential for a more robust theology of general revelation today—one that would no longer reduce God's wider revelatory Presence to little more than the "footprint" of God's past activity, or subsume general revelation under special revelation, creation theology under salvation theology, the work of the Spirit in Creation under the Spirit of Christ. But this, of course, is to get ahead of the argument.

Given the witness of those within and without the church as to the present Presence of God's Spirit in their lives—given, that is, the witness of many to revelatory experiences through creation, conscience, and culture—we need to again rethink our theology of general revelation. Thus, in chapters 2 and 3, we will first listen carefully to the testimonies of many, not prejudging their merits before hearing them out. We will then need to reread the Scriptures as to what they might be saying to us in this regard. We need to ask, What would it mean for our biblical interpretation to wear the "spectacles" of our wider experiences of God as we read through the text? How might we reread the

Scriptures so as to fall prey neither to a natural theology that eliminates the present in-breaking of God's revelatory Presence, finding only traces of past activity, echoes of God's earlier involvement, footprints of God's previous Presence, nor to a redemptive triumphalism that reduces general revelation merely to the grounds by which humankind is declared guilty by God and in need of his saving grace? Those biblical narratives that describe divine revelation outside the people of God, or without reliance on prophet or temple, Christ or his church, do not allow such soteriological heavy-handedness. They will be the focus of chapters 4 and 5.

As we seek a robust two-way dialogue between (1) our actual experiences of Transcendence outside the church and (2) the Scripture's authoritative descriptions and discussion of God's wider revelation, are there theologians who can help us? In chapter 6, we will look at the church's traditional understanding of general revelation, one rooted in limited readings of Romans 1 and Romans 2. We will then turn to three historic theological discussions that have relevance for our topic: the heated dialogue that took place more than a half century ago between the theologians Karl Barth and Emil Brunner; the apologetic theology of Friedrich Schleiermacher, which was written two centuries ago to his secular friends in the Romantic movement in Berlin; and the autobiography of C. S. Lewis, who described a series of divine encounters that he had beginning as a child. Here are resources from the church's tradition that can help guide us in our investigation of God's wider revelatory Presence.

Having attempted to redress that which has resulted too often in a paltry understanding of God's wider revelatory Presence outside the church and without direct reference either to Jesus Christ or to Scripture, we will then turn in chapter 7 to three theologians who can help us build a more vibrant constructive theology—the missiologist John V. Taylor, the Protestant Jürgen Moltmann, and the Roman Catholic Elizabeth Johnson. They will help us explore the theological role that the Spirit plays in God's wider revelation. It is the Spirit who is God's revelatory Presence in the world. It is not Christology, but pneumatology, that provides the primary direction and insight for our theological explorations. If we are truly trinitarian in our theology with regard to God's revelation beyond the walls of the church, are we open also to moving from Spirit to Word in our theological pilgrimage, as well as from Word to Spirit? And more particularly, are we open to the testimony of the Spirit of Life in and through creation, conscience, and culture, as well as the work of the Spirit of Christ in redemption? It is the same Spirit.

With this as our orientation, we will turn in conclusion in chapter 8 to again consider traditional notions of God's wider revelation that have flowed out of creation, conscience, and culture. Such a reconsideration of the traditional loci for God's wider revelation will help clarify our constructive theological proposal. Finally, we will take up as a case study for a constructive theology of God's wider revelatory Presence a theology of religions. What might be the practical consequence of a reconstituted and more robust constructive theology of general revelation? Obviously, the ramifications of a reappraisal of the scope and significance of God's revelatory Presence throughout humankind extend to the whole of one's Christian theology. But one example will prove instructive of its potential: How are we to understand God's revelatory Presence in and through other religious traditions? Such a study, however brief, will serve both to illustrate the book's constructive theology and to integrate praxeologically our various theological probing—experiential, biblical, and theological.

2

Experiencing God Today

Our Turn to the Spiritual

We all sense it: as the millennium has dawned, something has changed in Western culture, something that also has ramifications with regard to the Christian faith. Stated most simply, our *experience of God* is becoming at one and the same time *less centralized*, or institutionalized, in its various expressions, even while it becomes *more important* even than our theological positions. Increasing numbers of Christians are choosing to question religious authority, are deciding for themselves what theological positions to hold, and are identifying more loosely with religious institutions, even while they are increasingly open to embracing Mystery and experiencing Transcendence outside of the worshiping community. While reason remains important, contemporary Christians respond increasingly more to the imagination than to logical argument, to story over proposition. While valuing divine revelation, they often discover its reality not only within the community of faith but also outside the boundaries of institutional Christianity. Depending on your age, geography, and/or present religious affiliation, you will celebrate or bemoan this marked trend. But its sociological reality seems a given. This book is one attempt, theologically, to speak into this trend, to learn from its strengths, to counter its erosions, and to suggest a way forward, both in our worship and in our mission.

Less Centralized

In 2009, John Meacham, writing in *Newsweek* magazine, declared the end of Christian America.[1] The phrase, while hyperbolic, nonetheless captured an important shift. Quoting the 2009 American Religious Identification Survey, Meacham noted that "the number of Americans who claim no religious affiliation has nearly doubled since 1990, rising from 8 to 15 per cent." In the same period, the number of self-identified Christians has fallen 10 percentage points, from 86 to 76 percent. Though the number of Christians remains large, two-thirds of the American public (68 percent) stated their belief that religion (and one could insert Christianity here) was "losing influence" in American society. This survey is in line with those already referred to in chapter 1. A poll by George Barna, for example, not only revealed that 20 percent of Americans turn to "media, arts and culture" as their primary means of spiritual experience and expression, but also suggests that if the trends continue, by 2025, the same number of Americans will look to the arts as to the church for their spiritual formation, a revolution surely in how faith has traditionally been encouraged.[2]

Clergy abuse scandals; a perceived intolerance with regard to homosexuality; the presence of ubiquitous and contradictory information on the internet; the church's typical disregard of non-church-based "spiritual" experiences; an awareness that the earth now has seven billion souls, most of whom are not Christian but many of whom are spiritual; a failure to attract top leadership within its institutions—various reasons for the institutional church's decline have been given and can be debated.[3] But few debate the basic shift that is occurring and at an accelerating pace—attendance on Sunday morning is now below 20 percent in the United States; Sunday school, particularly for adults, is an increasingly failed enterprise; a questioning of religious authority, even within the church, over issues of lifestyle and politics is taken for granted by many; and so on. The waning of institutional Christianity in the West is unmistakable.

Robert C. Fuller cites an important study conducted by 346 social scientists representing a range of religious backgrounds. Their goal was to clarify what people mean when they say they're spiritual but not religious. The study revealed that most spiritual-but-not-religious people ascribe negative

1. John Meacham, "The End of Christian America," *Newsweek*, April 13, 2009, 34.

2. George Barna, *Revolution* (Wheaton: Tyndale, 2005).

3. A parallel study in England by David Hay titled *Something There* summarizes the typical complaints against organized religion by those who were spiritual but not religious: religious institutions foster ignorance; they are rigid and authoritarian; they are narrow-minded, hypocritical; they damage people. David Hay, *Something There: The Biology of the Human Spirit* (Philadelphia: Templeton Foundation Press, 2006), 209–27.

connotations to the term "religious," associating it with such things as church attendance, the clergy, and adherence to traditional beliefs. "Spiritual people," on the other hand, reject traditional beliefs and forms of religion in favor of mysticism and nontraditional beliefs and practices. They are less likely, the study concludes,

> to engage in traditional forms of worship such as church attendance and prayer, less likely to engage in group experiences related to spiritual growth, more likely to be agnostic, more likely to characterize religiousness and spirituality as different and non-overlapping concepts, more likely to hold nontraditional beliefs, and more likely to have had mystical experiences.[4]

More Important

Yet occurring simultaneously with the "fall" of the Christian religion as seen institutionally has been the "rise" of interest in all things spiritual. Robert Wuthnow, in his "Arts and Religion Survey" taken in 1999 with a nationally representative sample of 1,530 adults, discovered that when asked "How important has it been to you as an adult to grow in your spiritual life?" 26 percent said "extremely important," 28 percent said "very important," and 23 percent said "fairly important"—for a total of 77 percent of adult America. Only 21 percent of the population asserted that spiritual growth was "not very important" or "not at all important." In America, interest in spirituality is widespread.[5]

Such present-day openness to divine Presence finds confirmation in Europe as well. Important evidence in this regard is presented by David Hay in his book *Something There* (2006). While referencing the unmistakable waning of institutional Christianity in Britain over the last 150 years (from 40 to 60 percent regular church attenders in 1850 to just 7.5 percent in 2000, and the rate of decline is accelerating), Hay, together with his colleague Gordon Heald, also notes an important countertrend. Studying people's reported spiritual or religious experiences, they discovered that 76 percent (almost identical to that reported by Wuthnow in his somewhat analogous America-based survey) of all Britons reported having a spiritual experience, up from the 65 percent he reported in 1979.[6]

4. Robert C. Fuller, *Spiritual, But Not Religious: Understanding Unchurched America* (New York: Oxford University Press, 2001), 5.

5. Robert Wuthnow, *All in Sync: How Music and Art Are Revitalizing American Religion* (Berkeley: University of California Press, 2003), 27.

6. Hay, *Something There*, 23; see the report of Hay's 1979 report in Alister Hardy, *The Spiritual Nature of Man: A Study of Contemporary Religious Experience* (Oxford: Clarendon,

As interesting as these impressive numbers was the corollary investigation by these scholars. Wanting a manageable list of types of spiritual experiences, they went to the library of the Religious Experience Research Unit (now called the Religious Experience Research Centre based at the University of Wales), founded in 1969 by Alister Hardy. Using material collected over a lifetime (he started collecting firsthand descriptions of humankind's transcendent experiences in 1925), Hardy had accumulated an archive of thousands of personal responses to the question: "Have you ever been aware of or influenced by a presence or a power, whether you call it God or not, that is different from your everyday self?"[7] Hay and Heald identified the eight most common types of experience that Hardy recorded. They also then compared their findings both with their survey in 2000 and with an identical study they had carried out in 1987. Their findings? Fifty-five percent of those in 2000 said they were aware of a patterning of events/synchronicity (up from 29 percent in 1987), 38 percent said they had had an awareness of the Presence of God (up from 27 percent), 37 percent had had a prayer answered (up from 25 percent), 29 percent had become aware of a sacred Presence in nature (up from 16 percent), 25 percent had had an awareness of the presence of the dead (up from 18 percent), and 25 percent had felt the awareness of an evil presence (up from just 12 percent). Hay concludes,

> The remarkable rise in reports of spiritual or religious experience in Britain during the last decade of the twentieth century is extraordinary and takes some explaining. My own guess is that in reality there has been no great change in the frequency with which people encounter a spiritual dimension in their lives.

1979), 126. See also Charles Taylor, *A Secular Age* (Cambridge, MA: Belknap Press of Harvard University Press, 2007), 727, where after noting our fractured expressivist culture where the language of transcendence is declining, he nevertheless recognizes, "The sense there is something more presses in." There is a sense of "something beyond flourishing," of "life beyond life" (726).

7. Cf. Hardy, *Spiritual Nature of Man*. In this book, Hardy states that he is not trying to prove God's existence or to support any one form of institutional religion or any particular faith, but simply to demonstrate "that a large proportion of people do have feelings towards a benign power" (2). In classifying these feelings, Hardy lists twelve main divisions including visions and voices, sensory experiences of touch and smell, extrasensory perception, enhanced or "super-human" power, and various affective states—e.g., peace, joy, awe, clarity, ecstasy, yearning, hope, fear, remorse, purpose. The triggers for these experiences are as varied as life itself—from work to play, worship to the arts, nature, physical activity, happiness and despair. Such experiences are fifteen times more likely to occur in childhood than old age, nine times more likely to stem from despair than from creative work, and twice as likely to be triggered by visual stimulus than from auditory. Twenty percent of the three thousand responses that were classified described a spiritual experience similar to what Otto described as the "numinous": a *mysterium tremendum et fascinans.*

What is probably altering is people's sense that they have social permission for such experience.[8]

That is, as we approached the new millennium, those in the West not only sensed the sterility of modernity's rationalism but also became more sensitive and open to spiritual events and powers in their own lives and felt they had permission to testify about these to others.

Hay points out that a parallel increase in reported interest in spirituality can also be found in the European Study of Values. The French sociologist Yves Lambert noted that for the nine countries that were studied, the rate of self-definition as a "religious person" among young people with no formal religion went up from 14 percent in 1981 to 22 percent in 1999; belief in God from 20 percent to 29 percent; and belief in life after death from 19 percent to 28 percent.[9] Lambert concludes,

> The development of this autonomous, diffused religiosity, detached from Christianity . . . is the most unique phenomenon. This "off-piste" religiosity is illustrated mainly through variables that are less typically Christian: "taking a moment of prayer, meditation, contemplation or something like that"; belief in a "life after death" (which can include diverse conceptions such as belief in reincarnation); belief in God as "some sort of spirit or life force"; and being led to "explore different religious traditions" rather than "stick to a particular faith."[10]

What has triggered this growing openness to spiritual experience? Hay references the classic study on atheism by the Jesuit scholar Michael Buckley.[11] Buckley notes that with the rise of the Enlightenment in seventeenth-century Europe, there also grew a skeptical tradition that questioned religious experience. Over time, this rise in skepticism eventuated in the long-term abandonment of and sense of personal relationship with an immanent God, replacing that with an intellectual conviction based in philosophical argument. (For example, religious apologetics moved away from appeals to personal experiences of relationship with the Transcendent to arguments for God based on design.) But as modernity has waned, such abstractions are increasingly coming up both sterile and bankrupt. In the process, there has begun to be

8. Hay, *Something There*, 11.
9. Ibid., 24. See Yves Lambert, "A Turning Point in Religious Evolution in Europe," *Journal of Contemporary Religion* 19, no. 1 (2004): 29–45.
10. Lambert, quoted in Hay, *Something There*, 25.
11. Michael Buckley, *At the Origins of Modern Atheism* (New Haven: Yale University Press, 1990).

a revaluing of long-abandoned religious experience. What was thought in the previous decades to be precious, private, without rational foundation, and mainly for children was again valued as holistic, human, spiritual. As Theodore Roszak had earlier suggested, the "wasteland" needed to come to an end—and it did.[12]

Hay and his colleague Kate Hunt interviewed three focus groups of people who had been preselected randomly at a Nottingham shopping center because they reported that they never went to church. Hay reports that for many, it was a confrontation with one's mortality, or an experience of being profoundly alone, that opened them to something spiritual. For others it was a shock, given the beauty of the world. He writes, "Intuitions of a spiritual dimension to reality were particularly likely to burst out in two kinds of extreme situation, deep distress and overwhelming delight. It is as though a lifetime's conditioning falls away in the face of unavoidable immediacy and, like it or not, the immediate response often amounted to prayer."[13] Hay and Hunt concluded that by far the most common and impressive phenomenon they encountered during their research was this: "Underneath the confusing variety of interpretation, ranging from explanations couched in the language of mainstream religious orthodoxy through to bizarre personal speculation, there loomed an all-pervasive sense of 'something there.'"[14] Thus the title of Hay's book. There was, he writes, a "virtual universality of this experience," even while the vagueness of description was problematic. Recall, for example, my reference in chapter 1 to John Updike's story, where David Kern encounters a dying cat while on his way home from the hospital where his wife is giving birth. David concludes that the experience was "supernatural mail on foreign soil"—it had "the signature, decisive but illegible."[15] Here is Hay and Hunt's findings, too.

Examples of "Supernatural Mail on Foreign Soil"

Lest we remain at arm's length from the experience of revelation, discussing it only in the abstract and limiting our comments to "words about other words," let us begin our study of revelation that is experienced outside the Christian community of faith's institutional forms by giving a sample of testimonials,

12. Theodore Roszak, *Where the Wasteland Ends: Politics and Transcendence in Postindustrial Society* (Garden City, NY: Doubleday, 1972).
13. Hay, *Something There*, 99.
14. Ibid., 115.
15. John Updike, "Packed Dirt, Churchgoing, A Dying Cat, A Traded Car," in *Pigeon Feathers and Other Stories* (New York: Knopf, 1962), 172.

first from Hay in his study, but also from students in my classes and from a variety of other witnesses.

Responding to Creation

In his study, David Hay interviewed a number of persons who did not go to church. He asked if they had ever had a transcendent or spiritual experience.

> One woman told of a spontaneous experience from her childhood: "My father used to take all the family for a walk on Sunday evenings. On one such walk, we wandered across a narrow path through a field of high, ripe corn. I lagged behind, and found myself alone. Suddenly, heaven blazed upon me. I was enveloped in golden light. I was conscious of a presence, so kind, so loving, so bright, so consoling, so commanding, existing apart from me but so close. I heard no sound. But words fell into my mind quite clearly—'Everything is all right. Everybody will be all right.'"[16]

Recall the similar description from C. S. Lewis in his autobiography, which I quoted in chapter 1: "It was as though the voice which had called me from the world's end were now speaking at my side. It was with me in the room, or in my body, or behind me."[17] We will return to Lewis's description in chapter 6.

Or again, Hay relates the story of someone who had a spiritual experience at home. The person testified:

> The experience itself is very difficult to describe. It took me completely by surprise. I was about to start shaving at the time, of all things. I felt that my soul was literally physically shifted—for quite a number of seconds, perhaps 15 or 20—from the dark into the light. I saw my life, suddenly, as forming a pattern and felt that I had, suddenly, become acquainted with myself again after a long absence—that I was, whether I liked it or not, treading a kind of spiritual path, and this fact demanded me to quit academics and enter social work. . . . I must stress here that prior to this experience, I never used to use the words such as "soul" or "salvation" or any such "religiously coloured" words. But in order to make even the slightest sense of what happened to me, I find it imperative to use them. Looking back it does seem as if I saw a kind of light, but I think that this might have been a metaphor I coined immediately after the experience.[18]

16. Hay, *Something There*, 14.
17. C. S. Lewis, *Surprised by Joy* (New York: Harcourt, Brace, & World / Harvest Books, 1955), 180–81.
18. Hay, *Something There*, 15.

Roy Anker makes use of this same metaphor to explain the experience of some moviegoers and the intention of some filmmakers.[19] We will take this up in the next chapter.

Or to reference Hay again,

> As a child (not younger than 6, not older than 8) I had an experience which nowadays I consider as kindred, if not identical with those experiences related by Wordsworth in *Prelude*, Bk I, lines 379–400. The circumstances were: dusk, summertime, and I one of a crowd of grown-ups and children assembled round the shore of an artificial lake, waiting for full darkness before a firework display was to begin. A breeze stirred the leaves of a group of poplars to my right; stirred, they gave a fluttering sound. There, then, I knew or felt or experienced—what? Incommunicable now, but then much more so. The sensations were of awe and wonder, and a sense of astounding beauty . . . that child of 6 or 7 or 8 knew nothing of Wordsworth or about mysticism or about religion.[20]

The description might remind its readers of the wind blowing across a grassy field in Andrei Tarkovsky's film *The Mirror* (1975). Or those who have seen the movie *American Beauty* (d. Mendes, 1999) might recall Ricky's description of his seeing a plastic bag suspended in the air, dancing in the wind, one pregnant fall day when snow was in the air. He says to Janie, "This bag was just . . . dancing with me . . . like a little kid begging me to play with it. . . . That's the day I realized there was this entire life behind things and this incredibly benevolent force that wanted me to know there was no reason to be afraid . . . ever." Ricky goes on, "Sometimes there's so much beauty in the world I feel like I can't take it . . . and my heart, she's going to cave in."[21]

Hay relates that one of his colleagues had a chance to interview more fully the man who had experienced these leaves stirring in the wind. Now in his fifties, he told Hay's colleague,

> It's very difficult to say that it revealed—what? The existence of infinity? The fact of divinity? I wouldn't have had the language at my command to formulate such things, so that if I speak about it now it is with the language and ideas of a mature person. But from my present age, looking back some half a century, I

19. Roy Anker, *Catching Light: Looking for God in the Movies* (Grand Rapids: Eerdmans, 2004); Anker, *Of Pilgrims and Fire: When God Shows Up at the Movies* (Grand Rapids: Eerdmans, 2010).

20. Hay, *Something There*, 16.

21. Alan Ball, the screenwriter, said in an interview that he inserted the scene of the plastic bag into the movie based on an experience he actually had. Ball says of that moment, some may think "it's just the wind." But for Ball, as for Ricky, it was more. Ball told the interviewer, "I suddenly felt this completely unexpected sense of peace and wonder." Quoted in Bob Longino, "'Beauty' Maker," *Atlanta Journal-Constitution*, March 26, 2000, sec. L, p. 4.

would say now that I did then experience—what? A truth, a fact, the existence of the divine. What happened was telling me something. But what was it telling? The fact of divinity, that it was good? Not so much in the moral sense, but that it was beautiful, yes, sacred.[22]

Occasionally in my systematic theology classes I will ask my students to write a brief reflection paper on an experience of transcendence or the divine that they have had outside the walls of the church. About 40 percent of the testimonials submitted are based similarly on an experience in nature, though the occasions are as varied as life itself: one woman reports walking in the foothills above the Air Force Academy in Colorado Springs as a lonely and marginalized freshman at that institution and sensing God was ever present like the wind; another, jumping off a high bluff into cool water after a long, hot hike and experiencing her dependence on God; others, gazing out over Yosemite Valley and encountering God the artist; seeing a sunrise on the Trans-Canada Highway while listening to Coldplay's "Swallowed in the Sea"; seeing the immensity of the boulders in Rocky Mountain National Park; watching the clouds and sky out an airplane window; walking for hours in the rain; seeing a shooting star. The experiences cannot be predicted, and even generalizations are at best provisional. The one constant is the sense of epiphany, of the numinous, of God that is mediated in and through creation. As Irenaeus observed long ago, "For man [and woman] does not see God by his own powers; but when He pleases He is seen by men, by whom He wills, and when He wills, and as He wills."[23]

Cardinal Avery Dulles, the recently deceased dean of American Catholic theologians, writes in his *A Testimonial to Grace* of his foundational experience of God's gracious Presence mediated in and through the natural. Leaving Harvard's library to get some fresh air one bleak February day when he was a young man, something impelled Dulles to look away from the melancholy of the scene to a young tree that was just beginning to bud. He writes:

> While my eye rested on them the thought came to me suddenly with all the strength and novelty of a revelation, that these little buds in their innocence ... were ordered to an end by the only power capable of adapting means to ends—intelligence—and that the very fact that this intelligence worked toward an end implied purposiveness—in other words, a will.

Dulles relates that as he then turned home that evening, he was conscious that he "had discovered something which would introduce me to a new

22. Hay, *Something There*, 16.
23. Irenaeus, *Against Heresies* 4.20.5.

life, set off by a sharp hiatus from the past. That night, for the first time in years, I prayed."[24]

Another type of creational experience is narrated by William P. Brown. He recalls a childhood epiphany that took place at the science museum in Seattle. Seeing a button to push, Brown obliged. On a screen flashed a scene of a young couple having a picnic in a Chicago park. But quickly the camera zoomed outward, first above the park, then the city, then Lake Michigan, the continent, and the globe out into the far reaches of space until the solar system was little more than an atom in size. Then, the process was reversed, and soon young William was looking at the couple in the park again. But this time, the focus was reversed as the camera bore in ever deeper, first to a hand, then a patch of skin, then to the cellular level, and on to the quark-scale level. Brown says he was mesmerized by the ride through the cosmos and back to the microcosmos. He says he saw things "I thought only God was privy to behold." It was only years later that he discovered that he had seen *Powers of Ten* (1977), the experimental film of Charles and Ray Eames. "The sum effect," wrote Brown, "of such wildly disparate perspectives was nothing short of transcendent."[25]

Or take the experience of Louis Zamperini, the well-known Olympic long-distance runner whose plane crashed in the Pacific during World War II in 1943. Over the next forty-seven days, he and his two buddies, adrift on an inflated raft, faced white sharks, enemy aircraft that strafed them, thirst, and starvation. As told by his biographer Laura Hillenbrand,

> One morning, they woke to a strange stillness. The rise and fall of the raft had ceased, and it sat virtually motionless. There was no wind. The ocean stretched out in all directions in glossy smoothness, regarding the sky and reflecting its image in crystalline perfection. Like the ancient mariner, Louie and Phil had found the doldrums, the eerie pause of wind and water that lingers around the equator. They were, as Coleridge wrote, "as idle as a painted ship upon a painted ocean."[26]

In her best-selling biography, Hillenbrand narrates that for the two surviving fliers, it was an experience of transcendence. The sky whispered like it was a pearl. "For a while they spoke, sharing their wonder. Then they fell into reverent silence. Their suffering was suspended. They weren't hungry or thirsty. They were unaware of the approach of death."[27]

24. Avery Dulles, *A Testimonial to Grace: And Reflections on a Theological Journey* (Kansas City: Sheed & Ward, 1996), 35.
25. William P. Brown, *The Seven Pillars of Creation: The Bible, Science, and the Ecology of Wonder* (New York: Oxford University Press, 2010), 1.
26. Laura Hillenbrand, *Unbroken* (New York: Random House, 2010), 166.
27. Ibid.

Zamperini recalled that as he watched this beautiful, still world, his thoughts at the time were drawn to another moment of transcendent beauty in nature that he had experienced. "Such beauty he thought was too perfect to have come about by mere chance. That day in the center of the Pacific was, to him, a gift crafted deliberately, compassionately, for him and Phil."[28] Several days later, while he and Phil continued to drift on the calm sea, Zamperini astonishingly heard singing. Though Phil heard or saw nothing, Louie saw human figures floating in a bright cloud, silhouetted against the sky. "They were singing the sweetest song he had ever heard." Zamperini knew what "he was seeing and hearing was impossible, and yet he felt absolutely lucid." This was, he felt certain, no hallucination, no vision. "He sat under the singers, listening to their voices, memorizing the melody, until they faded away."[29]

Responding to Creation, Conscience, and Culture Working Together

But lest one wrongly conclude from my selection of testimonials that nature/creation is the only source of such experiences of the Transcendent (something chapter 3 will redress more completely as it takes up our experiences of the Sacred through the arts), let me offer two final testimonials—testimonials of how creation can work alongside culture and conscience to convey God's revelatory Presence.

The first is from a recent doctoral graduate in theology at Fuller Seminary, Patrick Oden.[30] Writing on the theological aesthetics of Jürgen Moltmann, he began with a personal story from his college days. Away from home and on fall break with all of his friends away, Patrick decided to read through Milton's *Paradise Lost*. Finding an expanse of lawn and a large tree to sit under, he began to read. He says, "A breeze had picked up, giving voice to the various trees as their branches danced. Colors in the crisp, fifty degree air, oranges and reds and yellows, seemed brighter, more full. There were scattered, high clouds in the sky moving fast towards the west. And it was quiet. Wonderfully quiet." Oden says he began to read out loud, in a quiet voice, falling "into the rhythm of words and story, losing myself in the original human narrative as told by Milton." Several hours later, cleansed from the dross of a rough quarter of schoolwork, he felt his heart, soul, and mind lifted up into the story, "into a taste of heaven itself." Each day during the week, Patrick returned to the tree to read Milton, and each time after some adjustment, he again fell "in tune

28. Ibid.
29. Ibid., 167.
30. Patrick Oden, "Experiences of Beauty: Theological Aesthetics in the Work of Jürgen Moltmann" (unpublished paper, Fuller Seminary, Pasadena, CA, 2008), 2–3.

with life and eternity. Gorgeous nature all around me, masterful words and story going into me, my soul felt expansive, hardly able to be contained within any more. . . . It was a prolonged epiphany."

The second testimonial comes from Philip Mangano. For the last four decades, Mangano has worked to abolish tragedy among the homeless. Volunteering on a breadline for years, directing a city's homelessness response, leading a statewide homelessness/housing advocacy group, and finally serving as the director of the White House Interagency Council on Homelessness in Washington, DC, under President Bush, Phil says that this "trajectory of life, that calling from above, began in the middle of a row, down front," in a movie theater on Harvard Square. One day, on the spur of a moment, he went to see *Brother Sun, Sister Moon* (1972) with a friend because it was directed by Franco Zeffirelli, a favorite film director, though he had no idea what the film was about. It was only later that Mangano learned that the director had made this homage to St. Francis of Assisi because of a promise the director had made for a granted prayer.

As a conservative Protestant who had not gone to movies growing up, Mangano said he had never heard before that day of St. Francis of Assisi, that "young Italian who had a spiritual awakening and decided, against the demands of his father and the best wishes of his friends, to live his life in companionship with the poorest, lepers living near Assisi." Though he was a seminary graduate, he confessed that he had no reference point other than the Gospels themselves for Francis's decision "to give up everything in service to the most disadvantaged," nor any models for choosing a life of "abject simplicity." But Zeffirelli's film threw open the door to such a life, and Mangano walked through. He said, "As much as my life has failings and missteps, and it does, the Gospel and Spirit seized me that day and, like Francis Thompson's proverbial 'Hound of Heaven,' has been at my heels ever since." Having gone into the theater thinking one way about life, Mangano said he came out transformed by his encounter with God.[31]

Such testimonials are easily multiplied. The novelist John Updike, for example, as he has chronicled life in the last half of the twentieth century, provides a treasure trove of such accounts of revelational events that happen outside church and synagogue. Though fictional, Updike's stories also seem true to life (perhaps more so than the miraculous, but true, experiences in the life of Zamperini!)—that is their power. We have already referred to David Kern's experience of life juxtaposed with death as he came home from the maternity ward of the hospital where his wife was giving birth. Such fragile, but real,

31. Philip Mangano, personal correspondence, February 13, 2013.

revelation is described in others of his stories as well. In "Pigeon Feathers," it is the beauty of the individual patterns on the wings of the pigeons he has just shot in the barn that allows a younger David to be "robed in this certainty: that the God who had lavished such craft on these worthless birds would not destroy His whole Creation by refusing to let David live forever."[32] In his early novel *Of the Farm*, it is the pattern of rain on the window that opens out into an epiphany; in *Rabbit, Run*, the epiphany comes when Rabbit hits a perfect drive on the golf course; in Updike's story "Wife-wooing," that sense of the Transcendent comes within sexual intimacy; in *Marry Me, Marry Me*, an adulterous couple realizes that without a sense of the Transcendent, a "blessing," their adulterous affair will prove hopeless. In *Roger's Version*, the Transcendent is apparent to Dale Kohler, a computer programmer, as he reflects on the big bang theory. What all such events have in common, whether rooted in the human conscience, in creation, or in human culture, is that they are "supernatural mail"—they have "the signature: decisive but illegible."[33]

Testimony to the Presence of God in life is often the purview of poets. One of the best known is Gerard Manley Hopkins, someone who wrote few poems in his difficult and sheltered life, but whose poems are some of the most widely read in the English-speaking world. As a youth, Hopkins excelled in school, particularly in the arts, and he won prizes for his poetry. But while at Oxford, he converted to Roman Catholicism under the influence of John Henry Newman, and for the next nine years studied theology and philosophy, underwent spiritual discipline, and struggled to teach classics to the poor. A devout Jesuit, Hopkins totally committed himself to training in spiritual self-perfection, letting the Society regulate his vocation and intellectual interests. Not a particularly effective teacher and discouraged by the social work he engaged in, he often suffered depression, having a sense of personal futility. Moreover, not able to reconcile his poetry with his calling, he willingly sacrificed his art for his calling as a Jesuit. When he joined the Society of Jesus in 1868, he actually burned all the poems he had written up until that time, believing that he could not serve both his muse and his Master. And even at his death twenty-one years later, the few subsequent poems he wrote remained unprinted, even though they are today some of the best known ever written.

Though Hopkins never came to terms with how his poetry and his vocation as a Jesuit could be reconciled, he could not completely silence his muse

---

32. John Updike, "Pigeon Feathers," in *Pigeon Feathers*, 105.

33. John Updike, *Of the Farm* (New York: Knopf, 1965); *Rabbit, Run* (New York: Knopf, 1960); "Wife-wooing," in *Pigeon Feathers*; *Marry Me, Marry Me* (New York: Knopf, 1976); and *Roger's Version* (New York: Knopf, 1986).

either. Seven years after joining the order, and on the suggestion of his rector, he wrote "The Wreck of the Deutschland," a poem in honor of five Franciscan nuns who had died in a shipwreck. It was meant to commemorate their lives and death. But on an allegorical level, the shipwreck he wrote about was his own life—his hopes dashed in the storm of religious devotion. Two years later, Hopkins finished a small group of sonnets that reflected his sensitivity to God's Presence in and through creation. The poems revel in wonder and astonishment at the beauty of nature and of God its Creator who shines through his handiwork. Surely the best known is "God's Grandeur."

> The world is charged with the grandeur of God.
>   It will flame out, like shining from shook foil;
>   It gathers to a greatness, like the ooze of oil
> Crushed. Why do men then now not reek his rod?
> Generations have trod, have trod, have trod;
>   And all is seared with trade; bleared, smeared with toil;
>   And wears man's smudge and shares man's smell: the soil
> Is bare now, nor can foot feel, being shod.
>
> And for all this nature is never spent;
>   There lives the dearest freshness deep down things;
> And though the last lights off the black West went
>   Oh, morning, at the brown brink eastwards, springs—
> Because the Holy Ghost over the bent
>   World broods with warm breast and with ah! Bright wings!

Basic to the poems of Hopkins was his notion of "inscape," something he took from the writings of the medieval theologian Duns Scotus. "Inscape" was that pattern, or design, or unifying principle behind all works of art and of nature. It was "the outer form of all things, animate and inanimate, as it expressed their inner soul."[34] As his biographer writes, "He did not simply see things; he saw into them . . . he was confident that the form or inscape was significant of God's presence in all things. It was God's presence that 'individuated' the constellations of the sky, the motion of bird or wind, the forms of cloud, leaf and tree."[35] Having experienced God's revealing Presence in creation, Hopkins could not but portray that reality in his poetry, in the process re-creating the possibility of experiencing God's revelation for his readers as well.

34. James Reeves, ed., introduction to *Selected Poems of Gerard Manley Hopkins* (London: Heinemann, 1953), xxii.
35. Ibid., xxii–xxiii.

In his Nobel Prize lecture on literature, Aleksandr Solzhenitsyn summarized well the role of the artist in conveying the revelatory Presence of the numinous.

> Not everything can be named. Some things draw us beyond words. Art can warm even a chilled and sunless soul to an exalted spiritual experience. Through art we occasionally receive—indistinctly, briefly—revelations the likes of which cannot be achieved by rational thought. It is like the small mirror [in fairy tales]: you look into it but instead of yourself you glimpse for a moment the Inaccessible, a realm forever beyond reach. And your soul begins to ache.[36]

Here is what happens to some readers of Hopkins, just as it happened to Patrick Oden reading Milton under a tree and Phil Mangano watching Zeffirelli's *Brother Sun, Sister Moon* at a theater on Harvard Square.

Preliminary Observations on God's Presence

Several preliminary comments and cautions suggest themselves at this point, even as we continue our reflection on experience, though we will need to return to these observations in light of our later dialogue with Scripture and theology. As should be clear from this initial cross section of testimonies, many centering on creation, but others grounded in conscience or culture, the precipitating cause for experiencing God's wider revelation is both varied and unpredictable. There is no way of reliably "producing" it by our own effort. Revelation comes within the commonplace events of life; yet it comes at one and the same time from beyond us; it is transcendent to us, experienced as a gift and not a task. Here is our beginning point, as all the testimonials have reinforced.

Sociological and Phenomenological Descriptors

Though variety and individuation are clearly evident in the above testimonials and will again be seen in the reflections in chapter 3 on experiences of God's wider revelatory Presence triggered by the arts, sociologists and phenomenologists have nonetheless been able to offer certain generalizations. Two of the best come from Rudolf Otto and Peter Berger.

In his classic phenomenological work *The Idea of the Holy* (1917), Rudolf Otto describes several earmarks of experiences that are consistently described as sacred or holy. When the human spirit encounters the Spirit (or more

---

36. Aleksandr I. Solzhenitsyn, *East and West* (New York: Harper & Row / Perennial Library, 1972), 6.

precisely from a theological point of view, when the Divine Spirit enters into communion with the human spirit), there is a *mysterium* due to the Presence of the Other that has two defining characteristics: it is simultaneously *tremendum* (awesome) and *fascinans* (desirable).[37] Otto made his conclusions (the numinous is a "*mysterium: tremendum et fascinans*") based on evidence from the religious and spiritual experiences of peoples in a wide variety of places and times. But though he wrote as a phenomenologist, his conclusions were also informed by his Christian convictions. (He had written his dissertation, not inconsequentially, on Luther's understanding of the Spirit. We will return to a focus on the Spirit in chapter 7.) Put most simply: Otto recognized that throughout the biblical narrative, when God shows up, "we fall down." One thinks of Abraham (Gen. 17), Balaam (Num. 22), Joshua (Josh. 5), Ezekiel (Ezek. 1; 3; 44), and Daniel (Dan. 10). This is also true collectively as when all Judah "fell down" in response to the Spirit (2 Chron. 20) and when the twenty-four elders who sit in God's Presence fall down in worship (Rev. 4). The mystery experienced is both awesome and engaging, inviting reverence and response.

Otto's insights have continued to prove controversial, just as they were in his day, for he gives phenomenological validation to the spiritual experiences of those outside the church. (His conclusions were also attacked by Nazis, for they challenged the notion of a master race.) But his observations also find repeated confirmation in the testimony of many. Listen, for example, to the witness of John V. Taylor, who writes of his experience with African religion in his book *The Primal Vision*. A missionary in Uganda, Taylor recognized in those surroundings "the deep sense of a pervading Presence." This could be observed, he believed, in the ancient songs, proverbs, and riddles of the peoples he had chosen to live with. Taylor quotes David Livingstone's 1865 journal, *Expedition to the Zambezi*. Livingstone asked a Tswana, "What is holiness?" The answer? "When copious showers have descended during the night, and all the earth and leaves and cattle are washed clean and the sun rising shows a drop of dew on every blade of grass, and the air breathes fresh, that is holiness."[38]

Or listen to Deborah Buchanan, who in her doctoral thesis at Fuller Seminary argued that it is the Ring Shout, a West African circle dance that was common on plantations in the South during the period of slavery, where God could sometimes be seen as present to the participants. This dance allowed

---

37. Rudolf Otto, *The Idea of the Holy* (London: Oxford University Press, 1923), 12–40.
38. John V. Taylor, *The Primal Vision: Christian Presence amid African Religion* (Philadelphia: Fortress, 1963), 52, 139.

slaves to collectively grieve their losses, celebrate their joys, and experience religious freedom in the midst of captivity. The slaveholders thought such a dance the polar opposite of a spiritual practice, "an empty, frivolous, over-sexualized activity," and not the "sacred activity that the enslaved Africans experienced" it to be—a sacred activity rooted in freedom and justice, connecting them to one another, to deceased ancestors, and, as he deemed fit, even to God. These slave owners, who were chiefly European in background, believed dance to be empty of sacred content, but to these slaves who had come from Africa, it was sacred, a form of prayer. Here, argues Rogers, was a cultural practice, a dance that was "a vehicle for God's intentional, yet general, revelation to humanity."[39] In the Ring Shout, slaves testified to their experience of the Numinous.

Peter Berger has called this communion with the Divine, this sense of the Holy, *A Rumor of Angels*. Writing this classic work in 1970 during the height of modernism, when some trumpeted the supposed demise of the supernatural in our world ("God is dead!"), Berger argued that this was not the case. For "'in, with and under' the immense array of human projections, there are indicators of a reality that is truly 'other' and that the religious imagination . . . ultimately reflects." In short, Berger believed that there was possible an inductive approach to theology, an anchorage in fundamental human experiences—in "prototypical human gestures." There were experiences of the human spirit that pointed beyond that reality, that had "an immediacy to God." For Berger, these included our propensities for order, play, hope, damnation (for example, of Adolf Eichmann), and humor. He writes, "Both in practice and in theoretical thought, human life gains the greatest part of its richness from the capacity for ecstasy, by which I do not mean the alleged experiences of the mystic, but any experience of stepping outside the taken-for-granted reality of everyday life, an openness to the mystery that surrounds us on all sides."[40]

Preliminary Warnings

Otto's and Berger's inductive approach, like the one I am also following in this book, can be seen as well in N. T. Wright's recent popular apologetic *Simply Christian: Why Christianity Makes Sense* (2006), a twenty-first-century

39. Buchanan reports that there is documented evidence that the Ring Shout at times even led to Christian conversion. Deborah Johanna Buchanan, "Blue Tights, Dancing into a Life of Her Own: Facilitating Embodied Spirituality for African American Adolescent Girls" (PhD diss., Fuller Theological Seminary, 2008).

40. Peter Berger, *A Rumor of Angels* (Garden City, NY: Doubleday / Anchor Books, 1970), 45–75.

recasting of C. S. Lewis's classic *Mere Christianity* (1952).[41] In the opening
four chapters of *Simply Christian*, Wright suggests that there are four "voices"
that echo in the human subconscious: the longing for justice, the quest for
spirituality, the hunger for relationships, and the delight in beauty. That is,
Wright begins his apologetic for the Christian faith, not with special revelation,
not with a focus on Jesus directly, though that is where he ultimately turns,
but with our experiences of God's Presence in our everyday lives.

For Wright, these four creational voices—justice, spirituality, relationships,
beauty—point us toward God because they have their source in him; they are
expressions of the one voice that alone can lead us out of the multiple alien-
ations and frustrations of human existence into an authentic and specifically
Christian way of life. When we respond to these echoes, however faint they may
be, we are opening ourselves to the activity and the energy of the Spirit, who,
for Wright, knows no boundaries in reaching and restoring broken humanity.
These four "voices" may actually help us glimpse the glorious possibilities of
the new creation opened up to us in Christ. Perhaps, then, he thinks, we might
interpret these voices as echoes of the Spirit. To give but one of his examples,
Wright states, "Perhaps art can help us to look beyond the immediate beauty
with all its puzzles, and to glimpse that new creation which makes sense not
only of beauty but of the world as a whole, and ourselves within it. Perhaps."[42]

The Fear of Self-Deception

But though Wright's theological instincts are sound—recognizing in our
day and age the importance of beginning with our experiences of God outside
the church, Wright ends up being too tentative in his assessment of God's
revelatory Presence, whether in the artist, or in those who work for justice,
or in our reach for genuine spirituality, or in our struggle for redemptive relationships. While recognizing that in our post-Christian context, one needs
to begin not with abstract reasoning but with direct experiences of grace if
one is to get a hearing, Wright's focus on Jesus and that salvation offered in
him causes Wright to remain cautious about the nature and significance of
those numinous experiences that happen outside the church. Understanding
the Spirit's activity more in terms of redemption than of creation, Wright
limits the role that a creationally based revelation might play. His language
of "echoes" and "traces" suggests more the residue of God's past action in a
completed creation than the dynamic Presence of the *mysterium: tremendum*

41. N. T. Wright, *Simply Christian: Why Christianity Makes Sense* (San Francisco: Harper-
SanFrancisco, 2006).
42. Ibid., 236.

et fascinans. Wright remains hesitant to say much more than a "perhaps" when speaking of the revelatory role of art, spirituality, justice, or relationships. He states that these "echoes of a voice" do not enable us "to deduce very much about the world except that it is a strange and exciting place."[43] Really? The testimonies of those we have already listened to would belie his claim.

Behind Wright's excessive caution is his traditional evangelical emphasis on the reality of sin that clouds all human perception. As Andy Crouch writes in a similar vein in his concluding chapter to *Culture Making* (2008), which he titles "The Traces of God": "But how, exactly, is God involved? All efforts to pin down the details of where and when we can say that God is working in history are fraught with the danger of self-deception, if not outright blasphemy."[44] Yes, the danger of self-deception, if not outright blasphemy, is ever present and must be taken seriously. Wright and Crouch are correct. As I will argue, this is why it is crucial for one to have a full-orbed theological hermeneutic, a robust methodology that includes Scripture, tradition, and community as well as experience. One does not whisper "God" by shouting "man." The witness of God's revelation in Scripture is authoritative and the testimony and reflection of Christians through the ages foundational. But the danger for Christians is also on the other side. We can exclude by an overemphasis on sin and salvation the real, revelatory Presence of God through his Spirit that is the clear testimony of a vast majority of Westerners today. Though Alister McGrath is no doubt correct when he reminds us that "the human ability to discern God within the natural order is arguably fragile at the best of times," it has also arguably been present throughout history.[45] And the testimony of a rising number of Westerners today is that those experiences continue to be foundational and transformative, both centering and enriching life.

The Danger of Sloth (Acedia)

Self-deception remains a present danger for any who might focus on revelation in and through everyday experiences in life, but an overfocus on this possibility invites a complementary danger. Not trusting oneself to recognize the Divine in the quotidian can lead to the unintended consequence of sloth. Kathleen Norris speaks of this danger for Christians—of "spiritual torpor or apathy; ennui."[46] Norris suggests that "most of us, most of the time, take for granted

---

43. Ibid., 10.
44. Andy Crouch, *Culture Making* (Downers Grove, IL: InterVarsity, 2008), 202.
45. Alister McGrath, *A Scientific Theology*, vol. 1, *Nature* (Grand Rapids: Eerdmans, 2001), 291.
46. Kathleen Norris, *Quotidian Mysteries: Laundry, Liturgy, and "Women's Work"* (Mahwah, NJ: Paulist Press, 1998). See also Kathleen Norris, *Acedia and Me: A Marriage, Monks, and a Writer's Life* (New York: Riverhead, 2008), which Norris describes as "a longer meditation on

what is closest to us and is most universal. The daily round of sunrise and sunset, for example, that marks the coming and passing of each day, is no longer a symbol of human hopes, or of God's majesty, but a grind, something we must grind our teeth to endure." Norris writes, "The ordinary activities I find most compatible with contemplation are walking, baking bread and doing laundry." Norris wants us to recognize and savor "the holy in the mundane circumstances of daily life."[47] She wants to turn our everyday activities into "serious play." "But the grip of acedia on the human spirit is such that even the great beauty of this land and seascape can be rendered impotent and invisible" (she is referring to Hawaii).[48] The Greek root of *acedia* means "lack of care." Instead, she wants us to discover "the quotidian mysteries." She wants us "to keep up the daily practices that would keep us in good relationship to God and to each other."[49]

Here also is the emphasis of Kevin Vanhoozer and his students in their book *Everyday Theology: How to Read Cultural Texts and Interpret Trends* (2007). Taking as his definition of everyday theology "faith seeking understanding of everyday life," Vanhoozer says his "proof text for everyday theology is Matthew 16:1–3":

> The Pharisees and Sadducees came to Jesus and tested him by asking him to show them a sign from heaven. He replied, "When evening comes, you say, 'It will be fair weather, for the sky is red,' and in the morning, 'Today it will be stormy, for the sky is red and overcast.' You know how to interpret the appearance of the sky, but you cannot interpret the signs of the times."

We seek out certain kinds of knowledge, but in other areas we remain tentative and/or uninterested. In particular, we fail to take seriously the importance theologically of the cultural signs of the times—"the shared environment, practices, and resources of everyday life."[50] We fail to discover God in the midst of life.

The Denial of Mystery

Still another caution might be sounded as we begin this study, one that needs more elaboration. The thesis of Peter Rollins, in his book *How (Not) to Speak*

---

the subject of acedia. The word and the concept have fascinated me since I first encountered them many years ago in a monastery library" (author's note, n.p.).

47. Norris, *Quotidian Mysteries*, 16–17.

48. Ibid., 19, 29.

49. Ibid., 40–43. See Norris, *Acedia and Me*, 169–98.

50. Kevin Vanhoozer, "What Is Everyday Theology? How and Why Christians Should Read Culture," in Kevin J. Vanhoozer, Charles A. Anderson, and Michael J. Sleasman, eds., *Everyday Theology: How to Read Cultural Texts and Interpret Trends* (Grand Rapids: Baker Academic, 2007), 17, 28.

of God (2006), is: "That which we cannot speak of is the one thing about whom and to whom we must never stop speaking"[51] (xii). With the Christian mystics, Rollins approaches "God as a secret which one [is] compelled to share yet which [retains] its secrecy" (xiii). He believes that if the Western church is to prosper, it will need to engage with this ancient language. That is, even as we speak of God's wider revelation, we must also recognize ongoing mystery.

Rollins is helpful in reminding his readers that "concealment" is not the opposite of "revelation." Rather, revelation "has mystery built into its very heart" (xiii). Like Lewis's moments of Joy, Rollins understands that these experiences of God's revelational Presence are precritical, on this side of knowledge, too close to be seen, too plain to be understood. Rollins uses a variety of word pictures to get his point across. Some of his similes are relational: at its most luminous, he writes, revelation is analogous to the experience of an infant feeling the embrace and tender kiss of its mother. In this event, "the baby does not understand the mother" in the same way the infant is "known by the mother. In contrast, revelation is often treated as if it can be deciphered into a dogmatic system rather than embraced as the site where the impenetrable secret of God transforms us" (17). Rollins also uses the language of "hyper-presence." He writes: "God's interaction with the world is irreducible to understanding, precisely because God's presence is a type of hyper-presence. Hyper-presence is a term that refers to a type of divine saturation that exists in the heart of God's presence. It means that God not only overflows and overwhelms our understanding but also overflows and overwhelms our experience" (23). Such "hypernymity" "gives us far too much information. Instead of being limited by the poverty of absence, we are short-circuited by the excess of presence"[52] (24).

For Rollins, as we do theology, we must acknowledge not only the defining revelatory experiences of God's Presence but also the extent to which our language fails to adequately define who or what God is. Put most simply, any book on revelation must proceed humbly, aware that what can be said pales in significance to what lies beyond and behind our words. There is, for the person who has experienced God's revelatory Presence, "a God-shaped hole formed in the aftermath of God, a hole that compels them to seek after that which they already have" (52). Thus, at the beginning of this book, it is important

51. Peter Rollins, *How (Not) to Speak of God* (Brewster, MA: Paraclete, 2006). Page citations for all quotations from Rollins's book are given in the text. Rollins explains this "concealment" further in his follow-up book, *The Fidelity of Betrayal: Towards a Church beyond Belief* (Brewster, MA: Paraclete, 2008), 119–20.

52. God's hyper-presence, thinks Rollins, is "analogous to the idea of a ship sunken in the depths of the ocean: while the ship contains the water and the water contains the ship, the ship only contains a fraction of the water while the water contains the whole of the ship. Our saturation by God does not merely fill us but also testifies to an ocean we cannot contain" (ibid., 49).

to realize what we are not saying. Often general revelation is thought paltry because it is partial. But all revelation is partial. "Now I know only in part," writes Paul. "Then I will know fully, even as I have been fully known" (1 Cor. 13:12). Such an understanding of the limits of God's wider revelation should not lead to the conclusion that there is "a preference for absence over presence, seeking over finding, questions over answers, or hunger over nourishment; for in the absence," writes Rollins, "there is an icon of presence, in seeking there is evidence of having been found, in questioning there is a hint that the answer has been given, and in hunger there is a deep abiding nourishment" (52).

For Rollins, there is a silence that is part of the experience of God's revelatory experience, as Otto has also noted. He writes, "The silence that is part of all God-talk is not the silence of banality, indifference or ignorance but one that stands in awe of God. This does not necessitate an absolute 'silencing,' whereby we give up speaking of God, but rather involves a recognition that our language concerning the divine remains silent in its speech" (41). For Rollins, "God" cannot be colonized. Thus there is paradoxically a desire to say nothing, "to create sacred space," one that "opens up the most beautiful type of language available—the language of parables, prose and poetry" (42).

The Distraction of Clarity

Rollins's argument is similar to that of Charles J. Conniry Jr. in his book *Soaring in the Spirit* (2007).[53] Conniry writes, "We have inherited from the seventeenth century two primary approaches to Christian spirituality: *the way of knowledge* and its reactionary counterpart, *the way of piety*" (92). Here is one more manifestation of the Enlightenment's objective/subjective trap. Thus we have as a church tended "to conceive of spirituality in terms of accumulating religious knowledge" (93). Here is the *objective* fallacy. Discipleship has too often become little more than "the transmission of information" (93), and evangelism, an exercise chiefly in apologetics. One thinks of a book like Josh McDowell's *Evidence That Demands a Verdict*.[54] In this context, pietism became a "much-needed counterbalance to the sterile intellectualism of the Age of Reason" (94). But even here, pietism too often devolves into a *subjectivism* that "puts too much stress on godly behavior . . . defined for the most part in negative terms" (94). Here Conniry has in mind the church's "do's and don'ts"—"I don't smoke, don't chew, and don't go with girls who do." Today, we might say, "I don't support gay marriage."

53. Charles J. Conniry Jr., *Soaring in the Spirit* (Colorado Springs: Paternoster, 2007). Page citations for all subsequent quotations from Conniry's book are given in the text.
54. Josh McDowell, *Evidence That Demands a Verdict: Historical Evidences for the Christian Faith* (San Bernardino, CA: Campus Crusade for Christ International, 1972).

The problem with the Enlightenment's legacy—the way of knowledge and the way of piety—"is that we attempt to measure the quality of our spirituality in black-and-white terms: either by what we know or by what we do (and do not do)" (95). Here, in Conniry's words, is "the distraction of clarity" (170). Whether through knowledge or piety, there has been since the time of the Renaissance a "flight from mystery" (122). "For fifteen hundred years, mystics were just as influential as intellectuals in the formation of the church's theology and spirituality" (123). At times, they even superseded all else. Thomas Aquinas is a particularly interesting example. Near the completion of his magnum opus, the *Summa Theologica*, Aquinas had an experience of God's mystery that caused him to abandon his intellectual exercise. While worshiping at Mass one day in 1273, he said that he saw the things of God as never before—it was *a new creation*! Speaking afterward of the experience, he said, "All that I have written seems to me like straw compared to what has now been revealed to me."[55] At that, Thomas set down his pen, never again to write a word of theology. Writes Conniry, "A brief encounter with mystery was enough to displace a lifetime of studious theological reflection" (127).

Christianity's distraction of clarity, like its flight from mystery, has not only become ever more pronounced as we have entered the next millennium, but also produced, in turn, an understandable reaction. As we enter the twenty-first century, there has been as we have noted a significant turn to the spiritual rather than the religious. It is no longer necessary to convince people that there are many aspects of reality that are inaccessible to reason. Modernity's sterility has provided that lesson. Thus piety has taken a new turn, one more diffuse and often lacking in definable content, perhaps even substance. But though the wider culture has opened itself up to God's wider Presence in and through life, the Christian church is lagging behind in many quarters. Still encumbered by the inheritance of seventeenth-century thinking—of the dichotomous subjective/objective trap—we have found ourselves unable to hear the testimonies and entertain the call for new thinking with regard to God's revelatory Presence. Somehow, piety needs again to be connected to theology—to be given personal content. A third way—one that recognizes God's revelatory Presence in and through life in its fullness—is called for.

55. Thomas Aquinas, quoted in Conniry, *Soaring in the Spirit*, 127.

3

Reflecting on Experience

A Case Study—The Movie Event

> The cinema has done more for my spiritual life than the church.
>
> John Updike[1]

In 2012, the Oscars added a new component to their show. In addition to the jokes, the fashion, and the awards, they included a series of brief interviews with actors and actresses who responded to the question, "What is your favorite movie moment?" Christopher Plummer referenced *Snow White*. Janet McTeer referenced Christopher Plummer for his role in *The Sound of Music*. Several went back to their childhood when recalling their favorite movie moment—to seeing a car drive off a cliff in *Chitty Chitty Bang Bang*, only to be surprised as it turned out to be a flying machine. Kenneth Branaugh recalled, "It was a wonderful moment of cinema magic." So too was Judy Garland singing "Over the Rainbow" in *The Wizard of Oz*. Jessica Chastain confessed that it was while watching that movie that she "began my love affair with movies and my wanting to be a part of that wonder."

1. John Updike, quoted in Christopher Deacy and Gaye Williams Ortiz, *Theology and Film: Challenging the Sacred/Secular Divide* (Oxford: Blackwell, 2008), 38.

Experiencing magic and wonder is something at the heart of the moviegoing "event"—at least at its best. This magic and wonder is not merely a feeling; behind it is a heuristic intuition that something beyond us is being revealed/ revealing itself. There is a "reel spirituality" that sometimes takes place for the moviegoer. Viewers find themselves transported to another place or into the presence of another, or even an Other. In the process, they explore life's possibilities and contradictions, testing out solutions and even finding themselves surprised by joy . . . or sorrow, by love and pain and life itself. Given such events, it should not be surprising that commentators, both professional and lay, have explored since film's earliest days the spiritual dimensions of this experience. Could film-going be a particularly powerful example of the revelational possibility of art? It is such a question, a case study if you like, that this chapter will take up and explore. Again, our goal here is to root our larger theological conversation not in the theoretical or abstract, but in the testimony of people themselves who claim to have encountered God, to have received a revelation from God—this time, through watching a movie.

Perhaps the first example of a formal exploration of the theological possibilities of film was a pamphlet written by the Congregational minister Harold Jump in 1911, titled "The Religious Possibilities of the Motion Picture." Jump compared the function of the movies to Jesus's use of parables.[2] Here movies were understood more for their illustrative purposes. It was the poet Vachel Lindsay, writing in 1915, who perhaps first understood film's possibilities in more mystical terms: "The real death in the photoplay is the ritualistic death and the real birth is the ritualistic birth, and the Cathedral mood of the motion picture which goes with these and is close to these in many of its phases, is an inexhaustible resource."[3]

The Claim of Theology and Film Writers

Not all who have followed after Lindsay and Jump have been as sure of the spirituality of the movie event—whether affective or declarative. But since the advent of the VCR in the late 1970s, which allowed for the re-viewing of film on demand, and the subsequent invention of the DVD, Netflix, and other forms of internet delivery of movies, a growing number of commentators, both

2. Herbert Jump, *The Religious Possibilities of the Motion Picture* (New Britain, CT: South Congregational Church private distribution, 1911), reprinted in Terry Lindvall, *The Silents of God: Selected Issues and Documents in Silent American Film and Religion, 1908–1925* (Lanham, MD: Scarecrow Press, 2001), 54–78.

3. Vachel Lindsay, *The Art of the Moving Picture* (1915; repr., New York: Modern Library, 2000), 176–77.

professional and lay, have continued the exploration of the depth and extent of film's spirituality. Particularly important for our purposes in this book on God's revelation outside the church has been the repeated claim that the film event can, at times, be revelatory.

To reference just the last decade, since the turn of the millennium a number of books have come out, each making the assertion that movie viewing can be the occasion for God to be revealed. Andrew Greeley wrote in *The Catholic Imagination* (2000) that the sacramentality of creation can be "a revelation of the presence of God," and followed this up the same year with a book cowritten with Albert Bergeson, *God in the Movies* (2000).[4] In that book, and in his earlier *God in Popular Culture* (1988), Greeley argues that film was especially suited for the making of sacraments and the creating of epiphanies. In fact, the filmmaker (as artist) at times discloses God's Presence "even more sharply and decisively" than God has chosen to do through creation itself. "The pure, raw power of the film to capture a person who watches it, both by its vividness and by the tremendous power of the camera to concentrate and change perspectives, is a sacramental potential that is hard for other art forms to match." One such movie that became sacramental for Greeley was *Places in the Heart*, where the final scene of the communion of the saints became for him an occasion to again meet God.[5]

Ken Gire's popular study also from 2000 was titled *Reflections on the Movies: Hearing God in the Unlikeliest Places*. My own book *Reel Spirituality* came out first in 2000 and is now in its second edition (2006). In it, I argue that movies can be "a window through which God speaks." They can be "the occasion not only to know about God but to know God."[6] In the book I give a number of examples, including my own experience of hearing God call me into the Christian ministry while watching Richard Burton play Becket in the movie by that name. Edward McNulty's two volumes titled *Praying the Movies* (2001, 2003) seek for the readers "that elusive moment . . . an 'Aha!' moment, when the Spirit awakens us to something special in the film. It may be an act of one of the characters, a word, a song, an image, or the way all the elements of a shot or scene come together in the perfect way, making us aware that we are on holy ground."[7] David Dark's award-winning book in 2002 is titled *Everyday Apocalypse: The Sacred Revealed in Radiohead, The*

4. Andrew Greeley, *The Catholic Imagination* (Berkeley: University of California Press, 2000), 1.

5. Andrew Greeley, *God in Popular Culture* (Chicago: Thomas More, 1988), 245–50.

6. Robert K. Johnston, *Reel Spirituality: Theology and Film in Dialogue*, 2nd ed. (Grand Rapids: Baker Academic, 2006), 249.

7. Edward N. McNulty, *Praying the Movies*, vol. 2, *More Daily Meditations from Classical Films* (Louisville: Westminster John Knox, 2003), 13.

Simpsons, and Other Pop Culture Icons. In it he finds *The Truman Show*, *The Matrix*, and the movies of the Coen brothers to be stories that open unto epiphany.[8] Published in 2002, as well, was the article by Catholic film scholar Richard Blake, "From Peepshow to Prayer: Toward a Spirituality of the Movies,"[9] where he argues that the religious dimension of film is to be found not in the moviemaker's intention or in the overtly religious content of the movie but in the observer-critic's experience.

Gareth Higgins's reflection on movies that had personal significance for him is titled *How Movies Helped Save My Soul: Finding Spiritual Fingerprints in Culturally Significant Films* (2003); John Walsh, in *Are You Talking to Me? A Life Through the Movies* (2003), gives an autobiographical account of the power that film can have. Walsh affirms that "all my life I [have] been storing up images and dialogue and epiphanies from the movies that [have] come to mean more to me than my own true-life experiences."[10] The study guide Catherine Barsotti and I wrote in 2004 was entitled *Finding God in the Movies*. In 2010, Roy Anker's second book, *Of Pilgrims and Fire*, had as its subtitle, *When God Shows Up at the Movies*, certainly a more assertive subtitle than in his first volume on theology and film, *Catching Light: Looking for God in the Movies* (2004). But even in 2004, Anker could write that "when it does show up, grace befalls unlikely and unsuspecting people in surprising and unforeseeable ways that are quite beyond human prediction, conception, or charting."[11] In both his books, God's revealing Light is what allows Anker to focus clearly.

Gerard Loughlin's introduction to the anthology *Cinema Divinite*, edited by Eric Christianson, Peter Francis, and William Telford in 2005, is titled "Cinema Divinite: A Theological Introduction"; and Chris Deacy's and Gaye Williams Ortiz's book in 2008, *Theology and Film*, had as its subtitle *Challenging the Sacred/Secular Divide*. In the opening chapter, Chris Deacy argues that movies can perform a religious function "in a way that is no less enchanting, nourishing, emotionally intense, and transcendental [than in the church]."[12] And to annotate one last book, the subtitle of Craig Detweiler's

8. David Dark, *Everyday Apocalypse: The Sacred Revealed in Radiohead, The Simpsons, and Other Pop Culture Icons* (Grand Rapids: Brazos, 2002).

9. Richard Blake, "From Peepshow to Prayer: Toward a Spirituality of the Movies," *Journal of Religion and Film* 6, no. 2 (October 2002): n.p., www.unomaha.edu/jrf/peepshow.htm.

10. John Walsh, *Are You Talking to Me? A Life Through the Movies* (London: Harper-Collins, 2003), 12, quoted in Christopher Deacy and Gaye Williams Ortiz, *Theology and Film: Challenging the Sacred/Secular Divide* (Oxford: Blackwell, 2008), 39.

11. Roy Anker, *Catching Light: Looking for God in the Movies* (Grand Rapids: Eerdmans, 2004), 17.

12. Christopher Deacy, "Theology and Film," in Ortiz and Deacy, *Theology and Film*, 39.

second book on theology and film, *Into the Dark*, also published in 2008, was direct and to the point: *Seeing the Sacred in the Best Films of the 21st Century*. In his preface, Detweiler chronicles how and why he came to consider film a source of divine revelation, and then the book develops this thesis by considering movies from the list of top films on the Internet Movie Database (IMDB).[13] Moreover, Detweiler not only responds to the stories of these movies but also engages anecdotally with the IMDB's massive online community, looking for concrete evidence in the testimonials of their viewing events of God's Presence.

What all these books have in common (and I have listed a larger number than is perhaps necessary, so as to document that this understanding is typical within the field of theology and film and not unique to one or two authors) is the claim that movies can be a means of grace whereby God speaks to us. Film can, in the words of the filmmaker Paul Schrader, "take a viewer through the trials of experience to the expression of the Transcendent."[14] In the language of the Septuagint translation of the book of Exodus, they can be the occasion, or event, for us to "see the voice" of the Lord (Exod. 20:18). We will want to put this theological claim into conversation with biblical resources, the tradition, and contemporary theological scholars in the chapters that follow, but here our goal is to annotate and illustrate these claims with the testimony of filmgoers themselves.

Learning from Movie Viewers Themselves

The question might legitimately be raised: Though critics make the claim that film provides viewers an experience of God's revelatory Presence, is there much to substantiate the claim beyond a few anecdotal testimonials by those writing in the field? Have we perhaps confused the religious use of film with a religious experience through film? Have these critics simply read back into their experiences their theological beliefs, finding what they wanted to find? Have they simply offered a theoretical, or theological, hypothesis without adequate supporting documentation, or careful grounding of the film as film, a work of art? What evidence might one adduce to back up the critics' claim that God appears at the movies? In what sense might we understand "reel spirituality" to literally be a "real spirituality"?

13. Craig Detweiler, *Into the Dark: Seeing the Sacred in the Top Films of the 21st Century* (Grand Rapids: Baker Academic, 2008).

14. Paul Schrader, *Transcendental Style in Film: Ozu, Bresson, Dreyer* (New York: Da Capo, 1988), 169.

Too much of the reflection on theology and film in the initial decades (1980–2000) remained second-order abstraction, theologically freighted rhetoric that was largely independent of the experience of the filmgoer. When such criticism honestly engaged a film, moreover, it focused its reflection more on the "content" of the movie than on its reception. It spoke more "about" God than "of" God. This is, of course, understandable, for on one level the claim of God's Presence, of epiphany, in the artistic event can't be proven. There is no logical, formal, or evidential proof, as George Steiner has so eloquently argued.[15] Thus, it was far easier to ignore such judgments, particularly in the context of late modernity when a rationality modeled on the then-accepted norms of science and technology prevailed, "objectivity" being the approved standard of public discourse. But though a content-oriented criticism, when sensitively done, has a rightful place in theology and film studies, it becomes misleading and mistaken when it overlooks the experience of film watching itself, an experience that at times has included divine encounter. As Clive Marsh has argued persuasively, we "need to attend to what films actually do, rather than what religion scholars and theologians would like to think they do."[16] Only then can we be true both to film as a medium of communication/communion, and to theology, which arises out of a first-order experience with its Source.

Hearing the Critics' Own Stories

As noted in chapter 2, with the dawn of the new millennium, there has been a new willingness to engage spirituality in public discourse. It is this, I think, that lies behind the increased openness of theology and film authors during the last decade also to speak of film-going as the occasion for spiritual experience, for finding God at the movies. And not surprisingly, they have often referenced themselves and their own experiences as their starting point. We have noted Andrew Greeley, for example, who narrated how his watching the eschatological worship service at the end of *Places in the Heart*—where black and white, abused and abuser, are together—ushered him into the sacramental Presence

15. George Steiner, *Real Presences* (Chicago: University of Chicago Press, 1989), 214. Such is the final paradox of all discussion of God's revealing, sacramental Presence, of those "vibrations to the primal," to use Steiner's evocative phrase (ibid., 223). There will always be a sense in which we do not fully know what we are experiencing, nor do we fully know of what, or whom, we speak. As Steiner correctly asserts, "There is a sense in which no human discourse, however analytic, can make final sense of sense itself" (ibid., 215). The experience of the numinous is unprovable; but it is also foundational for all meaning in art.

16. Clive Marsh, "On Dealing with What Films Actually Do to People: The Practice and Theory of Film Watching in Theology/Religion and Film Discussion," in *Reframing Theology and Film: New Focus for an Emerging Discipline*, ed. Robert K. Johnston (Grand Rapids: Baker Academic, 2007), 146.

of God. His experience parallels my own, described in *Reel Spirituality*, when watching *Becket* was the occasion for me as a college freshman to hear God speaking.[17] Both of these movies have "religious" themes or subthemes.

A more "secular" example of a movie's numinous possibility might be the description Craig Detweiler offers in *Into the Dark*, where *Raging Bull* proved revelatory to Detweiler as a teenager. Detweiler relates how Robert DeNiro's haunting and brutal portrait of boxing champ Jake LaMotta left Craig beaten and bruised. As a high school "jock," he recognized far too much of himself in Jake. But after going through a figurative, if not literal, hell, the movie ends with the credits reading, "All I know is this, once I was blind, but now I can see." Detweiler relates that he did not at that moment understand fully this biblical text, nor did he comprehend that the boxing ring was a metaphorical re-creation of the crucifixion. Instead, this violent, R-rated movie simply put him on a spiritual search, for he had heard God asking him to open his eyes to his Presence all around him. This numinous event soon eventuated in his seeking to know more of God through attending a Young Life meeting. There, he says, he heard the gospel and responded to all he'd heard and read about Jesus.[18] And though not a common experience for Detweiler, this would not prove the only such film-forged theological event for him.

More recently, Detweiler has again written personally, this time of his experience watching Terrence Malick's *The Tree of Life*. After praising the artistic brilliance of this poetic meditation on a family's grief over the loss of their son, Detweiler commences a theological conversation. He not only puts the movie in dialogue with the Bible, from Genesis to Revelation, particularly focusing as Malick did on the book of Job, but he also becomes personal about what the viewing did to him. Writing about the mother's final surrender of her son to God, as the music of Berlioz's "Agnus Dei" sounds forth and a field of sunflowers appears, Detweiler writes,

> The power of her surrender snuck up on me. Having lost my sister in a car wreck, I am well acquainted with the grief central to the story. Yet I did not anticipate how purgative *The Tree of Life* would become. I had never encountered such purity in a movie. The film did not insist. It hardly coerced. It merely offered a comforting, divine possibility. How can all dross be removed from a movie frame? The mystery left our audience in stunned silence. No one moved. A spirit of peace washed over the screening room. We wanted the sacred stillness to linger.[19]

17. See Johnston, *Reel Spirituality*, 37–39.
18. Detweiler, *Into the Dark*, 13–14.
19. Craig Detweiler, "*The Tree of Life*: Cinema in Conversation," http://www.patheos.com /blogs/dochollywood/2014/02/tree-of-life-from-genesis-to-revelation/.

The "after-image" of Roman Catholicism in *Raging Bull* and the Christian beliefs of Terrence Malick in *The Tree of Life* might still suggest that a certain subset of "religious" movies is operative when we speak of a transcendent experience that viewers might have. And certain movies do seem to be referenced more often than others when viewers recall those movies through which they have seen the Divine as present. But interestingly, the movies named are rarely those with explicit Christian content—those that stray into the field of propaganda too easily. Rather, it is those movies that tell a good story that seem to find deep resonance among some of their viewers. For Roger Ebert, it was the Japanese movie *Ikiru* (d. Kurosawa) that spoke to the core of his being.[20] For Jeffrey Overstreet, it was *The Story of the Weeping Camel* (d. Davaa and Falorni).[21] These are anything but "religious" movies. Similarly, it is hard to label Quentin Tarantino's *Pulp Fiction*, for example, a religiously themed movie, though Ezekiel 25:17 is referenced. Nevertheless, it was the event of seeing this violent movie that proved the occasion of Greg Garrett's experiencing God's revelatory Presence.

In his book *The Gospel according to Hollywood* (2007), Garrett testifies that he found while viewing *Pulp Fiction* those "glimmers of the gospel" through film, those "moments in popular culture narratives where we can find inspiration and spiritual illumination."[22] He says he had no idea that theologians and film critics would debate the significance of the movie.

> All I knew was that when I left the theater, it was as a slightly different person than I was when I went in—slightly more hopeful, slightly more open to the possibility that there might be a God (and to the possibility that he, she, or it might be moving in my life), and more than a little anxious to have that kind of experience with the holy again.[23]

Similar to John Updike (whose reflection opened the chapter), Garrett concludes:

> *Pulp Fiction* became a touchstone in my growing faith, more meaningful than most sermons I'd heard and most church services I'd sat through. Like many in church and even more outside it, I have found that God can sometimes speak to me as powerfully through elements of the culture as through a formal religious service or in a religious setting.[24]

20. Roger Ebert, preface to Albert J. Bergesen and Andrew M. Greeley, *God in the Movies*, vii–ix.
21. Jeffrey Overstreet, *Through a Screen Darkly* (Ventura, CA: Regal, 2007), 16–40.
22. Greg Garrett, *The Gospel according to Hollywood* (Louisville: Westminster John Knox, 2007), xiv.
23. Ibid., xv.
24. Ibid.

For Garrett, who teaches English at Baylor University, discretion and discernment are necessary in any claim of divine encounter, and one must always approach the sacred through the film narrative itself, with its plot and characters, image and tone. "But," writes Garrett,

> if we believe in incarnation—that is, both the Judeo-Christian belief that God created the world and the Christian belief that God willingly entered into creation as a human being—then the world is indeed, as Gerard Manley Hopkins wrote, "charged with the grandeur of God," and with wisdom, prayer, and persistence we can discern God in the works of God's creation and in our own creations as well.[25]

Listening to the General Moviegoer

Those writing about theology and film are one obvious source for data concerning the experience of hearing God's revelation through or at the movies. A second source is the testimonials of the average filmgoer. In an effort to capture something of this perspective of "the person on the street," I have solicited the testimonials of several hundred of my students over the last three years, asking them to write about a movie they watched that might have proven to be an important spiritual event for them. I also have found the recent doctoral dissertation by Jonathan Brant to be of help. Brant uses insights from Paul Tillich's theology of revelation to help identify and understand the experiences of a sample of filmgoers at a Latin American cinema festival. It is to these two additional sources that we now turn as we hear testimonials of those who have sensed God's revealing Presence at the movies.

Student Testimonials

For the last three years, I have asked seminary students in my theology and film classes to write a two-page reflection paper on the one movie that was particularly significant to them spiritually. I asked, "Which movie has proven to be your most significant spiritual experience as a film watcher? Were there any?" The students were to describe the movie briefly, then give their experience spiritually with it, and end with what, if anything, resulted from their viewing. My question was put in writing so that all were given the same instructions. The language I used was also purposely left open-ended and ambiguous, with no definition of "spiritual experience" being provided. Rather than starting with a given film and then asking them to discuss its spiritual significance for them (something akin to what Chris Deacy and Craig Detweiler did in analyzing

25. Ibid., xviii.

the online responses of IMDB), I instead chose to begin with testimonies of students' spiritual experiences at the movies, however varied these might be, for I wanted to have recorded those particularly intense or important events at the theater when transformation and/or spiritual insight might actually have occurred. It was not the particular film that I was investigating in this case, but the variegated experience of "transcendence" that might occasionally be present for the moviegoer that I wanted to explore.

Partly stimulating my question was the story that Richard Viladesau narrates about an encounter between Albert Einstein and the violinist Yehudi Menuhin after a concert, a story I have already referenced.[26] Einstein met the virtuoso backstage and said, "Thank you, Mr. Menuhin; you have again proven to me that there is a God in heaven." What did the scientist mean? Were the words to be taken only figuratively? Or had Einstein had an experience of Transcendence, something music seems particularly able to do? In a similar way, would the students in their reflections speak of a Transcendent (capital *T*) experience mediated through a movie, or rather was their experience more akin to that transcendence (small *t*) that T. S. Eliot describes as a "still point in a turning world" or C. S. Lewis describes as "transcending myself"?[27] Would the respondents speak of something transformative in their lives, or simply numinous? Or both? Or neither? Would my initial question to them be understood in terms that proved spiritually educational or spiritually enlightening? The reason for the vagueness of the question was to allow such differentiations to surface. I wanted the viewers themselves to shape the nature of their response according to their own perception of their experience.

Interestingly, to the question "Which movie has proven to be your most significant spiritual experience as a film watcher?" the responses fell somewhat evenly into three groups, though in some of the descriptions, students moved freely back and forth between these differing meanings, and in a smaller number of cases, they were unable to identify any such experience:

(1) One group of students was quite sure that they had not had an encounter with the Divine through watching a movie, but nonetheless narrated a movie-watching experience in which a spiritual truth had been garnered or its understanding deepened. Often, but not always, such "educational" experiences were in response to movies with religious, or quasi-religious, themes— *Shawshank Redemption*, *The Ultimate Gift*, *The Passion of the Christ*, *A Walk*

26. Albert Einstein, quoted in Richard Viladesau, *Theological Aesthetics* (New York: Oxford University Press, 1999), 104.

27. T. S. Eliot, "Burnt Norton," *Four Quartets*, in T. S. Eliot, *The Complete Poems and Plays, 1909–1950* (New York: Harcourt, Brace & World, 1971), 119; C. S. Lewis, *An Experiment in Criticism* (Cambridge: Cambridge University Press, 1961), 141.

to Remember, Lars and the Real Girl, Lord of the Rings, Mother Teresa, Simon Birch, Signs—or movies that had clear Christ figures—*The Green Mile, The Dark Knight*, and so on. These students found such movies to function for them as theological parables. A sample of the language they used to describe the connection between the movie they saw and the experience they had makes clear the intellectual nature of the spiritual connection:

"whispered truth"	"was like"
"was representative of"	"exemplified"
"was symbolic of"	"demonstrates"
"reminded me of"	"is telling me"
"highlighted"	I "was moved to reevaluate"
"forced me to consider"	"I learned from"
"was deeply informative"	the movie's themes "allowed me to reflect"
"allowed me to picture"	"provided space for theological reflection"
"helped me to understand"	"led to deep reflection"
"taught me"	"allowed me to wrap my head around"
"caused me to discover"	"I got a glimpse of"

(2) Others wrote how they perceived through their moviegoing experience something greater, or other, or whole. They were unsure whether they had had a divine encounter or rather simply an experience that was enhancing to their own spirit. But in either case the watching of a particular movie proved life transforming. The language students used suggested that theirs was more of a "spiritual" insight through the story that had been experienced than a "Spiritual" experience of an Other that was revealing something to them. But sometimes the language was ambiguous (no doubt like the experience itself). They spoke of a "profoundly human moment," of "tears of identification" related to a particular movie event as bringing "personal fulfillment" or change. Their experiences were described as extraordinary and illumining, but not necessarily Divine. For these viewers the world and/or their personal lives took on spiritual depth and texture because of the movie they saw. But these moviegoers were reluctant to say they had actually met God at the movies.

(3) Last, a third group wrote how they had, they said, a divine encounter, an experience of the holy, which proved transformative in their lives. They were quite clear in their claims. What all the individuals in this group had in common, though they identified a wide variety of movies with no common genre or theme, was their clear sense of discovering themselves to be in the Presence of God, even as, or particularly as, they immersed themselves in the

film story itself. In each case, the movie's story had merged with their own stories, resulting in a divine encounter that changed their lives.

What these reflection papers suggest is that while asking filmgoers about a spiritual experience they might have had through film made sense to most people, the question also meant very different things to different people. Some remembered a film experience that was Spiritual (capital S); others reported of a movie that evoked a profound "spiritual" experience (small s); and still others found in a particular movie a parable of Christian truth that deepened their theological understanding of their faith. All three responses, though different, seemed genuine and unforced, if for no other reason than they were repeated in different groups at different times with different movies over a three-year period. Though it was certainly the case that not every movie my students saw would have evoked such responses (like all art, whether paintings, or novels, or music, the majority are forgettable or already forgotten, not to mention that what a viewer brings to the experience is equally important to any communion/connection that transpires), almost all of my students testified that they had had encounters with a "reel spirituality" that was indeed a real spirituality. In an analogous way, perhaps, to how Christians over the centuries have tried to describe natural theology (something we will take up in chapter 6), my students found in watching a particular movie either (1) a support for, or deepening of, their previous understanding of their faith; (2) the occasion for personal, spiritual growth, insight, or direction; or (3) an encounter with the Divine. Whether the movie was thought Transcendent, spiritual, or supportive of Christian truth, what stood out to the vast majority of students polled was the capacity of film to touch their spirit.

Though all the responses are valuable and fascinating (testimonials have a compelling power), it is those students' reflections who testified to revelatory experiences in and through a film event that will be our focus here, for theirs relate to the topic of this book. We will center on those who claimed to have had while watching a film an epiphany, an encounter with God. But so this third option can better be heard in its specificity, let me offer a brief sample from each of the other two categories, examples that would define film's spiritual power and meaning in alternate ways.

Receiving Theological Knowledge

Among those students who gave testimonials about a particularly meaningful spiritual experience through watching a movie, there were those who said that their experience of film was edifying because at the Cineplex they found in a particular film a parable, a visual reminder of Christian truth, a metaphor of Christian theology that proved compelling. Perhaps representative was the story of one student's experience viewing David Lynch's *The Elephant Man*. He related how that movie, based loosely on historical circumstance, allowed him to see more clearly, through eyes filled with tears, the God-given shape of the human. John Merrick was a badly deformed man, relegated to the circus sideshow in nineteenth-century England—that is, until he was rescued from its horrors by Sir Frederick Treves, a medical doctor at the London Hospital. Through a series of circumstances, including Treves and his boss overhearing John recite the twenty-third Psalm after years of silence (for no one thought he had anything worthwhile to say), John is rescued from his hellhole and becomes the talk of London society. When he is invited to have tea with Dr. Treves and his wife, John tells them that he wished his mother could see him now with his lovely friends: "Perhaps she could love me as I am. I've tried so hard to be good." As Mrs. Treves begins to cry uncontrollably given John's confession, so did my student. He wrote that every time he sees the scene, he realizes anew that he, like John, is a creation of God—that in fact, as Flannery O'Connor might say, "God is found most beautifully in the 'grotesque.'" For this student, John Merrick showed him "a full humanity: in suffering, in faith, in hope, and in love."

Receiving Transformative Spiritual Insight

Others who described a profound spiritual experience that they had had while watching a movie wrote of the movie event they experienced as not so much deepening their theological understanding as providing them spiritual insight, often accompanied with a personal transformation that had ongoing consequences. Two examples of the many testimonials to this end may suffice.

One woman, Jill, described a moviegoing experience she had as a high school student. She went to see Terry Gilliam's *12 Monkeys* (1996) with her boyfriend. She was a cheerleader and he, a star football player. The movie tells the story of survivors who fled beneath the earth's surface because of a contagion, but who send back a prisoner to gather information about what is going on. On his journey, James Cole (Bruce Willis) meets a psychiatrist (Madeleine Stowe) and an institutionalized mental patient (Brad Pitt). The musical score adds particularly to the story's dark and dramatic texture. As the young woman left the theater with her boyfriend, she says she felt a restlessness in her heart. She too sensed a contagion. The movie, she said, was smart, "brilliantly dark and deep." Her boyfriend, however, said, as he emerged into the light of the lobby, "That movie sucked. What a mess, I don't know what the hell it was even about."

The woman said that "something happened that night while watching *12 Monkeys*, which awakened my spirit." She said she realized she was living a cliché. "I realized, quite clearly, that I was capable, or better, that I was made to be someone other than who I had grown into." "Miraculously," she wrote, "and at the time inexplicably, it took only two hours to turn my life upside down, from the inside out. The revelation that I related more to the patients in the mental hospital than to my boyfriend sitting next to me finally forced me to stop ignoring this intrinsic pull to live my life differently and to allow myself to think about exploring life differently." This seminary student related that at the time she saw the movie, she was "not a Christian, not really interested in becoming one." But what those in the Methodist tradition might call the prevenient grace of God was at work. This student refrained from talking about this experience as the work of the Spirit, though it might have been. She did, however, conclude by saying that her life after that was never the same. "I didn't come to know Jesus until years after my exodus from that theater, and it required a lot of pain to get there. But as it would seem, Jesus was with me before I knew His name. Something miraculous, something transcendent, shifted in me that evening . . . and it was not the Army of 12 Monkeys."

Even more dramatic an account of a movie's potential for spiritual transformation was the testimony of a woman in her thirties, Carol, who in her twenties was the victim of a home invasion robbery during the Christmas season. Raped, robbed, kidnapped, pistol-whipped, and shot, she was left for dead in an empty lot. Over the next five years, as she attempted to send the perpetrator to jail, her life spiraled downward, out of control and in the clutch of post-traumatic stress disorder. Depressed and self-medicating with drugs and alcohol, she entertained thoughts of suicide. Then, as it was Christmas and the anniversary of her assault once again, the Frank Capra movie *It's a Wonderful Life* came on the television. She had never seen it. Sitting in her alcoholic haze in front of the television screen, she identified with George Bailey (played by Jimmy Stewart), whose dreams had been dashed at every turn, though he had tried to help others all of his life. She too had always tried to be good, though living in a borderline-abusive household she could never live up to her parents' expectation. Her dreams, and theirs, given the assault, had been crushed, just as George's had. Like George, she had thought, "It would have been better if I had never been born."

However, as she watched a gentle Angel named Clarence show George that all his simple acts of kindness had been important to the community where he lived, my student said her perspective on her own life also began to shift. "The gift this movie provided me with," she wrote, "was small hope." She explained,

> Following this period I no longer entertained thoughts of quitting life, but [had] a desire to find meaning in what had occurred to me. If the daily decisions

that George Bailey made had such a profound influence on those around him, [maybe] the decisions that I was making, even the smallest, most insignificant, [might] have a profound influence on those around me.

The student concluded her reflection by saying that though she was unsure whether the movie experience was "a divine encounter" or simply something that was "spiritually enhancing," she had no doubt that it was "life transforming." That day she realized that, like the movie reveals, all life has a rippling effect both for good and bad. While the trauma and its effects continue to ripple through her life today, she realized that "the good news is that those righteous decisions we make ripple just as profoundly as the negative ones."

Encountering God

There was in some of the student testimonials an ambiguity as to whether their viewing of a movie had been the occasion for the Spirit of God's inbreaking into their world or rather whether it had been a profoundly moving experience of the re-centering and grounding of their spirit. But for perhaps a quarter of the students, there was no doubt as they described their movie-viewing experience that they had encountered God—that God had revealed his Presence to them through the truth, beauty, and goodness portrayed on the screen, or the lack of it. And the result was consistently transformative, whether immediately or more gradually.

One older student, John, recalled seeing *Easy Rider* with his friends three times one Saturday afternoon in 1969, soon after the movie came out. He spoke of the movie in detail some forty years after his viewing experience. He wrote, "I walked into the film as one person and exited virtually as another, awakened to new ideas and options." This iconic film about two counterculture bikers who travel cross-country from Los Angeles to Mardi Gras in search both of America and of meaning in their own lives is a classic road movie. Thus, there is not much plot, with meaning coming in the form of the interaction of the "buddies" both with each other and with those they meet along the way. Captain America (Peter Fonda) and Billy the Kid (Dennis Hopper) encounter hitchhikers, bigotry (given their countercultural lifestyle), jail, and even the death of a friend. They pick up a drunken lawyer played by Jack Nicholson (his breakout role). And they visit a gentle hippie religious commune in New Mexico. There, they encounter a group of single adults and young families who have rejected the materialism and consumerism of their past (the American dream) for a return to the earth. The travelers watch as the community puts on a costumed play and plants crops in hard soil. They also observe those in the commune as they clasp hands, praying for "simple food for our simple tastes." My student wrote, watching the hippie commune, "I felt a remarkable sense of calm and well-being, as if a cool hand were put upon my brow."

When Fonda leaves with Hopper "on a quest towards Mardi Gras nothingness," John wrote that he felt a "visceral sense of dread, what I would now describe as a panic attack, a tightening in my chest as if a hand squeezed my heart." Moreover, he said, "a voice in my head compelled me to say to a comrade, 'Man, they just blew it.'" Both his friend and this student were later startled when near the end of the film's uneasy ride, Captain America speaks these identical words—of "blowing it," of not finding that meaning they had set out to find. Though the movie leaves it ambiguous as to how they precisely "blew it," it was crystal clear for this viewer. Though John had never lived in community, the next day, a Sunday, he boarded a bus for downtown Washington, DC, in search of a similar community. Here surely was where Jesus would live. He says, in that movie, "there was a depiction of faith that my spirit craved." These idealistic Jesus hippies made such an impression on him that his journey toward Jesus began that day. Forty years later, he still lives communally as a Christian. *Easy Rider* had proven revelatory.

Some who wrote of their spiritual experience in and through a movie said it was difficult to only pick one, for there had been "so many profound experiences." They identified themselves as "extremely easily moved" and thus experienced "God's presence in nearly every film" they saw. Laura wrote this summary:

> Movies can help us experience God. . . . Throughout my life I have gone through periods . . . when I struggle with my relationship with God. I doubt his presence in my life and am angry that things are not different for me. Each time I have found myself in this uncomfortable place with God, I am brought back into close relationship with Him through films. Here is a brief list of a few of the movies that have helped restore my relationship with God: *Magnolia*, *About Schmidt*, *Dancer in the Dark*, *Bella*, *Maria Full of Grace*, and *City of God*. Each of these films spoke to me at very specific points in my life. With all of these movies, when I arrived at the theater . . . I had no idea that I was about to experience significant transformations and messages. One may think I am exaggerating when I say transformation, but I honestly can say that a number of these films have completely changed the way I view my interactions with others, my humanity, the power of love, the beauty of forgiveness, and grace. I truly believe God can be experienced these ways and numerous others through art, but specifically movies.

Others admitted that they would describe "very few of them as transcendent." Jessica wrote, for example: "I do not typically experience film in a deeply personal and spiritual way. However, last summer I was pleasantly surprised when I encountered God unexpectedly in, of all places, a children's film. Disney Pixar's *Toy Story 3* was the last place I expected to have a transcendent experience with a film, yet the unassuming packaging of a children's movie provided the perfect opportunity for an unexpected spiritual encounter." What connected with Jessica in the film was the theme of growing up and moving on from one's childhood. She had been a fan of Woody, Buzz, and the rest of Andy's toys since as an eight-year-old she had seen the original *Toy Story* (1995). Expecting only a fun, simple little movie, she instead experienced through Andy's character "a reflection of my own childhood and transition to adulthood." As Andy handed down his toys to little Bonnie, she said she "experienced a sudden and unexpected rush of emotions, which ultimately resulted in crying." For Jessica, too, was also about to embark on a major life transition of her own—she had just gotten engaged. "Seeing *Toy Story 3* allowed (me) to express and confront those bittersweet emotions associated with making a major life transition." Here, she said, was God's way of helping her process her feelings and telling her it is okay. "I learned from this experience," she wrote, "that God can speak to you and meet you in the most unexpected places, for who would have ever thought that a 23-year-old woman would have seen herself in a fictional, animated, 18-year-old boy who was giving his toys away."

Others who shared their testimony of a particularly meaningful spiritual experience at the movies spoke of the divine consolation they experienced as they dealt with the divorce of their parents while watching *Now and Then*, or the divine invitation they sensed to be reconciled to their father as they watched the endings of *Field of Dreams* and *Big Fish*. (Both of these movies were cited multiple times.) One student said he "encountered the divine" while experiencing a poverty far exceeding anything he knew in *Slumdog Millionaire*. The movie helped him find his calling in assisting "the least of these" in our global village. And echoing the same theme of calling (as might be expected from a sample of young adult writers), another student now enrolled in Fuller's doctoral program in psychology described how the movie *Lars and the Real Girl* was the occasion for hearing God call her to serve God by helping those like her brother who had serious mental illness.

Some Tentative Conclusions

It is, of course, both difficult and perhaps dangerous to generalize on these unique testimonies. Experience is particular. But there are also commonalities (and the lack of such) among the many reflections that we have observed. Four observations might prove instructive. First, personality type, while a factor, seems not to have been determinative as to whether someone had a numinous experience. Whether the students said they had had many transcendent experiences at the Cineplex or few, whether they cried easily or very rarely, encounters with the Divine seemed to transgress all such borders. In almost every case, what was important, instead, was the deep resonance the viewer felt between something in the film narrative (or image or music) and the viewer's own present life. A connection, a parallel, was felt.

Second, the theme of the movie that proved significant in the lives of these student viewers was sometimes religious and sometimes not. The movie's "religious" content seems not to have been the critical factor, though it might be present. David, for example, was not a Christian when he saw *The Last Temptation of Christ*. Indeed, he was skeptical of all things Christian, and identified it with Pat Robertson, Jerry Falwell, Jim Bakker, and Tammy Faye. If he was to believe, he said, "I needed a breakthrough; I needed something amazing, transcendent, beautiful beyond anything I'd ever seen. I also needed a reason to convert to Christianity." Scorsese's cinematography and Peter Gabriel's musical score in the movie proved for him transcendent; the film's atmosphere lent itself to a spiritual experience. "This beauty was a breakthrough for me," David wrote, "a counter to the ugly side of Christianity that was holding me back." The movie event also influenced this student theologically, giving him a "reason" to believe. If Jesus was tempted in every way possible, Satan appearing to Jesus as a little angel and asking why he couldn't live a sexually fulfilling life like the rest of humankind, and yet did not succumb, then here was someone worthy of belief. David testified that the movie changed the course of his life, causing him to accept Christ as his Savior. But if some movies that opened out into a transcendent experience were explicitly theological, an equal number were not. The movie *Crash* made God immanent to one of the students in my classes, while *Up* provided a transcendent and spiritual experience for another (do we risk saying a "high"?). It spoke to the student, reminding her to relax and enjoy the gift of life.

Third, many of the movies that became transparent to the divine were classics that will endure—they appear on many of the all-time best lists: *Wings of Desire*, *The Tree of Life*, the *Star Wars* trilogy, *Shawshank Redemption*, *Magnolia*, *It's a Wonderful Life*, *Up*, *Finding Nemo*, *Toy Story 3*. The quality of a film matters . . . but, again, not always. Other movies that became the occasion for a divine encounter were assuredly not artistically significant: *Man on Fire*, *Matrix: Reloaded*, *I Heart Huckabees*. The experience of transcendence mediated within and through the created world that is central to both *Wings of Desire* and *The Tree of Life* produced a desire "to live in a constant state of wonder" for two of my students. But equally powerful was the metaphor of two distinct realms in *Matrix: Reloaded*. As Jessica left the movie theater after seeing it, she knew that she must learn to see the supernatural in the natural on a consistent basis. She testified that she had received "a transcendent experience that positively influenced my spiritual life."

Last, some, in reflecting on their experience of watching a movie, made clear use of the language of other Christian theologians. That is, though we can for purposes of theological discussion disconnect the Spirit's revealing Presence in the church and through Scripture from that which occurs outside the church and without reference to the Christian faith, we also know that there is but one Spirit. Church and world, special and general revelation, actually intersect and merge in our lives. And they did in the student reflection papers as well. Christopher, for example, coming from the Reformed tradition, wrote of his "worldview" being challenged by *Shawshank Redemption*. Just as Red had become institutionalized, so he had become institutionalized in his thinking and dreaming. He needed to be shocked alive into realizing that "the kingdom of God was a hope that reminds Christians that there are places in the world that are not made of stone."

Or to give a second example, Jonathan's reflection on the original *Star Wars* trilogy, something he didn't see until its rerelease in 1997, filled him with a divine sense of awe and wonder. In describing his experience, interestingly and I think perceptively, he references the notion of "Northernness" in C. S. Lewis's *Surprised by Joy*. In chapter 6, I will broaden our conversation to similarly dialogue with Lewis and other theologians who have tried to understand God's Presence and revelation in the world. But here it is enough to note that some of these seminarians who experienced the transcendent in a movie event already came to that experience with theological categories that helped them to describe and understand it. But again, not all. There were also those like Matt, who in watching *Magnolia* discovered that his understanding of God was too small. Matt's theology had not found a place for God to be present and intimately involved in the dirty lives of addicts, misogynists, child molesters, ex–child stars, and other losers. It wasn't until he watched the frogs fall from the sky, changing the destiny of so many in that movie, that he realized that God was not only active in their lives but also that "God's hand is intimately involved in the dirty life of mine also." He says *Magnolia* forced in him a change in his theology: "I realized that something of God could be learned through a movie that involved transparent portrayals of sin." There were also those like Jill who encountered God's Presence watching *12 Monkeys* and John who experienced God's revelation watching *Easy Rider*, or another who met God watching *American Beauty*. None of these individuals had any theological background or understanding. Instead, as with the Athenians whom Paul addressed in Acts 17 (and whom we will reflect on in chapter 4), God revealed himself to them not from out of the Judeo-Christian tradition but in terms of the light that they had.

Some who have just read this reflection based on the testimony of close to two hundred students as to one particularly meaningful spiritual experience they have had watching a movie might well respond that such experiential sightings are anecdotal and from a skewed sample, far too random and un-systematized to provide any sure foundation for doing theology. Alternate explanations can be offered for much that the students have concluded, and Christian theological presuppositions (after all, they are seminarians) have too often colored their judgments for any of these testimonies to be thought reliable. These might just as possibly be human projections, however sincere.

While we will indeed need to test these testimonies by putting them into theological conversation with both biblical insight and the Christian commu-nity's theological reflection, and this we will do in the chapters that follow, it is important to note at the outset that such autobiographical reflections do square with the testimony of the wider culture we live in, as we have seen. They are culturally congruent with the reflection already developed in chapter 2. In that chapter, we noted Hay and Hunt's comprehensive report on the "Soul of Britain Survey" (2000), where 76 percent of the population acknowledged they had had a spiritual encounter (whether an awareness of the Presence of God, or receiving help in prayer, or experiencing the Presence of evil or, perhaps, a sacred Presence in nature, and/or an experience that all things are "one").[28] We also noted George Barna's survey in the United States (also 2000) that 20 percent of Americans turned to "media, arts and culture" as their primary means of spiritual experience and expression, and the trajectory suggests that this number might rise to 30 or 35 percent by 2025.[29] Moreover, what is being claimed here is not that all the judgments are correct, only that here is a meaningful beginning point for a reflection on general revelation. It is the case that approximately one quarter of the students sampled said that they encountered God while watching a movie.

28. David Hay and Kate Hunt, "Is Britain's Soul Waking Up?," *The Tablet*, June 24, 2000, 846; and David Hay and Kate Hunt, "Understanding the Spirituality of People Who Don't Go to Church, a Report on the Findings of the Adults' Project at the University of Nottingham," August 2000, http://www.churchofscotland.org.uk/_data/assets/pdf_file/0006/3678/understanding _spirituality_report.pdf.
29. George Barna, *Revolution* (Wheaton: Tyndale House, 2005), 48–49.

Here then is a second answer to the question, Can a reel spirituality be a real spirituality? The testimony of moviegoers, like that of theology and film scholars, would suggest an affirmative answer to the question. Both are analogous to typical discussions of natural theology, where definitions remain debated and debatable, and the shape of the answer therefore varies significantly. But such comparisons will need to await a later chapter. Here, we turn in conclusion of this chapter to consider the research of Jonathan Brant, who, finding a helpful analogue in Paul Tillich's theology of revelation through culture, uses Tillich's categories to investigate the possibility of such revelation through film among attendees at a film festival in Montevideo, Uruguay.

Film Watchers in Latin America

Complementing my informal polling of students in my theology and film classes at Fuller Seminary is the careful doctoral work Jonathan Brant has recently done at Oxford University, subsequently published in 2012 as *Paul Tillich and the Possibility of Revelation through Film*. Conversant with those, like myself, who are writing in the field of theology and film, he desires to test our claim that film can be "not just a helpful conversation partner for the theologically pre-informed but a possible medium of God's presence."[30] Quoting, among others, from my book *Reel Spirituality*, he asks whether "art forms help us not only to know about God, but to actually experience God."[31] In seeking an answer, Brant focuses his empirical research on the viewing experience of a group of moviegoers who are part of a cinema club in Montevideo, Uruguay. His interest in his research, like mine in this chapter, is in describing the way film functions in and influences its viewers spiritually.

In his investigation Brant chooses to use Paul Tillich's theology of revelation through culture as "a heuristic lens" to investigate and analyze the particular experiences of these urban filmgoers.[32] He says he found Tillich's account compelling "because of its phenomenological attentiveness to real-life experience, notably his [Tillich's] own experience, of the power of art."[33] But would filmgoers agree that they had experienced what Tillich described as "revelation"? Here was his research question. Brant believed that by developing a grounded account rooted in qualitative research, he would be able to answer this question.

30. Jonathan Brant, *Paul Tillich and the Possibility of Revelation through Film* (New York: Oxford University Press, 2012), 7.
31. Johnston, *Reel Spirituality*, 17, quoted in ibid., 7.
32. Brant, *Paul Tillich*, 8.
33. Ibid., 14.

In spelling out Tillich's theology of revelation, Brant deals rightly with four stages in its development: (1) Tillich's autobiographical statements; (2) his preexilic German writing before he came to the United States while fleeing the Nazis; (3) his mature discussion as reflected particularly in his three-volume systematic theology; and (4) the critical debate Tillich's theory has generated. Not all of this need concern us here. But central, surely, is Tillich's testimony to his experience of art's revelatory possibility as he came back from the horror of World War I and gazed in a Berlin museum at the Botticelli painting *Madonna with Singing Angels*. I have already referenced this event in the opening pages of this book. One of Tillich's several accounts of that event, written in 1955 for *Parade* magazine, a weekly insert in newspapers across America, is worth repeating here in detail, however, both because of its relevance to this chapter's theme and because Brant handed it out to the filmgoers he was about to interview. Tillich wrote:

> Strangely, I first found the existence of beauty in the trenches of World War I. To take my mind off the mud, blood and death of the western front, I thumbed through the picture magazines at the field bookstores. In some of them I found reproductions of the great and moving paintings of the ages. At rest camps and in the lulls in the bitter battles, I huddled in dugouts studying this "new world" by candle and lantern light.
>
> But at the end of the war I still had never seen the original paintings in all their glory. Going to Berlin, I hurried to the Kaiser Friederich Museum. There on the wall was a picture that had comforted me in battle: *Madonna with Singing Angels*, painted by Sandro Botticelli in the fifteenth century.
>
> Gazing up at it, I felt a state approaching ecstasy. In the beauty of the painting there was Beauty itself. It shone through the colours of the paint as the light of day shines through the stained glass windows of a medieval church.
>
> As I stood there, bathed in the beauty its painter had envisioned so long ago, something of the divine source of all things came through to me. I turned away shaken.
>
> That moment has affected my whole life, given me the keys for the interpretation of human existence, brought vital joy and spiritual truth. I compare it with what is usually called revelation in the language of religion. I know that no artistic experience can match the moments in which prophets were grasped in the power of the Divine Presence, but I believe there is an analogy between revelation and what I felt. In both cases, the experience goes beyond the way we encounter reality in our daily lives. It opens up depths experienced in no other way.[34]

34. Paul Tillich, "One Moment of Beauty," in Paul Tillich, *On Art and Architecture*, ed. John Dillenberger and Jane Dillenberger (New York: Crossroad, 1989), 234–35.

Tillich previously had described this event in his 1952 lectures at the Minneapolis School of Art as "revelatory ecstasy," as "an ecstatic feeling of revelatory character." He said, "A level of reality opened to me which had been covered up to this moment, although I had some intimations of its existence."[35] Looking back as an older man on the influence of that experience, Tillich recognized that the concept of a "breakthrough," which dominated his theory of revelation, came from that moment.[36] The experience, he said, was transformative, opening him to an element of depth in human experience that provided him a "potent analogue" for talking about religious experience more broadly.

Though these descriptions lack a certain precision, as Brant points out, there is also enough coherence across his various retellings to accept Tillich's claim of having experienced revelation through culture. As Brant describes it, Tillich's theory of revelation through culture had six aspects: the individual as the recipient; the artwork as the medium; the event itself; the content of the revelation; its effect on the recipient; and the relationship of such revelation to Jesus as the Christ, someone who was fully transparent to the Being itself.

In order to identify those who might have had comparable experiences to that of Tillich, Brant developed a survey document with questions that might suggest parallel experiences. Besides more general film-related questions and demographic information, he asked participants in the film club,

- "Looking back on your life, is there one exceptionally memorable occasion when a Latin American film shook, transformed, or healed your life?"
- "Was there any particular connection with your life? Did you identify with a particular character? The setting? A particular event?"
- "How long ago did the experience occur?"
- "How would you describe the nature of the experience?" (Participants were given four choices: Intellectual, Emotional, Aesthetic, Spiritual.)
- "At any point in the experience did you sense a presence or a power (it doesn't matter whether you would call it 'God' or not) that is distinct from your everyday life?"
- "How would you relate the experience to what was going on in your life at that time?"
- "Was there an impact on your life?"[37]

35. Paul Tillich, "Art and Society," in Tillich, *On Art and Architecture*, 12.
36. Paul Tillich, *On the Boundary: An Autobiographical Sketch* (New York: Charles Scribner's Sons, 1966), 28.
37. Brant, *Paul Tillich*, 237–42.

Based on the results of these questionnaires, Brant identified from his larger group eleven filmgoers who seemed to have had analogous experiences in the cinema to what Tillich described at that Berlin museum. To test his hypothesis, he then gave to these individuals a brief description of Tillich's life, thought, and understanding of revelation, together with autobiographical paragraphs quoted above from *Parade* magazine. He then proceeded to ask these moviegoers a series of qualitative questions with the intent of discovering whether they, like Tillich, believed that art, in this case cinema, could function as "revelation," transforming, shaking, or healing their lives. Would they be happy to describe their experience(s), like those they had discussed regarding a particular film they had seen, as revelatory? Had there been a breakthrough? And would they, after reading Tillich's encounter with Botticelli, say they had ever experienced something similar?

Not surprisingly, Brant notes that those interviewed, like Tillich, could identify the medium, the event, the content, and the effect of their experience. The event was triggered by a particular film; moreover, the event was not merely "subjective," for it had an objective component, too, even if it remained a mystery (Tillich's terms in his systematic theology are "ecstasy" and "miracle.")[38] And though the film had specific content, this must "become transparent or must be ruptured at the moment of revelation in order to provide access to the religious depth or substance beneath."[39] The moviegoers said the impact of the experiences was *me ha marcado*—"it has marked me." There was, in Tillich's phrase, a "breakthrough."

Thus, alongside my informal survey of students and complementing it, Brant's empirical research chronicles much the same experience as my own students narrated. Both his quantitative surveys and then his qualitative research confirm the same experiential contours a number of us working in the field of theology and film have posited. For some, film provides an experience of "reel spirituality."[40] God can be found in popular culture.[41] God is heard in the unlikeliest places.[42] Movies can at least metaphorically help save one's soul—that is, can heal and transform.[43]

38. Paul Tillich, *Systematic Theology*, 3 vols. (Chicago: University of Chicago Press, 1967), 1:124–30.

39. Brant, *Paul Tillich*, 198.

40. See Johnston, *Reel Spirituality*.

41. See Craig Detweiler and Barry Taylor, *A Matrix of Meanings: Finding God in Popular Culture* (Grand Rapids: Baker Academic, 2003).

42. See Ken Gire, *Reflections on the Movies: Hearing God in the Unlikeliest of Places* (Colorado Springs: Cook Communications Ministries, 2000).

43. See Gareth Higgins, *How Movies Helped Save My Soul: Finding Spiritual Fingerprints in Culturally Significant Films* (Lake Mary, FL: Relevant Books, 2003).

Here then is an experiential witness to put alongside the repeated witness of those who encountered God through experiences in nature. Whether in creation or culture, God's wider Presence is experienced by many. But how can this be understood theologically and biblically? Are we simply baptizing the neo-Romantic claims of our post-Christian age?

4

Broadening Our Biblical Focus, Part 1

I n Psalm 19, the psalmist combines two quite distinct expressions of praise for God's revelation of himself into one song. The first half, which most commentators believe originally stood alone as its own hymn, focuses on God's revelation through creation: "The heavens are telling the glory of God" (vv. 1–4). With speechless speech their voice is nonetheless clear. Here is praise for what John Updike describes as "supernatural mail." It had "the signature: decisive but illegible."[1] Though no audible words are heard, communion is achieved and knowledge communicated, even in its mystery. The second half of this psalm moves on to praise God's revelation of himself through the perfect law of God (vv. 7–10)—a law that revives the soul, rejoices the heart, and enlightens the eyes. God's Word is more desirous than fine gold; it is sweeter than honey. Uniting in one paean of praise two types of revelation that otherwise might seem distinct, and grounding each on its own solid footing, the psalmist ends with a prayer that recognizes both his own inadequacy and the mystery of God that remains. He hopes his words and his murmurings (two responses paralleling the two kinds of revelation he has experienced) will be acceptable to God (v. 14), who remains beyond him. Whether in creation or redemption, the psalmist has experienced God's transformative revelation.

1. John Updike, "Packed Dirt, Churchgoing, A Dying Cat, A Traded Car," in *Pigeon Feathers and Other Stories* (New York: Random House / Fawcett, 1963).

And while special revelation (the law/Torah) might reveal more and open one up to God as Redeemer, it does not cause the psalmist to be dismissive of his creationally based experiences that also have produced awe and wonder.

It is a similar experiential focus that offers the best potential for understanding a biblical theology of general revelation today—one that, while also giving praise for God's fuller revelation in law and gospel, does not reduce general revelation to little more than the "footprint" of God's past activity, or subsume general revelation under special revelation, creation theology under salvation theology, the work of the Spirit in Creation under the Spirit of Christ. Given the repeated testimony of the last two chapters, the witness of those both within and without the church as to the Presence of God's Spirit in their lives—given, that is, the witness of many to revelatory experiences that have occurred outside the walls of the church and without direct reference to salvation—we need to reevaluate theologically what has too often been ignored as "illegible" without recognizing the testimony of so many that it has also been "decisive." We need, in particular, to again read the Scriptures asking what they might be saying to us in this regard. We need to inquire as to what examples of God's wider revelation are found within Scripture's pages. Have we as a Christian community been guilty of ignoring God's witness to the wideness of his revelation?

In asking these questions of the Scriptures, we need to avoid falling prey either to a natural theology that reduces general revelation to mere traces of God's past activity embedded in creation or creature (such "footprints" are not revelation, but its remainder), or to a redemptive triumphalism that reduces general revelation merely to the grounds by which humankind is declared guilty by God and in need of his saving grace (this is not the experience of those who have been transformed by such experiences). In asking these questions, we also need to temporarily suspend any "hermeneutic of suspicion." We need instead to enter into a sympathetic reading of the biblical texts. Rather than seeking an "objectivity" in our inquiry, we need to recognize that we all come to the Bible with our own personal commitments and questions. In this case, we seek to discover how the God of the Scriptures might reveal himself in the wider world beyond the boundaries of the church. Such a perspectival reading of the Bible need not run roughshod over careful exegesis of the text, though this danger is always present in any interpretation. Rather, it seeks to provide focus and perspective on the texts themselves through the use of new "spectacles." As we bring to the Bible a set of specific concerns, we often see new truth.[2] Wearing new spectacles, we read fundamentally differently—or

2. A particularly telling example of this is John Stott's two editions of his pamphlet on the Holy Spirit. The first was written prior to the beginning of the charismatic movement in the

perhaps to better state the knowledge trajectory, the text is read fundamentally differently by us. The knower's perspective is crucial in the knowledge equation, as we know, but it is what is known (the text) that delimits the discussion. Phyllis Trible says it well: "While multiple readings are not *per se* mutually exclusive, not all interpretations are thereby equal. The text, as form and content, limits constructions of itself and does in fact stand as a potential witness against all readings."[3]

Walter Brueggemann, in his *Cadences of Home: Preaching among Exiles*, refers to Paul Ricoeur's three worlds of a text. There is first "the world behind the text." Here is the particular *provenance* of redaction criticism that seeks to re-create the text's setting-in-life (*Sitz im Leben*). There is also "the world in front of the text," what Brueggemann describes as "a world of possibility generated by the text, which inspires, empowers, and permits hearers of the text to live and act differently on the basis of the substantive claim of the text." Here is the focus of reader-response criticism. But for both Brueggemann and Ricoeur, like Trible, most crucial is "the world in the text"—that is, "the dramatic transactions that are offered within the confines of the text wherein the several characters of the text—including Yahweh, the God of Israel—interact with each other in ways that 'the world behind the text' would never permit. It is the primary work of interpretation, so Ricoeur urges, to live in 'the world in the text,' in order to see what is permitted and required by the transactions given there."[4]

My aim in this chapter as we reread the Bible perspectivally is to explore all three worlds of the text, while concentrating on "the world in the text." My goal is not so much technical precision as it is insight and illumination. George Steiner has it right in quoting as his epigraph in *Real Presences* the artist Georges Braque: *Les preuves fatiguent la vérité* ("proofs weary the truth").[5] In a similar vein, Bill Dyrness writes about his use of the Bible as not being so much like reading a blueprint as it is playing a musical score.[6] One can obviously make mistakes while playing a Mozart sonata, and there are certainly

---

1960s and before he hired a charismatic minister as one of his colleagues at All Souls Church in London. With a new focus on the present power and in-breaking of the Spirit, Stott rewrote his pamphlet, not removing much if anything that had been written before, but adding a new understanding of the power and Presence of the Spirit today.

3. Phyllis Trible, *God and the Rhetoric of Sexuality* (Philadelphia: Fortress, 1978), 11.

4. Walter Brueggemann, *Cadences of Home: Preaching among Exiles* (Louisville: Westminster John Knox, 1997), 60.

5. George Steiner, *Real Presences* (Chicago: University of Chicago Press, 1989), epigraph.

6. William Dyrness, "How Does the Bible Function in the Christian Life?," in *The Use of the Bible in Theology: Evangelical Options*, ed. Robert K. Johnston (Atlanta: John Knox, 1985), 159–74.

wrong interpretations not allowed by the score—the score is not infinitely elastic. But scores are more than analytical instructions concerning technological precision. Robots or automatons might play music "correctly," but they will not enrapture. Their preciseness tends to produce sterility. Rather, a musical score provides the opportunity for nuance and collaborative creativity, one that continues its invitation anew in each new performance.[7]

Such perspectival readings will result in "thick descriptions," to borrow a phrase from the sociologist Clifford Geertz.[8] Again, Brueggemann can be helpful in charting our way. He speaks of the "practice of density" in our interpretation of a biblical passage. In our reading of Scripture, he believes, we have too often been guilty of

> a thinning of the text, so that the text is read only at the surface. On the one
> hand, thinning of the thick text and consequent loss of density has happened
> through theological reductionism, in which rich texts are flattened to serve creedal
> certitude. On the other hand, there is no doubt that historical criticism is [also]
> a thinning maneuver, designed to make irascibly complex texts amenable to
> Enlightenment rationality, to eliminate the haunting inscrutability of the text.

But despite such theological reductionism and biblical-critical thinning, "texts have persisted in their density, refused to be diluted, ever again available in richness, knowing that if denseness is uttered, 'they will come.'" Brueggemann writes of a God "who leaks out beyond good doctrine. However, the maddening leakage is there in the text, waiting to be spoken of in faith and in dismay." He says, "We know so little, having listened so poorly and hosted so carelessly. We are not ready to hear, but the text itself readies us."[9]

As we listen anew to the text (or see with new spectacles, to keep with our primary metaphor), our goal is to consider the theological significance of those biblical texts where God presents himself outside of sacred text, sanctuary, or prophetic utterance. It is a theological reading of the text that we seek. What might these texts teach us about God? In saying this, however, caution is needed lest we be tempted to say too much. As Psalm 19 reminds us, God remains mysterious, even in his revelation to us. Peter Rollins reminds his readers of the multiple biblical texts that speak of a "thick darkness" where God is, an impenetrable veil that shields us from God's unmediated Presence (see

7. A parallel might be observed in the current comeback of vinyl. According to many, "digital recordings are good on your iPod, but vinyl allows the music to be heard."

8. Clifford Geertz, "Thick Description: Toward an Interpretive Theory of Culture," chap. 1 of *The Interpretations of Cultures* (London: Fontana, 1993).

9. Brueggemann, *Cadences of Home*, 74–77.

Exod. 20:21). Even revelation is a concealment. There is mentioned at times in Scripture God's intentional hiddenness (see Isa. 45:15). Moses needs to be protected from God's Presence by hiding in the cleft of the rock (see Exod. 33:21–23). Gideon and Manoah also fear God's full Presence (Judg. 6:22; 13:22). Elijah covers his face before approaching the cave where God stands (1 Kings 19:13). Even the seraphim cover their eyes (Isa. 6:1–5). Psalm 97:2 describes God as having about him clouds and thick darkness. Again, in the New Testament we hear of God's invisible nature (John 1:18), inaccessibility (1 Tim. 6:15–16), inexpressibility (2 Cor. 12:4), and unsearchable nature (Rom. 11).[10] Though the topic at hand is God's revelation, God's mystery and inscrutability remain a given. Here is the biblical starting point of any theology of revelation, a humility before Mystery. God is beyond us, even as he is present with us.

The Old Testament Writings

Proverbs

As I have begun to reread the Bible with my experience of general revelation as my "spectacles," new texts have come to life. A beginning point has been the Wisdom literature of the Old Testament. Here the focus is reflection on the goodness of created life, not the narration of the story of salvation history, though later Jewish writers would eventually bring together creational and redemptive themes (see Sirach, Wisdom of Solomon, and the epilogue of Ecclesiastes). Job, Proverbs, Ecclesiastes, Song of Songs, and selected psalms focus on the "kerygma of life," to borrow the felicitous phrase of Roland Murphy.[11] These books, as Walther Zimmerli reminded modern scholarship fifty years ago, think resolutely within the framework of creation theology. Mention of God's saving acts in the exodus event is largely lacking. So too is appeal to the law. Instead the power and authority of these texts is rooted in the experience of life itself. And shockingly to some, these texts have as one of their sources the wisdom (do I risk saying "spiritual insight") of those outside of the covenant community of faith.

Proverbs, for example, is a collection of collections of proverbs. Its theological introduction (1:1–9:18) is followed by "the proverbs of Solomon" (10:1–22:16); "the words of the wise" (22:17–24:22); the "sayings of the wise" (24:23–34); "other proverbs of Solomon that the officials of King Hezekiah

10. Peter Rollins, *How (Not) to Speak of God* (Brewster, MA: Paraclete, 2006), 12–19.
11. Roland E. Murphy, "The Kerygma of the Book of Proverbs," *Interpretation* 20, no. 1 (January 1966): 3–14.

of Judah copied" (25:1–29:27); "the words of Agur son of Jakeh," followed by some numerical sayings (30:1–33); "the words of King Lemuel . . . that his mother taught him" (31:1–9); and a final description of a capable wife (31:10–31). That many of the proverbs are attributed to Solomon comes as no surprise. After all, Scripture records that "God gave Solomon very great wisdom, discernment, and breadth of understanding as vast as the sand on the seashore, so that Solomon's wisdom surpassed the wisdom of all the people of the east, and all the wisdom of Egypt" (1 Kings 4:29–30). We have recorded practical examples of Solomon's wisdom as seen in the narrative about the two women fighting over whose child it is who was still alive (1 Kings 3:16–28). But equally telling was his composition of proverbs and songs, and his ability both to "speak of trees, from the cedar that is in the Lebanon to the hyssop that grows in the wall," to "speak of animals, and birds, and reptiles, and fish" (1 Kings 4:32–33). Solomon's wisdom was of such repute that the queen of Sheba visited him to pay homage (1 Kings 10), and the biblical text records that he wrote three thousand proverbs and over a thousand songs (1 Kings 4:32).

Equally interesting as the collection of proverbs attributed to Solomon, however, are three of the other smaller collections, each having their origin outside Israel's believing community—each, that is, sensitive to and building on God's wider Presence. Each merits our particular attention.

1. The words of Agur (Prov. 30:1–14). What is surprising about the multiple collections of sayings that make up the biblical book of Proverbs is not Solomon's presence, but the stated sources of other proverbs. No one knows who Agur is. He is not mentioned in any biblical or extrabiblical texts. The identity of Jakeh is similarly unknown. But almost all biblical scholars are in agreement that these are not Israelites, and there is no indication that the source of Agur's wisdom is to be interpreted as coming from within the covenant community of Israel. Most likely, these two are from the tribe of Massa. The title in verse 1 is traditionally translated, "The words of Agur, son of Jakeh. An Oracle." But the majority of scholars today think that the Hebrew word translated as oracle (*massa'*) should actually have a minor emendation made to it, since "an oracle" seems redundant after "the words." If this emendation is made, then the text is actually saying, "The words of Agur, son of Jakeh, a Massaite," and Agur's location becomes known. Agur, then, is a member of a tribe in Arabia related to the Israelites and mentioned in Genesis 25:14 and 1 Chronicles 1:30. Others think "an oracle" should remain as the translation, and that it indicates perhaps that Agur is a foreign prophet, like Balaam (see Num. 24:3–4 and the discussion below). But in either case, this collection of fourteen verses (or perhaps of all thirty-three verses in the chapter, for one overarching theme runs throughout the chapter) comes from outside of the people of God.

It is important to note that Agur's words are in a different style and tone than most of Proverbs. They remind one more of Ecclesiastes and Job, suggesting perhaps the collection was one of the last included in this collection of collections. Rather than signal a detached confidence in their understanding of the world that God has made, Agur's words signal a weariness and caution before the mystery of God, given the limits of human understanding. He writes,

> Surely I am too stupid to be human;
>   I do not have human understanding.
> I have not learned wisdom,
>   nor have I knowledge of the holy ones [or Holy One].
> Who has ascended to heaven and come down? (Prov. 30:2–4)

Some debate why these verses are included in Proverbs at this point. But it would seem they are here near the end of the book to remind readers of the need for humility. Proverbs are not to be interpreted in a dogmatic fashion. Wisdom is based not in our ability to figure everything out, but in trust in God. We might wrongly conclude from the chapters of wisdom sayings in Proverbs that we can confidently understand the world and how to live in it. Our observations mistakenly become rules. But life's enigma remains and God's mystery endures. Here in the penultimate chapter of the book, Agur reminds us not to divorce the quest for human wisdom from its source—God. There is a need for humility.

It must be said, however, that such a message, one that finds parallels in the Mesopotamian Dialogue of Pessimism and presages Job and Ecclesiastes, though surprising in this context, is not the biggest theological surprise in this text. Rather, what is shocking is that here Israel has recognized in the international wisdom of one of its neighbors God's revelatory truth and has thus included Agur's proverbs as part of its holy Scripture. It is not just that non-Israelite wisdom has been put into conversation with Israel's wisdom, which is thought superior to it (1 Kings 4:29–34). Rather, in and through Agur's words, God's people heard God speaking—heard divine revelation in the words of this Arabian wise man. They thus included his reflection as part of the inspired Scripture, a text judged "on par" with the words of the prophets. Here, general revelation and special revelation have been conflated.

2. The words of King Lemuel . . . that his mother taught him (Prov. 31:1–9). In a similar way, King Lemuel's words, based on his mother's teaching, seem also to have an international source. The list of Israel's kings makes no mention of a "Lemuel." Yet the wisdom his mother taught him was thought by Israel to be God's revelation to them. Rabbinic tradition associated Lemuel

with Solomon, telling the tale of Solomon marrying Pharaoh's daughter on the day of the temple dedication. Others have hypothesized that Lemuel was the name Solomon was called by his mother! But such apocrypha is without foundation. As with the opening sentence of the sayings of Agur, if the Hebrew word translated as "oracle" (*massa'*) is given a minor emendation, then the text actually identifies Lemuel as a Massaite, a member of a tribe in Arabia. But whether this is true or not, it seems to be the case that Lemuel's mother's instruction is from outside the Israelite community. Here again is God's inspired Scripture, divine revelation, given through someone outside the believing community.

With Lemuel's mother's instruction, we have a "royal instruction," a genre common in Egyptian wisdom as well. Like other such instruction, Lemuel is warned against women who can destroy him and drink that can pervert his thinking, making him insensitive to the poor and needy.

> Do not give your strength to women. . . .
> It is not for kings to drink wine. . . .
> Or else they will drink and forget what has been decreed,
> And will pervert the rights of all the afflicted. (Prov. 31:3–5)

Distinctive of this collection is the fact that its advice comes not from the king but from the queen mother. Few other portions of Scripture are authored by a woman. But more distinctive surely is the fact that such advice comes not from an Israelite queen but from someone who does not worship Yahweh. God's revelation to his people is thus seen as not being limited to the law (Torah) and the prophets. It does not come only from those who worship the God of Abraham, Isaac, and Jacob. Instead, the poetic speech of a foreign queen mother is also recognized by the believing community as inspired and God-breathed. Here, special revelation and general revelation become one.

3. The words of the wise (Prov. 22:17–24:22). It is not just these two collections of proverbs by "outsiders" that have become part of the book of Proverbs' sacred canon, moreover. Most scholars are in agreement that the compiler of Proverbs also made intentional use of a third collection of non-Israelite proverbs, this one based in the thirty sayings of the Egyptian Instruction of Amenemope (22:17–24:22).[12] Amenemope's sayings have been freely adapted to be sure. And it is in the opening verses of this section that one discovers most of the connections to this Egyptian work. Many scholars believe that perhaps the reliance on Amenemope ends with Proverbs 23:11. But regardless

---

12. See D. Winton Thomas, ed., *Documents from Old Testament Times* (New York: Thomas Nelson & Sons, 1958), 172–86.

of the freedom with which the Israelite writer adapted this Egyptian collection of proverbs for his purposes or whether he moved on to other matters later in the collection, it is also the case that the editor/collector of these proverbs does not hide the use of his non-Israelite source. Near to the beginning of his admonitions, he writes:

> Have I not written for you thirty sayings
>   of admonition and knowledge,
> to show you what is right and true,
>   so that you may give a true answer to those who sent you? (Prov. 22:20–21)

Translators struggled for centuries with the seeming non sequitur in these verses. Why in the midst of "the words of the wise" (22:17–24:22) would the writer mention "thirty sayings," since it is by no means clear to any reader of Proverbs where these "thirty" sayings are. Failing to find a meaningful referent and struggling with a disputed text, translators, even in the earliest of days, tried amending the word to help make sense of the text. Some thought it meant "formerly" or "previously"; others, that it meant "excellently" or "nobly." The Greek Septuagint and the Latin Vulgate translate the word as "triply," and then interpret the resultant adverb allegorically as meaning "excellently" or "fully." But almost all scholars today believe the most plausible translation of the Hebrew to be "thirty" (*salisi(w)m*; "sayings" has been added in the English translation for felicity of expression). And they reference the "thirty" by relating it to the Instruction of Amenemope.

The story behind this consensus is an interesting one. In 1922, Sir Ernest Budge, an Anglican Egyptologist working for the British Museum, finally got around to giving a short account of the papyrus roll containing the Instruction of Amenemope, one of the Egyptian wisdom writings confiscated over thirty years prior and put in the museum's collection. As he read, he noted what he thought were familiar-sounding proverbs. Turning to the Old Testament, he discovered repeated similarities with Proverbs 22:17–24:22. And Amenemope had thirty sayings! Ensuing study has established a strong linkage between the two collections of proverbs.[13] Amenemope dates from the period of Egypt's New Kingdom (1558–1085 BCE), most probably in the thirteenth century. The text is the instruction of an official, Amenemope, to his son who is serving

13. The first scholar to follow up on this discovery and argue that the text of Proverbs made use of Amenemope was Adolf Erman, "Eine agyptische Quelle der Spruche Salomos," in *Sitzungsberichte der preussischen Akademie der Wissenschaften zu Berlin, Phil. Hist. Klasse* 15 (1924): 86–93.

in the Egyptian bureaucracy. Thus, there is little doubt as to the direction of the borrowing; Amenemope was written long before Solomon or the rise of Wisdom literature in Israel.

Both Proverbs and Amenemope open the same way:

> Give thine ears, hear what is said,
> Give thy mind to interpret them.
> To put them in thy heart is beneficial. (Amenemope, chap. 1)

> Incline your ear, and hear my words,
>   and apply your mind [heart] to my teaching;
> for it will be pleasant if you keep them within you,
>   if all of them are ready on your lips. (Prov. 22:17–18)

The introductions of the two documents end similarly as well: "so that you may give a true answer to those who sent you" (Prov. 22:21) and "to bring back a report to one who hath sent him" (Amenemope, preface). Other sayings influenced by this Egyptian wisdom writing follow. In fact, six of the nine opening sections in the Proverbs collection begin with a word or phrase that finds its exact counterpart in Amenemope. The second chapter speaks of "robbing the wretched" (cf. Prov. 22:22, "rob the poor"). Proverbs 22:24 begins, "Make no friends with those given to anger, and do not associate with hotheads," while Amenemope chapter 9 states, "Associate not with the hot-head." Other sayings in Proverbs reference Amenemope's "remove not the landmark" (cf. Prov. 23:10) and "labor not to seek for increase" (cf. Prov. 23:4). Where Proverbs says, "for suddenly it [wealth] takes wings to itself, flying like an eagle toward heaven" (Prov. 23:5), Amenemope chapter 7 says, "They have made themselves wings like geese and are flown away to heaven." Though there has been adaptation and recontextualization to be sure, the similarities are striking.

Here again, we note God's general revelation from outside of Israel as discovered in human observations (through "conscience," "creation," and "human creativity"). This time it is Egyptian culture that has been brought into Israel's life and even made a part of its special revelation—the Scripture that Jesus himself used. Egyptologists, in examining Amenemope, have sometimes noted its religious tone, a "quality of inwardness."[14] Perhaps here is why Hebrew

---

14. Miriam Lichtheim, quoted in Roland E. Murphy, *The Tree of Life: An Exploration of Old Testament Wisdom Literature*, Anchor Bible Reference Library (New York: Doubleday, 1990), 24; see the introduction to "The Teaching of Amenemope," in Thomas, *Documents from Old Testament Times*, 174: "Amenemope has a special message to convey. Morality matters, and the source of true morality is religion."

wisdom was open to this work. But whatever the reasons, we can conclude that the final redactors of the book of Proverbs recognized God's voice in these sayings. God was here revealing aspects of the sacred shape of created life to those neither part of the covenant community nor believers in Yahweh.

This revelation as received was not seen by Israel as oppositional to the law. In fact, those late in Israel's history would understand the law and such wisdom as having the same source—the Most High who was both "the Creator of all things" and the giver of "the law that Moses commanded us" (Sir. 24:8, 23). But in Proverbs these two sources of Yahweh's revelation are kept distinct—creation is not yet combined with redemption.

Chronicles

A more careful reading of the biblical text through the "spectacles" of God's revelation outside his redemptive community also brings to light new perspectives on Chronicles. Both Proverbs in its final form and Chronicles reflect a similar *Sitz im Leben* (setting in life) for its authors/editors—the postcaptivity period. At that time, questions about Israelite faith and life included not only the need to explore the shape of the human and a renewal of worship life, but also the role of Israel's God given the presence of and interrelationships with neighboring cultures that did not worship Yahweh. These Old Testament writers/editors had a similar question in mind: In what sense was Yahweh to be understood as God of the whole world, as well as the covenanting God of his people? They also had similar answers—ones that were more inclusive and accommodating than other portions of the Old Testament (e.g., Ezra-Nehemiah).[15]

One important means by which the Chronicler addressed this more international concern was by reshaping the stories of how Israel's kings interacted with other royalty in the ancient Near East. Three accounts in particular invite a closer reading, for they have been altered from or have been added to their original source material in 1 Kings, and in this way have been reshaped theologically to address new concerns.

1. King Neco of Egypt (2 Chron. 35:20–27). The first is the account of King Josiah and King (Pharaoh) Neco in 2 Chronicles 35:20–27. Here the Chronicler both refocuses and adds material to the brief account of Josiah's death that is recorded in Kings (2 Kings 23:29–30). After narrating the "faithful deeds" of this great monarch, the writer of Kings concludes by saying that King Josiah

---

15. See G. N. Knoppers, "Intermarriage, Social Complexity, and Ethnic Diversity in the Genealogy of Judah," *Journal of Biblical Literature* 120, part 1 (2001): 15–30. See also Louis Jonker, *1 and 2 Chronicles* (Grand Rapids: Baker Books, 2013), 62–63.

went to meet Pharaoh Neco, who was traveling through Israel to Assyria. Neco met him at Megiddo, but killed him (v. 29). His servants then took Josiah's dead body by chariot to Jerusalem, where he was buried, and a new king was appointed (v. 30). It is all very matter of fact.

The Chronicler, on the other hand, expands this brief description of "what is written in the law of the Lord" in the book of Kings, shifting the roles of the protagonists and having Josiah not die until he is carried back to Jerusalem, where he is universally mourned. The writer adds to the sparse description in Kings the account of King Neco (the word "pharaoh" is not used), who, while on his way to fight in Carchemish on the Euphrates (modern-day Iraq), sent envoys to Josiah saying that he was coming to fight not Judah but rather the "house with which I am at war," and "God [*elohim*] has commanded me to hurry" (2 Chron. 35:21).[16] The envoys conveyed Neco's message, saying, "Cease opposing God [*elohim*], who is with me, so that he will not destroy you" (v. 21). That is, let me pass through your territory unopposed, for this is God's will.

But Josiah, who had always done "what was right in the sight of the LORD [Yahweh]" (34:2), who had "repair[ed] the house of the LORD his God" (34:8) and had "found the book of the law of the LORD given through Moses" (34:14), who was penitent and had "made all who were in Israel worship the LORD their God" (34:33) and keep "a Passover to the LORD in Jerusalem" for the first time since the days of Samuel (35:1), this king did not believe Neco could be conveying an authentic message from God. After all, it was Josiah who knew Yahweh by name, not Neco; it was Josiah who had rediscovered Israel's Scriptures, the Lord's special revelation to his people, and had them read it, not Neco; and it was Josiah who worshiped the Lord in Jerusalem, not Neco. By what possible logic could he conclude that Neco was speaking accurately about God's desire for Josiah? Surely his words were based in deceit or projection, or so Josiah reasoned. And even if Neco had heard these words, they were to be referenced to Neco's own god, someone impotent before Josiah's God. And so King Josiah rejected Neco's words as being from Yahweh and instead disguised himself in order to fight. And then the text reflects: "He [Josiah] did not listen to the words of Neco from the mouth of God [*elohim*], but joined battle in the plain of Megiddo" (35:22), and Josiah was killed. The Chronicler

16. Most scholars believe Neco was going to lend support to Assyria in its battle with Mesopotamia. From the Babylonian Chronicles, we learn that indeed Neco came *on behalf of* Assyria, not against Assyria, which might be assumed from the brief description in the book of Kings. The Chronicler drops this confusing reference in Kings as he tells the account. A number of scholars believe that the Chronicler must have had access to some other information. See Sara Japhet, *1 and 2 Chronicles: A Commentary* (Louisville: Westminster John Knox, 1993), 1045, 1056.

relates that all Jerusalem mourned the passing of Josiah, even Jeremiah, who uttered a lament (v. 25, cf. Jer. 22:15–16).

What is telling in this recounting of Josiah's actions is the theological failure of Josiah to recognize that Yahweh might also be revealing himself to and through an Egyptian pharaoh, perhaps even through an Egyptian pharaoh's "false" religion. Neco's description of a "generic" spirituality—his reference to *elohim*—or, worse, his reference to his own Egyptian god, seemed paltry and surely mistaken, given Josiah's lifetime of covenantal faithfulness. It was the people of God who should be telling this pharaoh what it was that the Lord (Yahweh) desired, not vice versa. After all, Israel read the law. After all, it was they who worshiped God aright in Jerusalem. Would many in the church today think any differently?

But the Chronicler moves in another direction. He is at pains to remind his readers that the Lord is God of the whole world, even Egypt, and he reveals himself to others including King Neco, not just to the covenant community. King Josiah, despite his exemplary, reforming activity and his personal piety, was not beyond criticism in Scripture. He joins a long list that includes Noah, Abraham, David, and Solomon. His failure to listen at a critical juncture to Yahweh through the testimony of King Neco cost him his life. Josiah's conception of God was too small.[17] Josiah, who had been a youthful zealot and lifetime follower of God's revelation (the Book of the Law), and who just one chapter earlier (2 Chron. 34:22–28) had willingly consulted the prophet Huldah, ironically dies because he is not open to hearing God's revelation as mediated through the spirituality of King Neco.

Interestingly, the retelling of Josiah's life story does not end with the Chronicler. First Esdras, one of the Old Testament apocryphal books, opens with still another recounting of Josiah's life. Like Chronicles and Ezra-Nehemiah, which are its sourcebooks, the interest in 1 Esdras is in the worship life of postexilic Israel, something that 1 Esdras considers as having its foundation in the reforms of Josiah. And so the story is told still a third time. But while the Chronicler had King Neco be the messenger of God—of Israel's God—despite the fact (or because of the fact?) that Neco worshiped his own deities and was not a believer or perhaps even a sympathizer in Yahweh, the writer of Esdras finds this a scandalous thought. So he puts Yahweh's message of

17. It is interesting to note the many similarities between the Chronicler's retelling of Josiah's encounter with Neco and his narration of King Ahab's death. In both, (1) the king disguises himself, (2) is wounded in battle, (3) by an archer, (4) requests that he be "taken away, [(5)] for I am badly wounded," and (6) is put in a chariot. If this comparison is intentional, it only reinforces the tragic ending of a very good king who closes his ears to God at a crucial time and pays the price.

warning to Josiah into the mouth of Jeremiah: "Josiah . . . did not heed the words of the prophet Jeremiah from the mouth of the Lord" (1 Esd. 1:28).[18] Moreover, rather than reference *elohim*, the generic Hebrew word for God, Esdras uses "the Lord" (*kyrios*, vv. 27, 28, as we have only Greek versions of the book, or translations from the Greek) and "the Lord God" (v. 27).

For the Chronicler, God is God of the whole world, from beginning to end (note that the book's narrative extends from Adam to Ezra). Moreover, as John Goldingay argues, this comprehensive past is presented not in a dispassionate, objective sense, but in order to provide a relevant understanding for the present. The Chronicler's historical interest, that is, has two poles: the events of the past and his present community. Josiah's life is meant to be seen as a lesson for the postexilic faithful. As a historian, the Chronicler is "a preacher and theologian."[19] Part of his theological agenda has to do with the retooling of Israel's worship life, which he anchors in David and Josiah, "insiders" par excellence. But important as well is the recognition that God is God over all, over the "outsider" too. God thus reveals himself not only to those like Jeremiah but also to those outside the community of faith—to foreigners such as Neco, and as we will see below, King Huram of Tyre (cf. 2 Chron. 2) and King Cyrus of Persia (see Isa. 45:1; 2 Chron. 36:22–23; Ezra 1).

2. King Huram of Tyre (2 Chron. 2:3–16). That the Chronicler was interested for theological reasons in noting God's involvement with those outside of his chosen people is reinforced by his narration of a second encounter between one of Israel's kings and a neighboring one. The Chronicler records in 2 Chronicles 2:3–16 how King Solomon asks King Huram of Tyre to send "an artisan skilled [the root is *hokhmah*, "to be wise at"] to work in gold, silver, bronze, and iron, and in purple, crimson, and blue fabrics, trained also in engraving, to join the skilled workers who are with me in Judah and Jerusalem, whom my father David provided" (v. 7). And so King Huram sends Huram-abi, a skilled artisan. He is said to be "the son of one of the Danite women, his father a Tyrian" (v. 14). What is telling in this recounting is that the Chronicler has intentionally altered the description of Huram-abi from his source material in Kings at three points: Huram-abi's arrival time in Israel, the skill set he is said to possess, and his ancestry. Rather than report having Huram-abi (now alternately named Hiram) come from Tyre *after* the temple has been built to make a large number of bronze works for the temple—innumerable pillars,

18. A similar reorientation is apparent in the later rabbinic literature as well. See *Lamentations Rabba* 1:61 and *Ta'anit* 22b. See Zipora Talshir, *1 Esdras: A Text Critical Commentary* (Atlanta: Society of Biblical Literature, 2001), 50.

19. John Goldingay, "The Chronicler as a Theologian," *Biblical Theology Bulletin* 5, no. 2 (June 1975): 112.

bas-relief, basins, pots, bowls, and so on (1 Kings 7:15–47)—the Chronicler has him come at the beginning to help with all phases of the construction (v. 13). Rather than have Hiram simply be an artisan working in bronze (1 Kings 7:14), the Chronicler gives instead the greatly expanded list of skills noted above (v. 14). And rather than his mother being "a widow of the tribe of Naphtali" (1 Kings 7:14), she is now "one of the Danite women" (v. 14).

Why would these changes be made by the Chronicler? And why would it matter? It seems probable that here was a way for the Chronicler to connect Huram-abi with another skilled artisan, Oholiab, who worked not on the temple but on an earlier house of God, the tabernacle, as Bezalel's assistant. The Chronicler is projecting a continuity in Israel's worship between the time of Moses and that of David/Solomon. When Solomon requests of the king of Tyre a skilled craftsman, it is not just for a metalworker; his list of desired skills is extensive, identical to that given in Exodus with regard to Bezalel and Oholiab (Exod. 35:30–36). Moreover, Oholiab is described in Exodus as being of the tribe of Dan (Exod. 31:6; 35:34) and his skill (literally, *hokhmah*) as a divine gifting that comes from God (Exod. 31:6; 35:35). The Chronicler's readers learn that Huram-Abi's mother is also a Danite, and they are to infer similarly that his skill/wisdom as an artisan (his *hokhmah*) is like Oholiab's, a wise gifting (2 Chron. 2:13).[20] Just as Oholiab assisted Bezalel, so Huram-abi will assist Solomon. The comparison between building the tabernacle and building the temple is made even more explicit by the Chronicler, as Solomon and Bezalel are also compared. Solomon received his wisdom only after seeking God at the altar built by Bezalel (2 Chron. 1:5–6). Both leaders are from Judah, and both are singled out as being filled with the Spirit of God (Exod. 31:2–3; 2 Chron. 1:7–12). And while in Kings, Solomon's wisdom/skill is manifest in his judicious decisions, wise observations, and artistic expressions, in Chronicles, his skill is more akin to Bezalel's, the ability to do practical things, to build a magnificent temple.[21]

Thus, an artisan from outside of the people of God, Huram-abi, one gifted (*hokhmah*) with a divine skill, would join Solomon who was himself also gifted (*hokhmah*) by God in jointly constructing the house of God.[22] That such is the probable meaning of the text is reinforced by the astonishing words of King

20. A parallel instance of the Chronicler modifying the received history with regard to ancestry has Samuel being included in the Levite lineage (1 Chron. 6:1, 28), whereas in 1 Samuel 1:1 he is said to be of the tribe of Ephraim.

21. I am indebted to Raymond Dillard for noting many of these similarities. See Raymond Dillard, *2 Chronicles*, Word Biblical Commentary (Waco: Word, 1987), 4–5.

22. Given his Danite mother, Huram-abi is, in one sense, both an insider and an outsider. But his political affiliation with Tyre would seem to place him outside the religious community of Israel, particularly as he is represented as King Huram's contribution to the building of the

Huram who, in dispatching Huram-abi to Solomon, writes: "Blessed be the LORD God of Israel, who made heaven and earth, who has given King David a wise [*hokhmah*] son, endowed with discretion and understanding, who will build a temple for the LORD, and a royal palace for himself" (2 Chron. 2:12). The letter is much more elaborate and theological than the business-like parallel in Kings. Echoing what Solomon himself has said in his letter to Huram (2 Chron. 2:4–6), it can be compared with the queen of Sheba's praise (2 Chron. 9:7–9), as well as that of King Cyrus of Persia (2 Chron. 36:23). With his much more theological intention in mind, the Chronicler has King Huram of Tyre recognize Israel's God as the Creator of heaven and earth. It is that God who has gifted both Solomon and Huram-abi, "a skilled artisan, endowed with understanding" (2 Chron. 2:13). God is God over all the world, bestowing similar gifts on Israelites and non-Israelites alike.

3. King Cyrus of Persia (2 Chron. 36:22–23). A third example of the Chronicler's theological interest in recognizing that God reveals himself to the Israelite and non-Israelite alike is his reference to King Cyrus of Persia, which ends his book. Wanting to make a connection to the books of Ezra and Nehemiah, the Chronicler ends his history not with the fall of Jerusalem to the Chaldeans—who burned the temple and destroyed the wall of Jerusalem, taking those who escaped the sword captive—but following the establishment of the kingdom of Persia, as Jeremiah had predicted, with a surprising and brief reference to King Cyrus.

> In the first year of King Cyrus of Persia, in fulfillment of the word of the LORD spoken by Jeremiah, the LORD stirred up the spirit of King Cyrus of Persia so that he sent a herald throughout all his kingdom and also declared in a written edict: "Thus says King Cyrus of Persia: The LORD, the God of heaven, has given me all the kingdoms of the earth, and he has charged me to build him a house at Jerusalem, which is in Judah. Whoever is among you of all his people, may the LORD his God be with him! Let him go up." (2 Chron. 36:22–23)

And thus the book ends much like it has begun, with God the Lord of the whole universe. Just as the Israelites' story began for the Chronicler with Adam, it ends with the ruler of all the kingdoms on earth revealing to Cyrus that he should assist the Israelites in relocating to Jerusalem and rebuilding their temple there.

These final two verses are clearly borrowed from the first four verses of chapter 1 of Ezra. The text, through the end of the first sentence of the edict,

---

temple. This does not seem to be a situation like Daniel, for example, who retained his Jewish identity while in service of a foreign king.

is quoted almost verbatim. Then the third verse is shortened and edited poorly, and the text ends abruptly without the rest of the edict being given. Readers need to turn to Ezra for that. The fuller companion text in Ezra reads:

> Any of those among you who are of his people—may their God be with them!—are now permitted to go up to Jerusalem in Judah, and rebuild the house of the LORD, the God of Israel—he is the God who is in Jerusalem; and let all survivors, in whatever place they reside, be assisted by the people of their place with silver and gold, with goods and with animals, besides freewill offerings for the house of God in Jerusalem. (Ezra 1:3–4)

The repetition of Ezra's opening verses, though now in awkwardly edited form, might be an indication that Chronicles, Ezra, and Nehemiah were once one book and that when broken apart, the Chronicler, or a later editor, felt the need to end Chronicles not on a down note, but with a message of hope. Or perhaps the Chronicler has borrowed from Ezra-Nehemiah? Cyrus is God's means of fulfilling his word to Jeremiah (see Jer. 25:11 and 29:11) about moving beyond the seventy-year time of punishment for Israel. Though Israel's kingship is at an end, the king of Persia now becomes the new anointed, someone who will bring forward the reign of Yahweh not only in Israel but throughout the nations. As Raymond Dillard concludes in his commentary on Chronicles: "The book ends with a new exodus at hand: not because God forced the hand of a reluctant Pharaoh, but because he moved the heart of a Persian king."[23]

Interestingly, in Isaiah, Cyrus is labeled by God "my shepherd" (Isa. 44:28). The focus is internal, on Israel and its needs; though the exact meaning of the metaphor "shepherd" is unclear, it would seem that Cyrus is to be seen in this text as the one who is caring for Israel. In Isaiah 45, Cyrus is again mentioned as one helping Israel at the instigation of Yahweh himself.

> For the sake of my servant Jacob,
>   and Israel my chosen,
> I call you by your name,
>   I surname you, though you do not know me.
> . . . .
> I have aroused Cyrus in righteousness,
>   and will make all his paths straight;
> he shall build my city
>   and set my exiles free,
> not for price or reward. (vv. 4, 13)

23. Dillard, *2 Chronicles*, 302.

Significantly, Cyrus is portrayed almost as a pawn of the Lord's in this text.

> I am the LORD, and there is no other;
>   besides me there is no god.
>   I arm you, though you do not know me,
> so that they may know . . . (vv. 5–6)

But Yahweh also has Cyrus in mind. He begins his prophecy to Cyrus by telling him that God will go before him to subdue nations and strip kings of their robes, to break down doors and level mountains, "so that you may know that it is I, the LORD, the God of Israel, who call you by your name" (vv. 1–3). Cyrus is God's "anointed," the only time in the Old Testament where the messianic term is applied to a foreign king. Otherwise, the term is used only of priests, prophets, and kings of Israel, and of course it becomes Israel's name for its expected deliverer.[24] It is this foreign king that God has taken by the hand (v. 1) and called by name (v. 4).

But though Cyrus is said in Isaiah not to know God, in Chronicles (and Ezra) we get a different picture. There has been a fast-forward in the story. Cyrus has, through Yahweh's empowerment, built his empire. He has conquered kings and subdued nations. And as a result he has come to know that God has called him by name. Thus Cyrus is no longer one who "does not know me." Rather, he can say, "The Lord, the God of heaven, has given me all the kingdoms of the earth, and he has charged me to build him a house at Jerusalem, which is in Judah" (2 Chron. 36:23). Here, as the book of Chronicles ends, we hear a witness to the power and faithfulness of God coming not from one of the people of God, not, to speak anachronistically, from someone in the church, but from someone who has heard God speak outside the community of faith. Like King Neco and King Hiram, King Cyrus is a witness to the power and Presence of God, the Creator of heaven and earth.

What can we conclude about these three foreign monarchs?[25] Although these kings are necessarily to be perceived as foreign (that is the whole point—Neco

24. See Lev. 4:3; 1 Sam. 2:10; 16:6; 24:6; 26:9, 11, 23; 2 Sam. 19:21; 1 Chron. 16:22; Ps. 18:50; 105:15; Hab. 3:13.
25. A more comprehensive listing would also include King Pul of Assyria (another name for Tiglath-pileser), whom the Chronicler recounts as taking Israel into exile after "the God of Israel stirred up the spirit" of this king (1 Chron. 5:26). This language is unique to the Chronicler and is the same that is used to describe King Cyrus ("the Lord stirred up the spirit of King Cyrus," 2 Chron. 36:22). Such a listing might also include the visit of the queen of Sheba to Solomon (2 Chron. 9).

and Cyrus represent the two main powers in Israel's larger world, and Horam is Israel's immediate neighbor to the north), readers and rereaders of the texts will recognize, to use Ehud Ben Zvi's words, "a sense of 'sameness' in the human world populated by Israelites and foreigners. It is not only that these alien monarchs all speak 'typical' Hebrew, but, even more significantly, that their words include allusions to biblical Hebrew texts and expressions. . . . Moreover, [they] uphold positions [and behaviors] that are expected of 'pious' Israelites."[26] Ben Zvi sees in these accounts the tendency to "Israelize" the foreigner. If this is perhaps an exaggeration, Louis Jonker is certainly correct when he concludes, "the kind of social identity being negotiated here seems to be inclusive and accommodating, rather than defensive."[27] These three kings, even in their foreignness and surely in their uniqueness, are each positive characters whom the narrator supports. Moreover, they play significant roles in the narrative, communicating important theological messages and assisting in (re)building the temple. If these foreign monarchs have the potential to receive God's revelation and to act consistently with the knowledge they have received, then readers of the text will be led to assume that, at least potentially, all people have such a possibility. Rather than assume that any knowledge of God that is given to those outside the community of faith is veiled at best and serves only to render these individuals inexcusable before God, there is, instead, presented in these texts a positive interpretation of what those outside the community of faith can know of God.

Psalms

Both Proverbs and Chronicles are part of the third section of the Hebrew Scriptures, the Writings. Before leaving that portion of Scripture and looking at the Law and the Prophets for further descriptions of God's revelation beyond temple and text, it will be helpful to also more briefly look at the Psalms, the largest portion of the Hebrew Writings. In particular, we need to consider the creation psalms, those hymns of praise to God (e.g., Pss. 8; 19; 29; 104; 148). Some of these hymns of praise say nothing about God's revelation. Psalm 148, for example, does not mention anything of general revelation, instead calling the people of Israel to praise God who is Creator of heaven and earth. Rather than finding in this psalm nature speaking directly to the psalmist, one can hear behind the psalmist's words the sacred text of Genesis. Similarly, Psalm 8

---

26. Ehud Ben Zvi, "When the Foreign Monarch Speaks," in *The Chronicler as Author*, ed. M. Patrick Graham and Stephen L. McKenzie (Sheffield: Sheffield Academic Press, 1999), 224–25 (see also 209–28).

27. Jonker, *1 and 2 Chronicles*, 62.

is not words of praise to God who has revealed himself to his people through creation, but words of address to God the Creator, given the wonder of creation. It is creation itself that causes the psalmist to praise the Creator. Here is not revelation but the echo of God's past activity, the artifact left behind after the builder (v. 2) and artist (v. 3) has departed.

But two other creation psalms do provide further perspective on God's revelation:

1. Psalm 19. We have mentioned above Psalm 19. Those who read this psalm in light of a traditional understanding of Romans 1 find the psalm to show only the insufficiency of God's revelation through nature. John Calvin is representative here. Commenting on this psalm and what we can learn about God the Creator from revelation through his creation, he writes:

> While the heavens bear witness concerning God, their testimony does not lead men so far as that thereby they learn truly to fear him, and acquire a well-grounded knowledge of him; it serves only to render them inexcusable.[28]

James Hoffmeier, in his article "'The Heavens Declare the Glory of God': The Limits of General Revelation" is slightly more positive with regard to how Psalm 19 portrays God's revelation through creation. But only slightly. In the psalm, creation, "the work of his hands," can reveal the glory of God (*El*), he thinks, but it is "veiled information," not sufficient to know God in any intimate or salvific way.[29] Quoting Peter Craigie, he finds that the real value of general revelation is the fact that it points to special revelation.

> To the sensitive, the heavenly praise of God's glory may be an overwhelming experience, whereas to the insensitive, sky is simply sky and stars only stars; they point to nothing beyond. In this hymn of praise, it is not the primary purpose of the psalmist to draw upon nature as a vehicle of revelation, or as a source of the knowledge of God apart from the revelation in law (Torah); indeed, there is more than a suggestion that the reflection of God's praise in the universe is perceptible only to those already sensitive to God's revelation and purpose.[30]

Hoffmeier and Craigie are not alone in turning to Calvin in order to distance general revelation from the present illumination/inspiration of God through

---

28. John Calvin, *Commentary on the Book of Psalms*, trans. James Anderson (Grand Rapids: Eerdmans, 1948), 1:317.

29. James K. Hoffmeier, "'The Heavens Declare the Glory of God': The Limits of General Revelation," *Trinity Journal* 21, no. 1 (Spring 2000): 17–24.

30. Peter Craigie, *Psalms 1–50*, Word Biblical Commentary (Waco: Word, 1983): 181, quoted in Hoffmeier, "Heavens Declare," 21.

the Holy Spirit. For them, one needs to know the Creator first through his special revelation in order to perceive God's praise in creation. Their Lutheran counterparts also question the nature and extent of creation's witness. Hans-Joachim Kraus, in his commentary on Psalms, understands Psalm 19 to be "a poem in which the mysterious life force in nature and the stars and the sun appears before us as witness to the glory of God."[31] And fellow Lutheran Claus Westermann writes of this witness to God's glory as ongoing, but only as "the echo [that] goes on reverberating: day to day pours forth speech." He writes:

> Commentators on these verses have often spoken of "creation as revelation" here, from which a "natural theology," a *theologia naturalis*, could be derived. But what Psalm 19 is saying at this point has nothing to do with revelation, quite apart from the fact that a general concept of revelation is unknown in the Old Testament.[32]

The issue these four scholars raise is this: is it the world on its own that witnesses to God as Creator, or is it the Spirit who continues to reveal/illumine God in and through creation? In the one, "general revelation"—if one mislabels it as such—is but a remainder, an echo that continues to reverberate through the cosmos and that humanity can perceive. However, it is paltry and insufficient. Only as one knows the Creator first can one fully understand God's creation and respond in praise. In the other, general revelation is actual revelation, the self-revealing of God's Spirit in and through creation. Here creation's revelation is seen as robust and engaging. One indication that Psalm 19 means it to be the latter is the almost universal acknowledgment that the first part (vv. 1–6) of Psalm 19 was first an independent hymn of praise to God. Relevant as well is the fact that in the first part, it is the Hebrew name *El* that is used, the designation for God as the Creator of all, and not Yahweh, Israel's Redeemer who is also the Creator. Perhaps most importantly, in these first six verses, the vibrancy of the description of creation's proclamation gives no hint that this revelation is disappointingly incomplete or lacking. Though it might be inaudible, it is nonetheless decisive, something Job also discovered in his encounter with the Creator (Job 38–40).

The recognition that the heavens declare the glory of God, that there is a real knowledge of God even through speechless speech, is not dependent on the psalm's second part, which references the law. It is not Scripture, but nature, that is the psalmist's text, as the Spirit speaks through it. The Roman Catholic biblical scholar Richard Clifford is surely correct in recognizing the

---

31. Hans-Joachim Kraus, *Psalms 1–59: A Commentary* (Minneapolis: Augsburg, 1988), 275.
32. Claus Westermann, *The Living Psalms* (Grand Rapids: Eerdmans, 1984), 254.

first stanza of this psalm to be "an illustration of Otto's famous phrase, '*mysterium tremendum et fascinans*.'"[33] The psalmist, through and in creation, has encountered Mystery—a mystery that is at one and the same time awesome and inviting, fearful and fascinating.

2. Psalm 29. Psalm 29 is a second creation hymn that is relevant to our investigation. The psalm speaks of the Lord (Yahweh) showing his majesty through a thunderstorm (vv. 3–9). There is thunder, lightning, and destructive winds. The focus is not on the storm, however; it is on God.

> The voice of the LORD is over the waters;
>   the God of glory thunders,
>   the LORD, over mighty waters.
> The voice of the LORD is powerful;
>   the voice of the LORD is full of majesty. (vv. 3–4)

Though we possess no extant examples of Canaanite psalmody, many scholars today are convinced that Psalm 29 was originally a Canaanite hymn. They think this because of obvious parallels with Canaanite texts that speak of a "storm" god. The only difference (though a significant one) that was adopted in this foreign text is that "Yahweh" was inserted in eighteen of the twenty-three lines! Whether such a formal adaptation of a Canaanite psalm can be claimed in the absence of hard evidence in one sense doesn't matter. What does seem clear is here is an example of an adaption of the surrounding people's understandings of Baal—a god of thunder and conqueror of the mighty waters—that was able to contribute to the description of faith in Yahweh. Though the Canaanites might have gotten it wrong in worshiping God as Baal, that God was the fierce Creator who still providentially and mysteriously ruled the universe was correct (cf. Ps. 104:31–32). And Israel to its credit recognized this, even being unafraid to use the trappings of an idolatrous religion. (One might find in Acts 17, which will be discussed in the next chapter, a parallel "affirmation" of aspects of a foreign religion.)

The focus of Psalm 29 is on our "awe in the presence of the Creator and His word of power," says James Mays.[34] What is described is not just a "perfect storm" but a theophany that reveals Yahweh as the ruler of the universe. What is unique and surprising in this psalm, however, is the close identification of Yahweh with nature. In most other psalms, there is a strong distinction between Creator and creation. The account of Elijah comes to mind where God

---

33. Richard Clifford, *Psalms 1–72* (Nashville: Abingdon, 2002), 112.

34. James Mays, *Psalms*, Interpretation: A Bible Commentary for Teaching and Preaching (Louisville: John Knox, 1994), 136.

is not in the wind, earthquake, or fire (1 Kings 19:11–18). If there is a parallel Old Testament text, perhaps it is Job 38–40. Given Israel's context where the surrounding nations worshiped nature gods, Israel most often refrained from using phenomena in nature to directly describe God's glory. More often, God is praised for his actions in history—*Heilsgeschichte*. But here, the glory of the Lord is extensively and directly described as being revealed through natural occurrences. Psalm 29 describes a mighty epiphany of nature, something more typically heard by their Canaanite neighbors.

5

Broadening Our Biblical Focus, Part 2

God's people do not have a monopoly on divine revelation, as we have seen. Agur, King Lemuel's mother, Amenemope, King Neco, Cyrus, the Canaanite poets who first penned Psalm 29—all provide us with biblical examples of the extended reach of God's revealing Presence. God has made himself known to those outside the community of faith, as well as to those within. Scripture makes clear that God's means of communication extend beyond his revelation made known through the Jewish and Christian communities of faith and their Scriptures. It also includes his revealing Presence through nature and providence, dreams and conscience, observation and creativity.

All of the biblical examples in chapter 4 that highlight the reach of God's revelation were taken from the Writings, the third and final section of the Hebrew Scriptures. It is particularly in this section of the Old Testament that we find biblical paradigms of the extent of God's revelation beyond the borders of Israelite faith. This is most probably because the chiefly postexilic context for the final shaping of these documents made the issue of the breadth of God's influence a particularly relevant one. How was the small band of Jewish people who returned from exile to understand their God's relation to the more powerful nations that surrounded them? Was God also lord over them? Was he active in their context as well? And the answer given multiple times, as we have seen, is a resounding yes.

But it is not just in the Writings that God's wider revelation is evident. Turning to the Torah, a second unit in the Hebrew Scriptures, we find similar examples, particularly in the book of Genesis.

The Old Testament Torah

Genesis

1. Melchizedek (Gen. 14:17–20). Perhaps the most mysterious and enigmatic story narrating the revelation of God to someone outside of the covenant community is the account of Melchizedek, high priest and king of Salem, who comes to offer a blessing over Abram/Abraham, just prior to God's covenanting with him in Genesis 15. In Genesis 14 we read:

> And King Melchizedek of Salem brought out bread and wine; he was priest of God Most High [Heb., 'el 'elyon]. He blessed him and said,
>
>> "Blessed be Abram by God Most High,
>>   maker of heaven and earth;
>> and blessed be God Most High,
>>   who has delivered your enemies into your hand!"
>> And Abram gave him one-tenth of everything. (Gen. 14:18–20)

The larger context for this brief description in Genesis 14 can be easily summarized. Lot, the nephew of Abram, somewhat true to form, is taken captive by four kings during battle. Abram, with his own small army of 318, routs these kings, rescuing Lot and confiscating their goods. When the king of Sodom for whom Lot was fighting comes out to welcome them home, they are first met by another king, Melchizedek, who blesses Abram, for he is also a high priest. Abram responds in thanksgiving to this blessing (an "ordination" of sorts to his God-appointed task) by giving Melchizedek a tithe of everything. When the king of Sodom then asks Abram for the prisoners to be handed over to him and says for Abram to take all the goods for himself (which would make him wealthy), Abram refuses, not wanting to be perceived as becoming rich through the largesse of that king. Instead, Abram only asks that his men be given their rightful share.

While this account is thus easily told, most scholarship concerning the Melchizedek vignette has found this portion of the Abrahamic story anything but straightforward in its description. This has caused many to get lost in the trees and never see the forest as they discuss the account. They have asked, for example, (1) how the Melchizedek episode came to be located in its present context, given that the end of verse 17 and the beginning of verse 21 could otherwise be connected with regard to a description of the king of Sodom; (2) whether the word "Melchizedek" is a descriptor (the Hebrew literally means "the king of righteousness") for a nameless person, or whether it is a proper name that includes the name of a specific Canaanite deity; (3) whether "Salem" is a shortened form of "Jerusalem," or whether it might actually be a reference to the age-old religious site of Shechem (cf. an alternate reading of Gen. 33:18); (4) whether 'el 'elyon, maker of heaven and earth," is a Canaanite deity and the blessing, thus, a Canaanite religious blessing; (5) whether the bread and wine prefigures the Eucharist, is a customary Canaanite religious ritual/sacral meal, or both; and (6) whether the tithe is religiously motivated, and if so, what significance is to be given to the fact that Abram gives it to Melchizedek? With such questions, valid as they are, biblical commentators have more often fixated on the data of the story and have unfortunately spent little time on its larger theological meaning. (Or alternately, some have rejected the straightforward, theological meaning of the text and have thus spent their energies attempting to discover alternative reasons for casting its theology in a new light.)

Moreover, when the episode's theological meaning has been sought, too often it has been dictated by the need to either deny theological insight to Melchizedek or to make him a hidden believer. The latter is a reason that some think Jerusalem is Melchizedek's hometown and thus more "Israelite" in origin (Josephus), that Melchizedek is Noah's son Shem who transferred the priesthood to Abraham (the Targum), that Melchizedek is to be considered a symbol for the right principle, something like the Egyptian ma'at (Philo), and that the bread and wine is a type of Christ (several Christian scholars).

But in all these attempts to make Melchizedek somehow more acceptable as God's spokesperson, what is underemphasized is the fact that the conduit for God's blessing here is a foreign priest acting in the integrity of his own beliefs. There is in this small vignette the transfer of pre-Israelite religious traditions into Israel.[1] Of course the Canaanite model would be there. It was the only model these people had. God embraced this priesthood and built on it. This is to say that all theology emerges out of indigenous religious traditions that are embraced, purified, and extended. We have already seen this with Amenemope and Psalm 29. Here we find it again. With Abram (Abraham), the father of the Israelite people, there is no "elder" to "ordain" him as leader and prophet. So God calls Melchizedek, the high priest of Salem, for the task.

---

1. Technically, of course, prior to the birth of Israel, there are no Israelites, but I use this term to indicate the people of God who became part of the Abrahamic covenant.

And having received God's revelation, Melchizedek performs his priestly task, offering a blessing in the name of God, the Creator of heaven and earth, who has delivered Abram's enemies into his hand.

That Melchizedek's blessing is perceived as a legitimate religious rite is made clear by the tithe that Abram presents in return to him. That the prayer is genuinely received by Abram is also indicated by the fact that Abram responds to the king of Sodom using the same appellation, "I have sworn to the LORD, God Most High, maker of heaven and earth, that I would not take a thread or a sandal-thong or anything that is yours" (Gen. 14:22–23). In distancing himself from Sodom and its pattern of injustices, Abram is comfortable using the epithet for God that Melchizedek himself has used. Though this name for God is used only one other time by an Israelite (Ps. 78:35), Abram uses it here in solidarity with the one who graciously offered a blessing on him.[2] Perhaps Abram is like Paul on Mars Hill (Acts 17), knowing God in a fuller sense than Melchizedek? Perhaps in God's providence, Melchizedek has come to realize there is one supreme God? Or perhaps, as Robert Alter hypothesizes, "Abram elegantly co-opts [Melchizedek] for monotheism by using *'el 'elyon* in its orthodox Israelite sense (v. 22) when he addresses the king of Sodom."[3] But whatever the exact religious belief of Melchizedek, the text would have us understand that God has revealed to a foreigner the need to bless Abram, and this priest of Salem does so with full integrity and devotion. The episode ends with Abram showing his appreciation for Melchizedek's genuine act of faith and understands Melchizedek's blessing to be a genuine act of consecration. Without giving up his own religious identity, he can pay tribute to and learn from another tradition.

A final note. Melchizedek's name—whether the descriptor for an anonymous priest and king or the actual name of this priest of Salem—would have been heard by Hebrew readers of this text as "the king of righteousness."[4] To them, this would have indicated that righteousness and justice were outstanding characteristics of Melchizedek.[5] It could be that such a reference to "righteousness" by the one who blessed Abram for his future calling is

2. *El* is the proper name for the sky god in the Canaanite pantheon, and is commonly used as a general name for "god" in the Hebrew Scriptures. *'Elyon* is another name used with regard to Canaanite deities and is used by itself in Num. 24:16; Deut. 32:8; Isa. 14:14; Lam. 3:35, 38; Dan. 7:18, 22, 25, 27, as well as multiple times in the Psalter. It is also used, on occasion, as part of a couplet with *Yahweh* or with *elohim*.

3. Robert Alter, *The Five Books of Moses* (New York: Norton, 2004), 72.

4. In a famous English-language example of a proper name that carries with it a secondary interpretation, Mr. and Mrs. Hogg named their daughter "Ima."

5. In what follows I have been helped by the argument of Judy Klitsner, *Subversive Sequels in the Bible* (Jerusalem: Maggid, 2011), 75.

intentional in the text. It could indicate that Abraham actually learned from Melchizedek something of what God desired of him; that is, God used a foreigner to reveal God's self to Abram. For immediately following in chapter 15, God promises Abram an heir, and it says Abram "believed the Lord; and the Lord reckoned it to him as righteousness" (Gen. 15:6). Again in chapter 18, when the Lord takes Abraham with him as he pronounces judgment on Sodom, he says of Abraham, "I have chosen him, that he may charge his children and his household after him to keep the way of the Lord by doing righteousness and justice; so that the Lord may bring about for Abraham what he has promised" (Gen. 18:19). Abram's commissioning by "the king of righteousness" has to do with his own need to be righteous. That this is the writer's intention is illustrated immediately as Abram is baited by the king of Sodom with wealth, if he will but betray the just handling of booty from war. But reminded by Melchizedek of the need for righteousness, Abram responds to the king of Sodom by referencing Melchizedek's and his own "God Most High, maker of heaven and earth," the same God that Melchizedek said gave Abram the victory (Gen. 14:19–20).

2. Abimelech (Gen. 20). A second small narrative in Genesis that is relevant to our investigation is that of Abimelech's encounter with Abraham in Genesis 20. It has, to quote Walter Brueggemann, "a self-conscious theological tone."[6] The normal pattern throughout the Torah for God's revelation of himself to his people is stated in Numbers 12:6.

> When there are prophets among you,
> I the Lord make myself known to them in visions;
> I speak to them in dreams.

Dreams and visions were one way God chose to communicate to people in the Old Testament, particularly in the books of Genesis and Daniel. They function as a way of describing a religious experience.

Genesis 20 records Abimelech's dream about Sarah; Genesis 28 describes Jacob's dream at Bethel; in Genesis 31, Jacob is warned in a dream to flee, and then Laban is also warned in a dream; in Genesis 37 we have the record of Joseph's early dreams; in Genesis 40 we find the dreams of the cupbearer and baker; in Genesis 41, the pharaoh's dream; and in Genesis 46, a dream where Jacob/Israel is told to go down to Egypt. Other dreams include those of Nebuchadnezzar in Daniel 2 and 4; Balaam in Numbers 22; Samuel in 1 Samuel 3; and Solomon in 1 Kings 3:5–15. What is interesting about this

6. Walter Brueggemann, *Genesis*, Interpretation: A Bible Commentary for Teaching and Preaching (Atlanta: John Knox, 1982), 77.

list is the number of persons outside of the believing community of Israel who experience a revelation of God through dreams. Although some of the dreams are those of God's "prophets" (Jacob, Joseph, Samuel, and Solomon), and other dreams are symbolic and need interpretation by God's "prophets" (pharaoh's cupbearer and baker, as well as the pharaoh himself, by Joseph; and Nebuchadnezzar by Daniel), there are several revelations from God in dreams that do not fit this pattern. They all are recorded, as one might expect, by the "Elohist" ("E" source), who speaks of God using the public name for God, *elohim*. These dreams come to persons outside the Yahwistic community— Abimelech, Laban, and Balaam.

The episode of Abraham and Sarah with King Abimelech of Gerar is an especially fascinating example. Abraham had settled for a period in Gerar, a small city-state west of Beersheba in the Negev that was ruled by Abimelech. As was the case earlier when the couple journeyed into Egypt, we read that Abraham chose to call Sarah his "sister," thinking this might protect him/them. And so, as was the right of the king at that time, Abimelech took Sarah into his harem, perhaps trying to pin down an alliance through marriage with this new group of people that Abraham represented. But God intervenes, protecting Sarah from having sexual relations with Abimelech (and thus not making ambiguous the true father of Isaac, who is yet to be born) and Abimelech from incurring the judgment of God. The story plays itself out in several brief scenes: Abimelech takes Sarah into his harem (vv. 1–2), God warns Abimelech in a dream (vv. 3–7), Abimelech tells his advisers (v. 8), Abimelech confronts Abraham (vv. 9–13), Abimelech nonetheless gifts Abraham and Sarah (vv. 14–16), and Abraham prays for Abimelech (vv. 17–18).

There is a carefully crafted symmetry to the story, each bit of action followed by an interpretive dialogue. Abimelech's meeting with his advisers can be seen as the midpoint of the story, with God holding Abimelech responsible before this meeting and Abimelech holding Abraham accountable after the meeting. And though the reader of Genesis has already encountered a similar incident in which Abraham has hidden Sarah's identity as his wife from a pharaoh (Gen. 12), the story here is quite distinct.[7] While in Genesis 12, the pharaoh is cursed by God and eventually expels Abraham to avoid further pain, Abimelech is here affirmed as honorable by God, more than demonstrating this by compensating Abraham and Sarah for damages (though nothing transpired and his intentions were noble), and by inviting Abraham to settle in his land wherever it pleased him. There is no doubt in the telling

7. This point is generally missing in commentaries and other scholarship, which have typically emphasized their similarities.

of this sister/wife story where the sympathy of the reader is found, and it is not with Abraham.

But such a description fails to capture the heart of this account. Terence Fretheim, in a brief vignette in the journal *Word & World*, gets to the core of the story by identifying two major points: "(1) God initiates a conversation with an outsider; (2) the outsider, as both teacher and confessor, engages the insider in conversation."[8] Here is a text that is not in the Christian lectionary—that is, one that is never read in worship as part of the church year cycle. Why is this? Most probably because the outsider is seen as God's spokesperson to the insider, and not the reverse. In this account, it is Abimelech who is the exemplar, not Abraham. In Fretheim's words:

> Perhaps it's because the story gives such a positive portrayal of Abimelech, a person who stands outside the chosen community. We may also find the text unsettling in that it invites us to hear comparable stories from our world, wherein outsiders may at times be more in tune with God's purposes for the creation than we are.[9]

Abimelech, the outsider, when confronted by God for having a married woman in his harem, not only rightly claims he was pure in intention and chaste in action, but also hides nothing, immediately sharing the situation with his advisers. These outsiders immediately respond to God's warning, much like the sailors in Jonah's boat (Jon. 1:16). It is Abraham in this account that is the antiprophet. Abimelech, after hearing Abraham's defensive and self-serving response, nevertheless treats Abraham and Sarah with generosity and *hesed* (loving-kindness), restoring Sarah's honor, loading her with gifts, and giving Abraham the pick of his land. Abraham, on the other hand, makes an elaborate threefold defense of his deceit that seems little more than an ironic rationalization.

(1) First, Abraham says he acted to hide Sarah's true identity "because I thought, There is no fear of God at all in this place, and they will kill me because of my wife" (Gen. 20:11). That is, the people in Gerar would act without regard for human rights and would not show justice to the foreigner. But readers in the story already know that Abimelech has shown himself to be a righteous man, responding to God in the dream by saying that he was someone who had acted "in the integrity of my heart and the innocence of my hands" (Gen. 20:5). And God had excused his actions (cf. Rom. 2:14–15:

---

8. Terence E. Fretheim, "Conversation or Conversion? Hearing God from the Other," *Word & World* 22, no. 3 (Summer 2002): 304–6.
9. Ibid., 304.

"When Gentiles, who do not possess the law, do instinctively what the law requires, these, though not having the law, are a law to themselves. They show that what the law requires is written on their hearts, to which their conscience also bears witness; and their conflicting thoughts will accuse or perhaps excuse them"). One thinks of Abraham's experience with another outsider, Melchizedek, the king of righteousness. But Abraham had forgotten that experience and prejudged the situation wrongly. As a result, it almost cost Sarah her integrity, his lineage its clarity, and the people of Gerar their future.

(2) Second, Abraham claims on a technicality that he has not lied, Sarah was also his sister through a common father, something later legislated against but allowable at this particular time in Israel's development. Those of us who have lived through the Clinton era know too well about hiding behind "technicalities" regarding relations with women. Abraham's clear intention here is to evade the truth.

(3) And third, Abraham, not realizing the damning implication of his words, explains to Abimelech that on leaving Haran, he had asked Sarah to make a pact with him that she would say at each place they came that he was her brother. That is, Abraham did not trust God to protect him from harm, so asked his wife to lie (perhaps I should write "lay") for him. It is Abimelech who in all of this proves himself willing to listen to God, and Abraham, the one who needs to believe what God has previously told him and act righteously, knowing that God would guide and protect him (something readers of this narrative again see God do).

Abraham had assumed that God could not be present in Gerar. (Josiah had similarly assumed that God could not be present to King Neco.) But let me again quote Fretheim.

> God is present and active among outsiders; indeed they are surrounded by experiences of divine graciousness, whether they realize it or not. Even more, God takes the initiative and communicates with the outsider [the point of this chapter!]. Indeed, God engages the outsider in dialogue, and this bears fruit in the life of all concerned. . . . We may find it disconcerting that God engages such a one apart from the ministrations of the community of faith, but this story makes clear that God does not run a closed shop on who receives a word from God and who can engage it.[10]

Abimelech became Abraham's teacher, and through Abraham, the teacher of his descendants, including those of us in the church today. He did so by

10. Ibid., 306.

becoming Abraham's challenger, offering a "prophetic" word to Abraham whom in this text God calls his "prophet." The irony is clear to all who have eyes to see—God's people do not have a monopoly on his revelation.

Two Early Prophets

There are two accounts of early prophets, one from Israel—Elijah—and the other from outside the people of God—Balaam—that both focus on God's revelation outside the normal channels of prophetic revelation. Both prophets did not write down their prophecies, nor did they give them to a school of disciples who would follow them. Instead, these prophets were recognized, though in quite different ways, as holy men (one who worshiped Yahweh and one who worshiped other gods) who received a revelation from Yahweh.

1. Elijah (1 Kings 19:1–18). Elijah's confrontation with Yahweh on Mount Horeb (Sinai) is a well-known biblical narrative that has fascinated readers for centuries. Though the account's primary meaning has to do with Elijah's recommissioning as a prophet, it is the means by which Yahweh reveals himself and his desires to his prophet (the "still small voice") that has become the major focus of readers. The text reads,

> Now there was a great wind, so strong that it was splitting mountains and break-ing rocks in pieces before the Lord, but the Lord was not in the wind; and after the wind an earthquake, but the Lord was not in the earthquake; and after the earthquake a fire, but the Lord was not in the fire; and after the fire a sound of sheer silence. When Elijah heard it, he wrapped his face in his mantle and went out and stood at the entrance of the cave. (1 Kings 19:11–13)

The larger account (1 Kings 19:1–18) has to do with Elijah's burnout as a prophet. Following the spectacular confrontation with the prophets of Baal on Mount Carmel and the subsequent life-giving rain that miraculously ends Israel's drought, Elijah becomes a "wanted" man. The apostate queen of Israel, Jezebel, considers him an enemy of the state. So, fearing for his life, Elijah flees on foot to Beersheba, ninety miles south on the southern boundary of royal control. Worn out after his encounters, Elijah feels isolated and depressed, expressing, perhaps hyperbolically, a death wish. When he falls asleep, an angel brings him food to eat—cake and water. Then Elijah continues his travel southward into the Sinai Peninsula to Mount Horeb, where he comes to a cave and spends the night. Addressed there by God as to what he is doing, Elijah again complains of the futility of his zealousness. Forgetting that thousands of Israelites had responded to him on Mount Carmel by pledging their al-legiance to Yahweh, and that Obadiah had hidden a hundred prophets from

Jezebel's persecution (1 Kings 18), Elijah tells God that he alone is faithful, and they seek to kill him (1 Kings 19:10).

God then confronts Elijah with what has often been the context for a theophany, for a manifestation of the Spirit of God, whether in wind, earthquake, or fire. But the Lord is not in these manifestations of power. Rather it is the evocative "sound of sheer silence" (v. 12) which follows that causes Elijah to respond by standing at the entrance to the cave. There he "hears" God's voice recommission him as a prophet. Whether the voice is audible can only be conjectured. That it is a continuation of the speechless speech, of the evocative silence, is clear. In the pregnant silence, Elijah hears God's voice call him back into service. He is (1) to anoint Hazael, someone who would later oppress Israel, as king over Aram (what is today Syria). Elijah would thus be part of God's plan to judge his people's apostasy. He is (2) to anoint Jehu, someone who would rid Israel of the heretical dynasty of Ahab and Jezebel, as king over Israel. And he is (3) to anoint Elisha to succeed him as prophet. God ends his revelation to Elijah by reminding him of the seven thousand faithful Israelites who did not bow to Baal (v. 18).

The emphasis of the narrative is on Elijah's recommissioning. A burned-out activist is reenergized and given new purpose by the gracious, intervening, revelatory Presence of God. Much of the description of Elijah's reconfirmation as a prophet is put in language that recalls Moses at Mount Horeb. Elijah is symbolically reported as having traveled "forty" days to get to Sinai, even though the journey would or could have been shorter. And the wind, earthquake, and fire that Elijah experiences in the cave are reminiscent not only of the earlier theophanies in Sinai ("fire" in Exod. 3:2 and "thunder" in Exod. 19:16–18) but also of the description of Moses being put by God "in a cleft of the rock" while God's glory passed by (Exod. 33). Moreover, Elijah's call, like Moses's, is audacious. Elijah is to show that Yahweh is God over more than even Israel; Yahweh is supreme over all the earth. His new commission comes in the context of a revelation that leaves Elijah both awestruck and emboldened (recall Otto's description of an encounter with the numinous: *mysterium tremendum et fascinans*).

But though the account in 1 Kings is important to the larger narrative because Elijah's new commission prepares for the placing of the mantle of spiritual leadership on Elisha and foreshadows the confrontation between Aram and Israel that is to follow, it is the "sound of sheer silence" (1 Kings 19:12) that Elijah experiences that focuses the attention of readers. It is this powerful language of epiphany that continues to fascinate readers today. For they too have had such experiences of pregnant silence, or they long for such. The English translations of the three words of the Hebrew text vary, in part because the original writer also struggled to capture what exactly Elijah experiences. It is hard to put into words (as surely is the experience!): "a still small voice" (KJV and RSV); "a gentle whisper" (NIV); "the soft whisper of a voice" (GNT); "a low murmuring sound" (NEB); "a soft whisper" (NET); "the sound of a gentle breeze" (JB); "a sound of thin silence" (John Grey); "the sound of utmost silence," which can be "cut with a knife" (Samuel Terrien). Literally, the Hebrew means "a voice (or sound) of thin (or fine) silence (or quietness)." Rather than witnessing a spectacular in-breaking of Yahweh into history (cf. Hab. 3; Ps. 68; Judg. 5:4–5), Elijah experiences in the "sound of sheer, or thin, silence" the voice of God, a voice that commissions him anew.

What is being expressed by the text is similar to that fragile, audible silence that Eliphaz refers to in the fourth chapter of Job.

> Now a word came stealing to me, my ear received the whisper of it.
> Amid thoughts from visions of the night, when deep sleep falls on
>   mortals,
> dread came upon me, and trembling, which made all my bones shake.
> A spirit glided past my face, the hair of my flesh bristled.
> It stood still, but I could not discern its appearance.
> A form was before my eyes; there was silence, then I heard a voice:
> "Can human beings be pure before their Maker?" (Job 4:12–17)

Here are accounts similar to what mystics witness to. They testify that their direct encounters with God often occur in the stillness that follows privation or inner turmoil, or perhaps in a retreat into the isolation of nature or the experience of the night. And despite its paradoxical mystery, such "silence" still becomes the occasion for the numinous to speak to many of us today. One thinks of the account documented by David Hay in chapter 2 where a young girl, while walking in a cornfield, said that "heaven blazed upon me," or the young boy who experienced leaves stirred by a breeze as dusk faded, or Ricky's video of a plastic bag dancing in the wind one brisk autumn day in the movie *American Beauty*.

2. Balaam (Num. 22–24). The narrative account of Balaam is long and involved, taking up three chapters in the book of Numbers (Num. 22–24). The story divides into three parts: King Balak's summons of Balaam to curse Israel, Balaam's interaction with his donkey, and Balaam's four oracles to King Balak of Moab. It contains both real drama and not a little irony and humor. The story is a significant text biblically, as Moses (Deut. 23:4–6), Joshua (Josh. 24:9–10), and Nehemiah (Neh. 13:2) all refer to Balaam by name in their recounting of Israel's history. And although the New Testament

remembers Balaam chiefly in a negative light for his greed and pagan worship practices (2 Pet. 2:15–16; Jude 11; Rev. 2:14), he also is an important figure in the history of the early church. What most Christians and Jews remember when asked about Balaam is the description of his offish interaction with his donkey (the "seer" is unable to see). But the storyteller in Numbers also describes this non-Israelite prophet as a pragmatic person who possesses a basic integrity in relation to Yahweh and the Israelites as he interacts with the king of Moab. More pointedly, he is the one who becomes open to both hearing and delivering a divine message from Yahweh. Ultimately, the focus of the Balaam narrative is on Yahweh and his revelation, not on Balaam as a diviner. In Numbers, Balaam is simply the one who receives Yahweh's revelation (after all, his ass also received a message). But given the mysterious interaction between providence and free will, it remains significant that he did receive it and chose to act on it. (One needs only recall Jonah for an alternate example.)

We do not know where Balaam comes from, but his name is not Israelite, nor does the story allow for him to be an Israelite. The story begins with Balak, the king of Moab, being described as fearful that Israel will conquer his nation, given what they have just done to the Canaanites and the Amorites. He thus sends his messengers to Balaam, a seer, to commission him to curse Israel so that Moab might not be destroyed. Balaam meets his guests and responds by asking the emissaries to remain overnight while he seeks to divine an answer to their request. In particular, he is interested in learning whether Israel's God is blessing them, for if Israel's success is based on a blessing from their God, Balaam will not be able to undo this by his curse. And Yahweh does reveal himself to Balaam, saying that these people are indeed blessed. So Balaam declines the commission. King Balak is undeterred, however, sending "princes" this time to Balaam to ask a second time for him to curse Israel. Balaam initially refuses to go with them, saying that he cannot "go beyond the command of the LORD my God" (Num. 22:18). However, based on God's further instructions to him in a revelation at night, Balaam says he will meet with Balak.

When the retinue sets out, however, an angel of the Lord stands in the path of Balaam's ass three different times, causing the donkey each time to veer off the path. But surprisingly, Balaam doesn't see it. Angry, Balaam strikes the seemingly insolent animal. But after being struck for the third time, the donkey amazingly speaks (!) back to Balaam, having been empowered by God. The text states (Num. 22:31), "Then the LORD opened the eyes of Balaam." He finally sees the angel with his drawn sword, who tells Balaam that he has come to stop him. Confronted by the angel, Balaam confesses his sins for trying to oppose the angel. Though he is willing to turn back, the angel tells Balaam to proceed, but to make sure he speaks to Balak only what Yahweh tells him.

The third part of the story is the longest and records Balaam's encounter with the king. It recounts the four oracles from Yahweh, which he tells Balak. Coming to King Balak, Balaam tells the king that he will only speak "the word God [*elohim*] puts in my mouth" (Num. 22:38). Wanting to create a context in which Balaam will speak, the king takes this prophet to the high place of Baal, expecting Balaam to look out across the altars and finally curse Israel. But Balaam responds: "How can I curse whom God has not cursed? . . . Who can count the dust of Jacob?" (Num. 23:8, 10). As might be expected, the king is furious, for Balaam has turned out to bless Israel rather than curse it. But Balaam replies, "Must I not take care to say what the LORD puts into my mouth?" (Num. 23:12).

Undeterred, King Balak takes Balaam to a second location, where he again asks Balaam to curse Israel. But again Balaam responds, "God is not a human being that he should lie [i.e., not fulfill his promise]. . . . He has blessed, and I cannot revoke it" (Num. 23:19–20). Then, yet a third time, Balak tries to get Balaam to curse Israel (or at least not bless Israel!), but Balaam again ends up offering an extravagant, poetic blessing on Israel.

> The oracle of one who hears the words of God,
>   who sees the vision of the Almighty,
>   who falls down, but with eyes uncovered:
> how fair are your tents, O Jacob,
>   your encampments, O Israel!
> Like palm groves that stretch far away,
>   like gardens beside a river,
> like aloes that the LORD has planted,
>   like cedar trees besides the waters.
> Water shall flow from his buckets,
>   And his seed shall have abundant water,
> his king shall be higher than Agag,
>   and his kingdom shall be exalted. (Num. 24:4–7)

Balaam, like Elijah, looks out across the scorched plains of southern Palestine and, though there is no speech, hears God speak. And though there is no image, he sees the Almighty. He faithfully tells King Balak his experience.

Not surprisingly, King Balak is again furious. But Balaam is not through speaking. He repeats to the king in a fourth oracle that he has heard "the words of God, and knows the knowledge of the Most High." He has seen "the vision of the Almighty" and has fallen down, "but with his eyes uncovered: I see him, but not now; I behold him, but not near" (Num. 24:16–17). Balaam then goes on to declare that sometime in the future God will crush Moab and obliterate a series of other nations. Balak could not have imagined a worse response to his initial request.

This complex narrative has much that has interested commentators over the centuries. Balaam hearing his ass speak is surely (like the large fish in the Jonah narrative) what has first captured the attention of readers. And this narrative within a narrative is important to the narrative, for it functions as an ironic foil for the larger story: what is important is not one's abilities as a diviner, but rather to whom God chooses to reveal himself. And in this story, Yahweh chooses to reveal himself to the outsider Balaam, who practices his religion in a way that the rest of the Old Testament condemns.

The heart of this story is Balaam's encounter with Yahweh.[11] Thirteen times in the narrative, Balaam uses the personal name for Israel's God: Yahweh. Balaam's first words in the story (Num. 22:8), uttered to the king's emissaries who have come asking him to curse Israel, refer to Yahweh speaking to him. ("Stay here tonight, and I will bring back word to you, just as the LORD [Yahweh] speaks to me.") Twelve more times in the account that follows, Balaam mentions Yahweh. Is this simply a stylistic convention of the Israelite storyteller? Or has there been some recognition by Balaam that Yahweh is Lord of the whole world? Probably neither, at least in this first instance. Instead, Balaam has simply heard the name of Israel's God and has decided he is going to use it in his divination to discover whether Israel's god has blessed these people. Balaam will not attempt to curse Israel if Yahweh has blessed her. It will not work. So far so good. But readers struggle over what comes next—Balaam confesses in response to the second group of emissaries, "I could not go beyond the command of the LORD *my God*, to do less or more" (Num. 22:18, italics mine). Is Balaam now to be thought a worshiper? Has there been a "conversion"? No, as the narrative plays out, Balaam seems here to be speaking about the God who has revealed himself to him—Yahweh is in this sense "my God." Balaam is identifying the god he has personally sought answers from in his divination, and who has responded.

What is fascinating in both of these initial responses to Balak's emissaries is that Yahweh chooses to answer Balaam when he "consults" with him, even though Balaam is involved in divination procedures (Num. 22:12, 20). That is, Israel's God responds to the false, nighttime religious practices of a prophet outside of his people. In the second part of the story, as we have seen,

---

11. For an insightful discussion of the issues surrounding Balaam as a prophet, see Michael L. Barre, "The Portrait of Balaam in Numbers 22–24," *Interpretation* 51, no. 3 (1997): 254–66.

revelation happens even more improbably, through a talking donkey (Num. 22:28–30) and then through an angel (Num. 22:32–35). And in part three of the narrative, Balaam again hears Yahweh speak to him in the context of false religious practices—twice he has Balak build for him seven altars with a bull and a ram on each altar. He then has Balak stand beside his burnt offerings while Balaam goes "aside." And the text says that twice God "met Balaam," and, as a result, Balaam blesses Israel (Num. 23:4, 16). When Balak seeks a curse from Balaam still a third time, rather than again have Balak build him an altar, Balaam does not attempt to use divination practices as he seeks to hear God speak. The text reads:

> Now Balaam saw that it pleased the Lord to bless Israel, so he did not go, as at other times, to look for omens, but set his face toward the wilderness. Balaam looked up and saw Israel camping tribe by tribe. Then the spirit of God came upon him, and he uttered his oracle, saying:
>
>> The oracle of Balaam son of Beor,
>> the oracle of the man whose eye is clear,
>> the oracle of one who hears the words of God,
>> who sees the vision of the Almighty
>> who falls down, but with eyes uncovered. (Num. 24:3–4)

God chooses now to answer the non-Israelite religious practitioner directly, and the spirit of God comes upon him. Balaam indeed "hears" the spirit of God speak. A fourth and final oracle is introduced by Balaam's reiterating his commitment to be true to the revelation that Yahweh has indeed shown to him: "Did I not tell your messengers whom you sent to me, 'If Balak should give me his house full of silver and gold, I would not be able to go beyond the word of the LORD [Yahweh], to do either good or bad of my own will; what the Lord says, that is what I will say'?" (Num. 24:12–13).

Prophets

In turning to the section of the Hebrew Bible known as the Prophets, we might expect less interest by the biblical writers in revelation outside the covenant community, and this is indeed what we find. It is the revelation of God to and through his prophets that are the foci of these books. When dealing with those outside of Israel, the books are interested not so much in how these foreigners might be a source of general revelation to God's people as they are on how God's providential rule extends throughout the whole world. (The one exception, perhaps, is the "antiprophet" Jonah.) But in the prophets' discussion

of "the nations," there is also an indirect application to our discussion of revelation that is important to note.[12] Repeatedly, the prophetic books point out
that in God's actions, particularly regarding judgment for Israel's apostasy
and/or lack of faith, God will speak through the nations so that Israel will
repent and return to faith. God's providential rule, that is, has a communica-
tive intention. It is not disinterested, removed action that the prophets speak
of, but rather God's revealing himself to his people through his providential
rule. Consider these three examples.

1. Isaiah 10:1–20. The tenth chapter of Isaiah gives readers an example of
God's use of pagan culture to accomplish his purposes. Here the Old Testament's expansive notion of God's revelational possibilities in this world is
illustrated by his use of the Assyrians as his spokespeople. Judah (whose
people understood themselves to be "God's people") is besieged by pagan
Assyria (whose people certainly were not "God's people"). In such a situation,
one would expect the prophet to demand of God both judgment against the
evildoers (Assyria) and empowerment for God's people (Judah). God's glory
must be made clear. But no, the scenario is reversed. Isaiah states that God
would use pagan Assyria to communicate his judgment on "Jerusalem and
her idols" (Isa. 10:11). Only in this way might justice reign.

> Ah, Assyria, the rod of my anger—
>   The club in their hands is my fury!
> Against a godless nation I send him,
>   And against the people of my wrath I command him,
> To take spoil and seize plunder,
>   And to tread them down like the mire of the streets. (Isa. 10:5–6)

Assyria is described by God as "my" spokesperson. She will be "the rod of
my anger—the club in their hands is my fury!" (Isa. 10:5). Assyria will have

---

12. Gerhard von Rad, in his two-volume *Old Testament Theology*, notes a difference between
how the historical books of the Old Testament treat "the nations" surrounding Israel and Judah
and how the prophets describe them (Gerhard von Rad, *Old Testament Theology*, 2 vols. [New
York: Harper, 1962, 1965]). He believes that while in the historical books the nations are usually
mentioned only in terms of political stories or battles between Israel and the nations, in the
prophets God uses the nations much more concretely to bring into effect his purposes for both
judgment and salvation (1:161). Von Rad has somewhat overstated his case, as our explorations
of Gerar (Abimelech), Salem (Melchizedek), Tyre (Huram), Egypt (Neco), and Massa (Agur and
King Lemuel's mother) indicate. The nations are also used by God in the Law and the Writings
of the Hebrew Scriptures to bring about God's purposes. But though God is seen as God of the
whole world throughout the Scriptures, it is perhaps true that in the prophets, the nations are
more often used as a direct means of God's providential rule and as such an indirect means of
communication between God and his people.

no idea that God is communicating his judgment on Judah through her (Isa. 10:7). (Note: it is Judah that is called "a godless nation.") Assyria will be the unconscious instrument of a God in whom she does not believe. It doesn't matter; pagan Assyria is to be an expression of God's revelation to "believing" Judah.

In due season, God will judge Assyria for her hubris, too. But that is God's issue, not Judah's.

> When the Lord has finished all his work on Mount Zion and on Jerusalem, he will punish the arrogant boasting of the king of Assyria and his haughty pride. . . .

> Shall the ax vaunt itself over the one who wields it,
>   or the saw magnify itself against the one who handles it?
> (Isa. 10:12, 15)

But although Assyria and Yahweh have contrasting motives regarding Judah (world dominion versus communicating a just punishment to God's people through those who are not God's people), and though there are contrasting assessments of Assyria (her ability and success versus her pride and the need for punishment), Assyria is nevertheless God's chosen instrument. Here, in Isaiah 10, we have "one of the Bible's central utterances about the relation between heaven and earth in human history."[13]

I am indebted to Robert McAfee Brown for first calling to my attention the relevance of Isaiah's prophecy about the Assyrians to a theology of revelation as I sat in his classroom as a freshman in university.[14] The course was a class in religion and contemporary literature. Brown asked the question, "How might it be possible to hear God speak through the work of non-Christian artists today?" He answered by speaking metaphorically about the Assyrian in Isaiah 10. Just as Isaiah recognized in his day that God could speak a true word to his people Israel through the unbelieving, unethical Assyrians, so Christians might be able to affirm today that God in his freedom can speak not only through believers but also through novelists who are "Assyrians in modern dress."

2. Habakkuk. The book of Habakkuk "aims to involve its hearers in the reeducation of Habakkuk."[15] It is, in John Goldingay's words, "a dramatized

---

13. J. Alec Motyer, *The Prophecy of Isaiah: An Introduction and Commentary* (Downers Grove, IL: InterVarsity, 1993), 112.

14. See Robert McAfee Brown, "Assyrians in Modern Dress," in *The Pseudonyms of God* (Philadelphia: Westminster, 1972), 96–103.

15. Michael H. Floyd, *Minor Prophets, Part 2* (Grand Rapids: Eerdmans, 2000), 88, quoted in John Goldingay, "Habakkuk," in John Goldingay and Pamela J. Scalise, *Minor Prophets 2* (Grand Rapids: Baker Books, 2009), 50.

discussion of the nature of Yahweh's involvement in the world of international affairs, especially as these affect the people of Yahweh. We might then call it a discussion of theodicy, though that construct imports much modern baggage. And its stress on waiting and steadfastness, and its prayer (Hab. 2:3–4; 3:2, 16), indicate that it is not merely a discussion of a theological or apologetic question but a pastoral tract."[16] How are we to believe in the purposes and activity of God, given the world as it presents itself? There is sometimes a discrepancy between God and life, between faith and experience. Thus, the prophet seeks an explanation from God, and comes ultimately to declare his trust in what God intends to do.

The book begins with Habakkuk complaining twice to his God about the evil that persists around him, and twice Yahweh answers him in a vision. The prophet's first problem has to do with God's silence: Why is God not judging the "wicked" (Hab. 1:4)? How long must evil and violence continue? It is not completely clear who the "wicked" are, but whoever they are, the faithless are oppressing the faithful. Justice is being perverted. Why, God, don't you listen and intervene? Surprisingly, God does answer, but in shocking ways (Hab. 1:5–11). God says to his people through Habakkuk that he is, indeed, at work, but through the godless Chaldeans.

> For I am rousing the Chaldeans,
>   that fierce and impetuous nation,
> who march through the breadth of the earth
>   to seize dwellings not their own. . . .
>   Their own might is their god! (Hab. 1:6, 11)

The Chaldeans—those tribes in southern Babylon who took control of the state from the Assyrians in 627 BC and who sacked Asshur (614 BC) and Nineveh (612 BC) and defeated the Egyptians in 605 BC—will be Yahweh's instrument of justice against the unjust and violent in Judah. God will work through these people and, as verse 7 has it, "their justice and dignity" (such as it is) to accomplish his purposes. And in fact this is what happens. No event in history, it would seem, is godless.

But to involve God in the evil of Chaldean culture creates a bigger problem for this prophet, and for us. And so Habakkuk complains a second time. He asks of God, How could Yahweh, who is good and just, use an evil nation to judge a "less evil" nation? (Hab. 1:13). The Chaldeans were like fishermen with nets and hooks (Hab. 1:15–17) who delight in their killing, bringing in

16. Goldingay, "Habakkuk," 49–50.

helpless fish and rejoicing in their work. It was right that God had ordained, or marked, the wicked for judgment, but surely not by the evil Chaldeans. Such an unholy alliance could not be! So God responds a second time. The Chaldeans, too, will be judged in their own season. Those who rely on themselves will fail. To reinforce this point a series of five oracles of woe are included (Hab. 2:6–20). God promises that a righteous, faithful remnant will survive. But the Chaldeans, nevertheless, will be God's spokespeople for a season. Having heard that the proud who forget God will not live, Habakkuk ends his short book with a hymn. He has heard God's word of judgment. The divine Warrior will act against the wicked; Habakkuk will trust his God. He will "exult in the God of my salvation" (Hab. 3:18).

In the New Testament, Habakkuk's trust in a life of faith (Hab. 2:4) is picked up and quoted three times: in Romans 1:17, Galatians 3:11, and Hebrews 10:38. As such, the book is usually summarized as a book about faith, and so it is. Here is the core of the gospel as Martin Luther discovered in reading Paul's use of Habakkuk in Romans at the start of the Reformation. But what is too often overlooked is another and perhaps more central theme in Habakkuk. The central question for Habakkuk in the book is how *God* is to be understood as involved in this world. And the answer is clearly revealed. As in Isaiah 10, God speaks not only through the prophets but also through the actions of a ruthless, cruel nation. We cannot divorce God from the world and its culture. Rather, here as elsewhere, it is through human culture that God makes known his purposes for the world.

3. Jonah 1:4–16. In both Isaiah and Habakkuk, we see God's revelation manifest in his providential rule through the actions of the nations. While with Neco and Cyrus, Melchizedek and Abimelech, God speaks to the nations and their leaders and only then through them to Israel, with Assyria and the Chaldeans, God's revelation comes without their direct knowledge. They are the unwitting spokespersons of a God they refuse to accept. If there is a prophetic book where God's revelation is also made clear to those outside the covenant community, it would be the book of Jonah. Here, it is not the oracles of the prophet that are given priority in the text, as in the other prophetic books. Jonah's one prophetic oracle is only five words in the Hebrew. Rather, it is the story itself that provides readers its meaning. Although the setting of the story is the northern kingdom in the eighth century when Nineveh was a powerful Assyrian city, the book most likely was composed much later, perhaps during the postexilic period when, as we have seen, Israel was asking about their God in relationship with other nations and religions.

The narrative is familiar to most people, telling the story of Jonah, who is called by God to go to Israel's enemy, Nineveh, in order to call that city to repentance before God destroys it. But Jonah wants nothing to do with such a call, so flees in the opposite direction by boat (probably toward modern-day Spain). A storm on the sea arises, threatening the lives of all on board the ship. It is only when the sailors reluctantly throw Jonah overboard to appease his God that the storm abates. After three days in the stomach of a great fish that has "rescued" Jonah, Jonah prays and is spit out onto dry land. Called again to go to Nineveh by his God, Jonah goes, and exactly what he fears happens. The people recognize their sin and repent, and God relents from carrying out his punishment. Though Jonah has been "successful," this only makes him angry. The book ends as Jonah sits outside the city pouting, with God questioning him as to why he is angry.

For the purposes of our investigation into God's revelation outside the covenant community, it is Jonah's encounter with the sailors that is of particular interest (Jon. 1:4–16). Here, the major characters in the scene are the sailors and Yahweh. Throughout the book, God controls the forces of nature—the wind, the sea, the great fish, a fast-growing plant—in order to make Jonah carry out his prophetic task. Thus, when God brings on a mighty storm (Jon. 1:4), interestingly, it is not Jonah who recognizes God's involvement in their predicament but the non-Israelite sailors. They hear God speak through the wind and sea long before Jonah does (or at least long before Jonah lets on that he knows). Each cries out to his own god (Jon. 1:5). It is the sailors who wake Jonah up, demanding of him that he "Get up, [and] call on your god!" (Jon. 1:6). Only after the sailors decide to cast lots to ascertain who is at fault for this divine punishment and the lot falls on Jonah does Jonah respond: "I am a Hebrew. . . . I worship the LORD, the God of heaven, who made the sea and the dry land" (Jon. 1:9). When the sailors realize he is fleeing from the Presence of his God, Yahweh, they are afraid. When Jonah instructs them to throw him overboard and the sea will calm, they first resist and keep rowing. Finally, they pray to Jonah's God, asking to be spared from Jonah's punishment, and when Jonah is thrown overboard and the sea immediately calms, the sailors become even more afraid, and so the text relates, they "offered a sacrifice to the LORD and made vows" (Jon. 1:16).

The narrative, as written, is filled with irony (cf. Isa. 10). It is not the believer in Yahweh who acts in a godly way, but the pagan sailors: (1) they are the ones who are on deck working to save the ship while Jonah sleeps below; (2) they are the first to recognize that God is at work in the storm and pray to their gods; (3) they consult with Jonah and each other as to the best course; (4) even when Jonah gives up and says "throw me overboard," they continue to seek a more "ethical" solution; (5) and they cry out to Jonah's God for mercy for their contemplated action. But perhaps most important for our purposes,

(6) after tossing Jonah overboard and seeing the sea "cease from its raging" (Jon. 1:15), they offer sacrifice to Yahweh and make vows. Jonah's God has indeed revealed himself as "the God of heaven, who made the sea and dry land" (Jon. 1:9), and they respond in faith, the best that they are able. One would hardly expect the actions of non-Israelite sailors to be a model of wise and godly living for God's people, but such is the case. Is there any doubt that it is the sailors that the writer intends us to see as being models of faithful humanity? Lest we wonder, the text immediately notes that though Jonah is rescued by a big fish, it is not until three days later that Jonah is willing to bring himself to pray to his God. And even then, his prayer seems unduly centered on himself. (He makes twenty-four personal references to himself in just eight verses of text!) Jonah's self-absorption, moreover, continues throughout the story. Once God accomplishes his mission in getting Jonah to Nineveh, it is again a non-Israelite people, the Ninevites, who hear God and repent, while Jonah can only pout over his lack of shade.

Like the Isaiah and Habakkuk texts we have already looked at, the story of Jonah is not directly about revelation outside the covenant community. It is the revelation of Yahweh through the recalcitrant Jonah that is the basis for the repentance and belief of the king of Nineveh. Here is the focus of the story. But as an antiprophet, Jonah helps us see the extent of God's reach. God protects the sailors, having revealed something of his righteousness to them. God also changes the divine plan of judgment that was projected against the people of Nineveh. Perhaps we should say, as the story is told, it is as both Creator and Redeemer—it is both through general and special revelation—that God makes his will known.

The New Testament

Acts

Turning to the New Testament, the book of Acts provides us two narratives in which revelation outside the church and without reference to Scripture is made the basis of the apostle Paul's proclamation. Both have to do with Paul's mission to the gentiles. The focus is on the "outsider." Luke, the writer, provides his readers summaries of two encounters that Paul had with a purely gentile population, those who had no acquaintance with the God of Israel or with the Hebrew prophets. (Although Cornelius and his household provide a third Lukan example in Acts 10 of proclamation to the gentiles, Cornelius was a God-fearer who was well acquainted with the God of Israel and the Jewish Scriptures and thus understood revelation in light of Israel's faith.) In both cases, Paul does not directly reference the Hebrew Scriptures, nor does he build his apologetic around Jewish thought. Rather, he references the experiences of his gentile audiences and there finds points of revelatory contact arising from their own context.

1. Acts 14:8–20. In Acts 14, Luke records the first direct contact Paul had with a gentile population—the townspeople of Lystra. In this context, Paul does not root his presentation of the faith in terms of a fulfillment of Old Testament prophecy as he does with audiences who have a knowledge of the Jewish experience. Such an appeal to "authority" would be hard for the people of Lystra to accept, or even understand. Instead, seeking a point of contact, he appeals to God's revealing Presence in creation (though if there had been a Jew in his audience, he or she would have heard Paul's language as resonant with Old Testament descriptions). Some commentators speak of this as Paul addressing gentile audiences "through the light of natural revelation."[17] While potentially a helpful insight, the comment's usefulness depends completely on how natural theology is defined. We must avoid not only the idolization of nature but also its denigration. If by "natural theology" one means the footprint of God's creative activity that remains after after creation ends, a footprint built, or stamped, into the fabric of the universe, or—to change the metaphor—the echo remaining after the voice of God ceases speaking, then this is not Paul's meaning, as we will see. If, on the other hand, natural theology is placed "under the aegis of revelation," to use T. F. Torrance's felicitous phrase, then creation becomes the "theater" that displays the Presence of God. Here is a natural revelation in line with the apostle Paul's proclamation to the townspeople in Lystra.

Luke records that after experiencing hostility and threats from unbelieving Jews in Iconium, Paul took refuge in Lystra. The town was a small, rural Roman colony twenty miles to the south, where the Lycaonian language was still spoken in addition to Greek. The narrative begins with the description of a man who was lame, sitting and listening to Paul speak. Luke desires to emphasize the man's condition, so in the one description, he says, he "could not use his feet," "had never walked," and "had been crippled from birth" (Acts 14:8). The reason for this redundancy becomes evident as Luke records that Paul looked intently at him and discerned in him a faith to be healed. Paul then shouted in a *loud* voice, "Stand upright." And Luke writes, the man "sprang up and began to walk" (Acts 14:10). With such heightened language throughout the short description, readers are encouraged to understand the

17. See Michael Green, *Evangelism in the Early Church*, rev. ed. (Grand Rapids: Eerdmans, 2003), 180.

wonder of the event to those who were watching, and thus what follows is framed in a more believable context.

Part two of the story begins with the crowd beginning to shout out in Lycaonian, their local language, though of course Paul and Barnabas could not understand them. In their unsophisticated religiosity, the townspeople were saying that the strangers must be gods who had come among them in human form. Perhaps they were recalling a legend from their own area that Ovid, writing in his *Metamorphoses* less than a century before Paul, recounts. In the story, Zeus and Hermes in human form visit an old couple and later reward them for their hospitality. Most commentators project that this story was in the townspeople's mind as they called Barnabas "Zeus" (perhaps he was the bigger of the two?) and Paul "Hermes" (for he had been doing the speaking) (Acts 14:12). By the time the apostles realized what was going on, the local priest of Zeus had brought oxen and garlands, and the crowds wanted to offer sacrifices to the two. Paul and Barnabas were aghast; they tore their clothes and moved into the crowd where they shouted that they were not gods but mortals like the people, and simply had a message to bring them. They told the crowd that they should not worship them but "the living God [singular!], who made the heaven and the earth and the sea and all that is in them" (Acts 14:15). This Creator God, moreover, is not distant from them, but has continued to provide them a threefold witness of his care. In particular, God gives them rains, fruitful seasons, and food that fills their hearts with joy. (A Jew, if he or she had been listening, might have heard allusions to Exod. 20:11 and Eccles. 9:7, but to this gentile audience, the only reference they understood was their own experience of creation.) Luke writes that even with these words, however, Barnabas and Paul had trouble restraining the crowd from offering sacrifices to them.

To these rural and probably illiterate gentiles, Paul appeals neither to the Jewish tradition nor to the Greek thought of the academy. F. F. Bruce summarizes the situation well.

> To Jews and God-fearing gentiles, who already knew that God is one, and that he is the living and true God, the gospel [could be] proclaimed that this God had sent his Son as Messiah and Savior; but pagans had first to be taught what Jews already confessed regarding the unity and character of God. "God is one," the pagans of Lystra are told, "and has not left himself without a witness. His work of creation and providence show him to be the living God who supplies the needs of men and women; therefore abandon those gods which are no gods but empty figments of the imagination, and turn to the true God."[18]

18. F. F. Bruce, *The Book of the Acts*, rev. ed. (Grand Rapids: Eerdmans, 1988), 277.

Paul's emphasis here is on the ongoing providence of God as revelatory. In providing rainfall and harvest, food and rejoicing, God reveals his goodness and grace to all who will see. To a crowd who had been willing to recognize the work of the gods in healing a man who since birth could not walk, causing him to "spring up," Paul and Barnabas speak of a Creator who also showers them with divine blessing in other ways. We do not know how these apostles might have followed up their words if they had been allowed to finish their presentation. Would they, as in Acts 17, have turned to Jesus and his resurrection as proof that what they were saying could be trusted? We cannot say. Here was an unsophisticated audience unlike those highly educated Athenians at the Areopagus. But whatever their intention was, it is cut short as Jewish opponents from Iconium, who have tracked Paul and Barnabas to Lystra, come into Lystra and cause the crowd to turn on the two visitors. Praise turns quickly to anger, and, incredibly, the crowd ends up stoning Paul, leaving him for dead! But though the story ends badly, the initial reception of the apostles by the gentiles of Lystra, their openness to things spiritual, suggests that God is also preparing a gentile people for inclusion within the covenant community. And this happens in part through God's self-revelation as Creator through his creation.

2. Acts 17:16–34. The seventeenth chapter of Acts provides a second New Testament window into Paul's theology of general revelation. The text recounts Paul's speech about God's revealing Presence to a group of educated citizens in Athens. Along with Acts 14, it has been the only narrative-based text that theologians have typically used as they have developed their theology of revelation. (The Old Testament texts explored above have surprisingly seldom been considered by theologians of revelation.) Perhaps because this text has been recognized as pertinent to the theological discussion, or perhaps because as narrative there is a certain openness to the presentation that allows readers to let questions remain without pretending to "solve" all the issues, few texts in the New Testament have been as thoroughly explored or as variously assessed. Does it border on natural theology? If so, is that good, or is it deficient theologically? Is the description of Paul's speech Luke's idealized version of how one might speak the gospel to gentiles? If not, how can it be squared with what Paul writes in Romans 1? Was Paul perhaps not being fully forthright with his audience as he sought to make connection with them? Or has he effectively clothed biblical revelation in cultural argument? The questions have been numerous.

Those who have tended to want theologically to limit the role and extent of general revelation (it is but "a trace"—just enough to condemn people for not turning to God, but not enough to provide insight) have tended to be the ones who have had the most trouble understanding Acts 17. They have sometimes even questioned whether Paul's theology here is helpful or even adequate. Some commentators, uneasy with Paul's seemingly "soft" approach to idolatry (he begins his reflection by recognizing the Athenians as being "extremely religious" given their worship of an "unknown god," vv. 22–23), criticize Paul for not being more prophetic, more condemnatory of idolatry, and more forthright about God's judgment of their sin. Where is the Paul of Romans 1? No wonder, the critique goes, that Paul was not more successful in his preaching that day—after all, only a few responded. (In the interest of full disclosure, I write this while living in a radically secular Spain, where a few new converts in a local church are cause to celebrate God's faithfulness and power, not a situation to criticize or condemn. Context matters.) Contrast Paul's indirect apologetic here with Peter's more theologically rooted sermon where he preached that his Jewish listeners had crucified and killed Jesus, with the result that three thousand converts responded (Acts 2:41). One cannot afford to be soft on sin, so the judgment of certain commentators goes.[19]

Apart from the fact that there is no textual evidence to support such an interpretation that somehow Paul's is an example of "ineffectual" preaching, this interpretation also fails to recognize in the text itself the extent to which Paul affirmed the validity of God's revelatory Presence residing outside of the church, even among pagans. Paul is not simply being manipulative when he describes his audience as being "extremely religious." Certainly he is not saying something he doesn't really believe, nor something out of keeping with the first-century Athens we know from other records. Tellingly, in verse 28, Paul buttresses his argument that the Athenians should want to know more about this unknown God who wants them to find him by quoting with approval the poets Epimenides ("In him we live and move and have our being") and Aratus ("For we too are his offspring"). Aratus's line of text comes from his *Phaenomena*, which was a treatise in verse about astronomy. It had been written in the third century BC and shows many affinities with Stoic thought. Moreover, it had gained immense popularity over the years and was used for many generations as a schoolbook.[20] Thus Paul, in quoting this poet, would

19. See W. M. Ramsey, *St. Paul the Traveler and the Roman Citizen* (London: Hodder & Stoughton, 1895), 252; notes to the *New Jerusalem Bible* (Garden City, NY: Doubleday, 1985), 1829; Martin Dibelius, *Studies in the Acts of the Apostles* (New York: Charles Scribner's Sons, 1956), 57–63; for a fuller discussion, see J. Daryl Charles, "Engaging the (Neo)Pagan Mind: Paul's Encounter with Athenian Culture as a Model for Cultural Apologetics (Acts 17:16–34)," *Trinity Journal* 16 (1995): 47–49.

20. Kirsopp Lake, "Note XX: 'Your Own Poets,'" in *The Beginnings of Christianity: Part 1, The Acts of the Apostles*, ed. F. J. Foakes Jackson and Kirsopp Lake (London: Macmillan, 1933), 246–47.

have been signaling to his hearers that he was familiar with Athenian culture. He knew their textbooks and agreed with this poet's insight. Epimenides, the author of the other quotation, was considered one of the seven sages of Greece (perhaps the English equivalent to these two poets would be Shakespeare and Chaucer). Living around 600 BC, Epimenides is attested to by Plato, Aristotle, and Plutarch, among others, though much of what is known about him is legend. In Paul's day, Epimenides would have been understood to have penned the words Paul quotes as part of a laudatory speech put into the mouth of Minos on behalf of his father.[21]

Shockingly for many contemporary Christians, the classic poets that Paul affirms are not writing simply about a generic sense of spiritual well-being arising out of their humanity, or even about a general notion of God arising out of Jewish belief. These are not vague references to a general spirituality. No, these poets in their writings are referencing Zeus! The Cretan poet Epimenides puts on the lips of Minos, Zeus's son, these words:

> They fashioned a tomb for thee, O holy and high one—
> The Cretans, always liars, evil beasts, idle bellies!
> But thou art not dead; thou livest and abidest forever,
> For in thee we live and move and have our being. (*Horae Semiticae* 10)[22]

The last line is a common wordplay between the name Zeus and the Greek word *zao*, to live—that is, in the "living" (Zeus) we live.

And again, similarly referencing Zeus, Paul quotes from the Cilician poet Aratus (ca. 315–240 BC). The longer text reads:

> Let us take our beginning from Zeus, whom we men never leave
> Unmentioned; All highways are full of Zeus,
> All meeting-places; full are the sea
> And the harbours; everywhere we all have need of Zeus.
> For we are also his offspring; he is kind and to men
> Gives favourable omens. (*Phaenomena* 5)[23]

The Zeus that is being referred to by both of these poets is in all likelihood not the ruling head of the primitive pantheon of Greek mythology, a god that

21. Ibid., 247–51. Note: Paul probably also quotes from the same poem in Titus 1:12, another indication that Paul was familiar with this writer.

22. Quoted in F. F. Bruce, *Commentary on the Book of Acts* (Grand Rapids: Eerdmans, 1955), 359. See also Titus 1:12.

23. Quoted in Theophilus of Antioch, *Ad Autolycum*, trans. Robert M. Grant (Oxford: Clarendon, 1970), 35.

perhaps the illiterate citizens in Lystra were referencing when they attempted to offer sacrifices to Barnabas and Paul. Instead he is more likely the Stoic reinterpretation of Zeus as a life force in Greek philosophy. But whether a mythological figure or a life force, it is nonetheless a foreign and "idolatrous" god that Paul is referencing, someone or something far from the God he worships. Or is this true?

Rather than simply criticize the Athenians for their idolatry, an idolatry that Luke has already mentioned as being deeply distressing to Paul, Paul chooses to recognize that in their groping after God, the Athenians have evidenced a genuine sensitivity to God "who made the world and everything in it, he . . . is Lord of heaven and earth" (Acts 17:24). That is, these Greeks had received in truth God's revelation to them. As Paul develops the heart of his speech, he moves back and forth between affirmation and correction as he addresses the Athenians. He wants them to know that this God does not live in their shrines, nor does he need anything. Instead it is God himself who "gives to all mortals life and breath and all things" (Acts 17:25), as even their poets have recognized. That is, though their understanding of revelation is partial and confused, their poets have also sensed something profoundly right. Our lives are dependent on God who has made us and who continues to uphold us. Paul is not manipulating his hearers but seeking to build on a perceived common ground based in the revelation of God the Creator.

Such creational insight rooted in God's wider revelation is not for Paul sufficient for salvation. Given their evidenced ignorance and idolatry, Paul believes that the Athenians need to repent and believe in him who was raised from the dead (Acts 17:30–31). There is more to Paul's speech that Luke records than was the case in Lystra, where Paul was interrupted by hostile outsiders. But though Paul recognizes the need for the full revelation in Jesus Christ, he believes as well that there has been something correct, even profound, in what the Athenians have sensed, however partial or incomplete. The Creator has upheld them until now and invites them to know him further. In his preaching to a gentile audience with no context or background through which to interpret or understand the gospel message, Paul turns neither to Scripture nor to Christianity's Jewish background but to general revelation, to those intimations of spirituality experienced within the wider culture that, while partially confused, also reflect revelational sensitivity that Christians can build on. And the account concludes by confirming that indeed the bridge from general revelation to special revelation can be effectively traversed, that the two can be united, for "some of them [the Athenians] joined him and became believers, including Dionysius the Areopagite and a woman named Damaris, and others with them" (Acts 17:34).

A Conclusion to Our Biblical Discussion

In the last two chapters, we have undertaken a biblical overview of God's revelatory activity outside his saving acts and words and without explicit grounding in the Hebrew Scriptures or their worshiping community. We have seen repeated examples of God's present activity in his creation and through his creatures, chief of which is humankind. Of particular interest, perhaps, are the accounts of King Neco and of Balaam son of Beor. For in the narratives surrounding them that are given by the biblical writers, these two foreigners, both clearly outside of the people of God, nevertheless hear God speak to them directly. The texts do not allow for other interpretations. Although King Josiah is willing to consult the Hebrew prophet Huldah (2 Chron. 34), he is unwilling to hear Pharaoh Neco's word from God, asking the king to grant him safe passage: "He did not listen to the words of Neco from the mouth of God," and paid for his sin with his life (2 Chron. 35:22). Equally surprising is the story of Balaam, where after twice looking for omens within the context of worship practices to Baal, Balaam instead "set his face toward the wilderness" where the Israelites are camping tribe by tribe, and the biblical text says "the spirit of God came upon him" (Num. 24:1–2). Of course the writer has forewarned readers to be expecting something extraordinary to end this narrative about Balak's folly in trying to curse Israel, for we have already encountered a talking ass. But nonetheless, that God would be heard through a seer from one of the many false religions that surrounded the people of God who has himself seen/heard God reveal himself to him stretches conventional Christian theology to its limits. Unable to interpret away these texts, theologians have either ignored them or have labeled them "special revelation," a "one off" as it were, and then moved on to say that any meaningful revelation from God only occurs within the context of the people of God. Such an interpretation does not square with the biblical narrative. And as Phyllis Trible and Walter Brueggemann have reminded us, while a text can be read from a variety of perspectives, the text itself sets parameters around the interpretive possibilities.[24] It begs to be read for what it is.

Challenging, as well, for a Christian theology that has too often limited itself to reflection on the Word written, the Word incarnate, and the Word proclaimed is both the narrative of Elijah "hearing" God in the "sound of thin silence" (1 Kings 19:12) and the story of the priest and king of Salem, Melchizedek, giving a divine blessing to Abram (Gen. 14:18–20). The Creator's

---

24. Walter Brueggemann, *Cadences of Home: Preaching among Exiles* (Louisville: Westminster John Knox, 1997), 60; Phyllis Trible, *God and the Rhetoric of Sexuality* (Philadelphia: Fortress, 1978), 11.

wordless speech in and through creation that Elijah "heard" recalls Psalm 19: "Day to day pours forth speech, and night to night declares knowledge. There is no speech, nor are there words; their voice is not heard; yet their voice goes out through all the earth, and their words to the end of the world" (vv. 2–4). The sound of thin/sheer silence proved pregnant with meaning for Elijah, just as it often has for mystics down through the ages. With regard to the story in Genesis 14, we note that the priest of Salem's prayer to the God he knew, 'el 'elyon, was received by Abram as a genuine blessing, for Abram both gave Melchizedek the expected tithe for performing a sacred rite over him and used Melchizedek's same "name" for God, 'el 'elyon, when he spoke of the oath he had made when immediately afterward addressing the king of Sodom. The mystery of God's Presence is experienced, the text suggests, also by those of other religious traditions, something Paul would also later acknowledge in his speech to the Athenians as he recognized their "altar to an unknown god" and the truth, however partial, of their religious poets Epimenides and Aratus (Acts 17:22–23, 28).

We can, in the Elijah text (1 Kings 19) and in the psalms we have considered (Pss. 19; 29), recognize God's revelation in and through, first, his *creation*. Noting the wisdom and creativity of King Agur and of King Lemuel's mother (and grandmothers and their grandmothers, for wisdom is passed down through the generations) stretches our understanding of the breadth of God's revelation still further (Prov. 30, 31), recognizing, second, *human creativity*, wisdom, and observation as another context through which we experience God's revealing Presence. Consider also the poets Epimenides and Aratus. Perhaps the wisdom of Huram-abi's creativity fits here as well (2 Chron. 2). And third, we have noted the good *conscience* of both King Abimelech (Gen. 20) and King Cyrus (2 Chron. 36). They acted with integrity given the light they had been shown. (In the next chapter, the importance of conscience as a locus for revelation will again be made evident as we consider the *loci classici* for all discussions of general revelation, Rom. 1 and 2.) God speaks, even in his full mystery, whether through the human conscience, through creation, and/or through human culture. Here is a working description of general revelation's range.

Last, at times, God's revelation is indirectly "proclaimed," as with the Assyrians (Isa. 10) and the Chaldeans (Hab. 1). Christian theologians have too often wanted to "protect" God's purity from being sullied by any divine contact with the world and its sinfulness. "Surely," as Habakkuk reasoned wrongly, "God could not be in that place." But Robert McAfee Brown has it correct when he speaks of modern novelists (and we could say filmmakers, artists, scientists, astronomers, non-Christian religious leaders, and so on) as "Assyrians in modern dress." Sometimes it is not the "antiprophets" of any age, like Jonah (Christian leaders who, though wearing the trappings and speaking the talk reject aspects of the substance), but those, like the sailors who were transporting Jonah in the wrong direction, who prove sensitive to God's revelation (Jon. 1), at least the best they are able given the knowledge they have. Such indirection lies also behind Paul's words to the Athenians. As Paul suggests, "Athenians, I see how extremely religious you are in every way. For as I went through the city and looked carefully at the objects of your worship, I found among them an altar with the inscription, 'To an unknown god'" (Acts 17:22–23). These followers of an intellectualized Zeus were unaware of the source of their spiritual longing, but they had rightly sensed God's revealing Presence among them. Here is a revelational beginning to build on, particularly in a pre-Christian (and post-Christian?) context.

6

Engaging the Tradition

Thomas Oden, in his article "Without Excuse: Classic Christian Exegesis of General Revelation," summarizes questions surrounding the theology of general revelation that developed over the first millennium of the church's existence.

> The theme of general revelation is plagued by many controversies, hazards and potential misconceptions: Is Almighty God revealed clearly in creation and the providential ordering of the cosmos? Is this revelation intended for all and accessible to all? Is it saving knowledge? Does general revelation tend toward or lead to saving knowledge without further efficacious saving grace through the revealed Word?[1]

One will immediately note in this summary of issues the church considered early in its existence a disconnect with much of what the previous chapters have taken up. The early theologians of the church were more concerned with God's footprint stamped into creation's fabric than with continuing encounters with the divine through creation, conscience, and culture (and the same largely holds true today). Thus, when turning to general revelation, they had a different set of questions that were first taken up. The concern of this book, on the other hand, while also often labeled "general revelation" (the complement of "special

---

1. Thomas C. Oden, "Without Excuse: Classic Christian Exegesis of General Revelation," *Journal of the Evangelical Theological Society* 41, no. 1 (March 1998): 55.

revelation"), is not about that which can be known about God from the divine "footprint" left by God at creation (I will leave that to the philosophers), nor is it about that which is available to all people everywhere if they but had eyes to see. Furthermore, the focus of this book is neither on revelation as "saving knowledge" nor on sin that blinds. Rather, our interest is in the light that at times illumines. It is on those divine encounters that many witness to having only occasionally, but significantly, in their lives. Nevertheless, as general revelation has been the rubric under which our wider experience of God's revelation outside the church has typically been understood, a discussion of what has been traditionally labeled as "general revelation" in the history of the church will be important to consider as we continue.

Oden, in his essay, argues that the questions he poses were taken up by early Christian writers/theologians (those he describes as "pre-Protestant, pre-European, premedieval exegetes of the first millennium during the era of the undivided church") who came to something like a consensus on issues surrounding general revelation chiefly by exegeting Romans 1:18–22 and, to a lesser degree, Romans 2:14–15. Oden references Athanasius, Basil, Gregory of Nazianzus, John Chrysostom, Ambrose, Jerome, Augustine, and Gregory the Great in particular, but also cites other early church theologians including Tertullian, Origen, and Ambrosiaster. Thus, we begin our discussion concerning how theologians across the spectrum of the church have understood God's wider revelation to us by turning to Romans 1 and 2. For these texts have been, rightly or perhaps wrongly, the *loci classici* for a biblical understanding of that revelation that occurs outside the walls of the church.

Reconsidering Romans 1–2

It was Origen who set the pattern for subsequent theologians' understanding of general revelation by noting with Paul that in Romans 1, a "knowledge of God is plain from the very structuring of the world itself."[2] There is evident in creation, one could say, God's imprint that is both indelible and clear. If Origen were writing today, he might agree with those advocates of "intelligent design," who believe that the diversity of life that scientists document today demands the input of an external intelligence. Though God is invisible, he is known from that which is visible—the Maker being revealed in that which has been made. But—and for Oden this is of fundamental importance—though a knowledge of God is plain to both the wise and the uneducated, humankind has "contaminated the truth, at least as far as they are able" (the words

---

2. Origen, quoted in Oden, "Without Excuse," 58.

are Chrysostom's from the fourth century).[3] And so, writes Paul in verse 20, humankind is "without excuse." Writes Oden,

> If you assert general revelation without recognition that all are left without excuse, you have not read the whole sentence. If you assert divine judgment without making clear that it is based on what is clearly knowable to all humanity about God, you have condemned hastily.[4]

Central for the early church fathers in this description of general revelation based on Romans 1 is the following: (1) general revelation is tied salvifically to divine judgment and the history of sin; (2) general revelation is based on a refraction—an echo, a footprint, a trace—of the Creator in creation and is meant to reveal God's glory; (3) general revelation is rooted in reason (in Origen's words, "the God-given powers of the mind") so that by studying the visible world (the law of nature) we should be able to know the invisible.[5] Basic to this description, in other words, is the belief that general revelation is inextricably tied to issues of judgment and salvation, that it is based not on the present revealing work of God's Spirit but on the prior creational work of God, and that it can be discerned naturally by all humankind, using our God-given reason.

Although such an understanding of the text is arguably one possible interpretation of Romans 1, as Paul builds his case that "the wages of sin is death, but the free gift of God is eternal life in Christ Jesus our Lord" (Rom. 6:23), it also misses altogether the heart of that experience of divine Presence that is the testimony of countless Christians and non-Christians alike. It thus points out the limitation of using Romans 1 as the primary basis of one's understanding of God's revelatory Presence outside the walls of the church. For revelation, general or otherwise, as Karl Barth in particular has been quick to remind us, is based not on any divine footprint that we might choose to access independent of the present work of God through his Spirit. Rather, revelation is dependent on the Presence of the Revealer.[6]

---

3. John Chrysostom, quoted in Oden, "Without Excuse," 59.

4. Oden, "Without Excuse," 59.

5. Origen, quoted in Oden, "Without Excuse," 62.

6. Lacking any notion of the ongoing Presence of the Revealer, but only focusing upon what creation reveals to human reason, the discussion of God's revelation outside the church and without direct reference to Scripture or Christ in the Vatican II document *Dei Verbum*, 1.3, 6 (1965), is but a scant two sentences in nineteen pages of text: "God, who creates and conserves all things by his Word (see John 1:3), provides constant evidence of himself in created realities (see Rom. 1:19–20). . . . The holy synod professes that 'God, the first principle and last end of all things, can be known with certainty from the created world, by the natural light of human reason (see Rom. 1:20).'" Here the assumption is that revelation comes from creation itself, but, clearly, the topic is thought to be of minor theological importance given the scant attention it receives.

While there might be a knowledge of the Creator that can be inferred from creation, it only becomes revelation when the Spirit of God chooses to be present in and through that creation. This is what our descriptions of the experience of Transcendence in the opening chapters have reminded us of. When five persons see a sunset and only one of the five experiences God, it is not that the other four are sinfully blocking out the divine from their view, but that the one has been graced serendipitously with the Spirit's revelatory Presence. And when that person experiences the Transcendent in and through the sunset, their history of sin is not necessarily relevant (though we all are sinners in need of God's saving grace), for that person has been able to see God. Here surely is Paul's theological point in Romans 2.

Moreover, when general revelation is described phenomenologically, it is seldom (though it is occasionally) understood as the work chiefly of human reason, but more often as the experience of our imagination. Revelation is something, as Friedrich Schleiermacher so forcefully reminded his Romantic colleagues, that is primarily located not in reasoning (the "mind" as Hegel thought) or ethics (the "will" as Kant believed) but in our intuition and feeling. It is not that we by our own effort conclude or project by rational inference that God is a reality, but that we receive God's revelatory Presence in the midst of our lives.

Here is what happened to me while watching the movie *Becket*, or what the woman in my class who was brutally raped and shot subsequently experienced while watching *It's a Wonderful Life*. It is not that the Creator left behind clues or "tracks" in creation that our human reason then discerns, nor is it that as creatures shaped in the image of God, the *imago Dei*, that we have a vague unthematic awareness of God, a felt ignorance, a faint knowledge of something beyond that lacks any positive content. Rather, the work of the imagination that believers and nonbelievers alike describe is more fundamental and directional than this. They describe how God has personally revealed his divine Presence to them through the mediums of creation, conscience, and culture by his Spirit.

There is also a third problem with conflating Paul's argument concerning an awareness of God's existence through creation with that revelation that is experienced occasionally, but foundationally and at times transformatively, by individuals in the course of their everyday lives. Such revelatory moments are not, as in Romans 1, primarily about salvation and judgment, but rather about grace and encounter. Here was the experience of C. S. Lewis as he was repeatedly surprised by "Joy."

Even Origen recognized this, for in the continuation of his explanation of Paul's thought in the opening chapters of Romans, he writes concerning

Romans 2:14–15 that the law which gentiles keep (not killing one another, or committing adultery, or stealing from others, or bearing false witness, or dishonoring one's father or mother) is that which is "written on their hearts *by God*, not with ink, but *with the Spirit of the living God*"[7] (italics mine). It is interesting, as we will develop at length in the next chapter, that Origen rightly understands such revelation to be grounded pneumatologically. Revelation has to do with the Revealer—it is never a human possibility resident in creation but always a divine, present gifting. Such gifting is given by God through the Spirit, so that, in Paul's words, "their conflicting thoughts will accuse or perhaps excuse them."

Paul's words here cannot be explained away by claiming that Paul is speaking only hypothetically about being "excused" by one's works or is speaking only to gentile Christians, as if those outside the church are not Paul's focus.[8] There is simply no textual evidence for either viewpoint—that it is either hypothetical or limited to gentile Christians. Moreover, there is much that would point in a contrary direction.[9] How then are we to understand Paul's reflection? N. T. Wright is unsure, believing this text to be simply "a puzzle."[10] And certainly scholars have struggled with its meaning. Perhaps it is best to see with Origen this judgment as a rehearsal of our final judgment. But what is key for our purposes here is not the larger meaning of this text, but Paul's stated belief that some might be "excused." Since the whole point of Paul's opening chapters in Romans is to say that Jew and gentile alike "have sinned and fall short of the glory of God" (Rom. 3:23), Paul cannot be speaking here of an exoneration at the final judgment. If so, the text would lack any internal consistency. Rather, Paul must be referencing the fact that all, including those outside the church, do at times hear the Spirit and respond to that divine grace authentically, and are judged so by God. They do good works, for as Origen

7. Origen, in Oden, "Without Excuse," 68.

8. That Paul is only speaking about gentile Christians is Karl Barth's position, largely following Augustine's theological exegesis in *De Spiritu et Littera*. The "nature" of gentiles who have been transformed by God's grace in Christ Jesus has been radically changed, argues Barth. They have been given a new heart, the Holy Spirit now speaking to their inward parts, so his commandments are self-evident to them. This is who Paul references. See Karl Barth, *Church Dogmatics* II/2, 604; IV/1, 33, 395; IV/2, 561; IV/4, 7. Though Barth makes these assertions about what the text might mean, he fails to ground his theological interpretation in any careful exegesis of the text or answer the most basic problem associated with his hypothesis: how does limiting Paul's statements to gentile Christians fit with Paul's overall purpose, which is to show all humankind as equally in need of the grace of God?

9. See Klyne Snodgrass, "Justification by Grace—to the Doers: An Analysis of the Place of Romans 2 in the Theology of Paul," *New Testament Studies* 32 (1986): 72–93.

10. N. T. Wright, *Paul for Everyone: Romans, Part 1, Chapters 1–8* (Louisville: Westminster John Knox, 2004), 35.

says, the law has been "written on their hearts by God, not with ink, but with the Spirit of the living God" (see Rom. 2:26).[11]

Paul is not saying that some will experience salvation through *always* being sensitive to the Spirit of God (after all, Paul's whole point in the first three chapters of Romans is that we all have sinned and can only be "justified by his [God's] grace as a gift" [Rom. 3:24]). But though it is true that all fall short of the glory of God, it is also true that the Spirit, in and through creation, reveals God's glory such that those both within and outside the church perceive this revelation and at times act authentically on it. As a result, "such a person receives praise not from others but from God" (Rom. 2:29).[12]

A biblical example of Paul's reasoning can be found in the tenth chapter of 2 Kings, where King Jehu is described as "doing well" in the sight of God by killing Ahab and cunningly summoning other worshipers of Baal, only to then kill them and to destroy their temple. The text states:

> Thus Jehu wiped out Baal from Israel. But Jehu did not turn aside from the sins of Jeroboam son of Nebat, which he caused Israel to commit—the golden calves that were in Bethel and in Dan. The LORD said to Jehu, "Because you have done well in carrying out what I consider right, and in accordance with all that was in my heart have dealt with the house of Ahab, your sons of the fourth generation shall sit on the throne of Israel." But Jehu was not careful to follow the law of the LORD the God of Israel with all his heart; he did not turn from the sins of Jeroboam, which he caused Israel to commit. (2 Kings 10:28–31)

Jehu is rewarded by God for having "done well in carrying out what I [God] consider right, and in accordance with all that was in my heart" (v. 30), even though he continued the idolatrous practices that had begun with King Jeroboam.[13] Although the text makes it clear that the overall assessment of Jehu is

11. Origen, quoted in Oden, "Without Excuse," 68.

12. Augustine wrote, "What then is God's Law written by God Himself in the hearts of men, but the very presence of the Holy Spirit, who is 'the finger of God,' and by whose presence is shed abroad in our hearts the love which is the fulfilling of the law, and the end of the commandment?" But it also must be noted that Augustine believed Paul's statements in Romans 2 were pertaining only to gentile Christians, not all gentiles. See Augustine, "On the Spirit and the Letter" 36.21, in *Nicene and Post-Nicene Fathers of the Christian Church*, vol. 5, *Saint Augustin: Anti-Pelagian Writings*, ed. Philip Schaff (New York: Christian Literature Company, 1887), 98.

13. In 1 Kings 12:25–33, Jeroboam is described as trying to consolidate his power by changing the place of worship from Jerusalem to the twin centers of Dan and Bethel, changing the time of year when the Feast of Tabernacles is celebrated, widening the priesthood to include those not of the tribe of Levi, and by instituting the worship of golden calves as in Egypt. The text states that these changes in Israel's worship, regarding time, place, priesthood, and objects of worship, "he [Jeroboam] alone had devised" (v. 33). This act of apostasy based in self-interest

that he failed to follow the law of the Lord, he did do what was in accordance with God's will—he did follow the promptings of the Spirit—in killing all who were associated with the evil of King Ahab. And thus he is "excused" for his action.

Here is an analogous situation to what Paul had in mind when he wrote: "When Gentiles, who do not possess the law, do instinctively what the law requires, these, though not having the law, are a law unto themselves. They show that what the law requires is written on their hearts, to which their own conscience also bears witness; and their conflicting thoughts will accuse or perhaps excuse them" (Rom. 2:14–15). Though those who do not possess the law are included part and parcel in Paul's summary judgments ("There is no one who is righteous, not even one" [Rom. 3:10]; that "the whole world may be held accountable to God" [Rom. 3:19]; and that "all have sinned and fall short of the glory of God" [Rom. 3:23]), Paul can also say that like Jehu, in some of their actions, gentiles may be excused, for they have been sensitive to the Spirit of the Living God and have done well in carrying out what God considers right.

What can we conclude from this brief description concerning Romans 1 and 2? First, that what Paul is speaking about in Romans 1 is not our *locus classicus* for discussion about God's revelatory Presence outside the church and without direct reference to Jesus Christ. We need to turn elsewhere, as we have done, for that. Even if we conclude that Paul in Romans 1 assumes the present revealing work of God's Spirit, speaking in and through creation—assumes, that is, that God's creational footprint is not experienced independently of God's continuing providential and revelatory Presence (surely a theologically more probable interpretation of the text, one more in keeping with the Bible's general description of revelation and providence, but not an interpretation that the early church adopted)—Paul's focus in this opening argument in Romans is elsewhere. He is focused not on those occasions when God's revelatory Presence breaks through and we respond in awe and obedience, but rather on humankind's selfishness in regularly closing off such awareness of God's Presence. Romans 1 has its sights set on other things—on sin and salvation—and it is thus not directly addressing our topic.

Second, Romans 2 is not concerned with that "general revelation" that is universally accessible to all people everywhere at all times through their natural reason (that "divine discourse delivered through the medium of creation, there to be 'read' at all times and places" as Kevin Vanhoozer describes

---

became the "shorthand" judgment for the writer of Kings in describing the apostasy of many of the kings of Israel and is used twenty-one times in the book.

general revelation[14]). Its concern, rather, is on those occasions when we are sensitive to that which the Spirit writes on our hearts and act in accordance with that. Such revelation is only recognized sometimes and in some places by some people. But when it is, it is an authentic encounter with the Spirit of God. As Leonard Cohen sings in "Anthem":

> Ring the bells that still can be rung
> Forget your perfect offering
> There is a crack in everything
> That's how the light [Light] gets in.[15]

Nevertheless, because of the importance of Romans 1 and 2 in the church's understanding of God's revelation outside the church, and because this has been linked through the ages to a particular understanding of general revelation, one that must be questioned based both on our discussion in the first half of this book on the reported revelational experiences of others and on multiple strands of the biblical record that we have explored, it is important to slow down our discussion at this point and pause to consider the basis for our critique of this link between general revelation and the opening chapters of Romans. In particular, I will turn to three theologians whose writings bear directly on our argument, and whose positions have often been summarized succinctly in one or two words each: (1) Karl Barth's famous and terse *Nein* ("No"), written seventy-five years ago in response to Emil Brunner's volume about natural theology, *Nature and Grace*; (2) Friedrich Schleiermacher's use not only of *Gefühl* ("feeling") but also of *Anschauung* ("intuition") in *On Religion*—his collection of speeches at the turn of the nineteenth century to his skeptical colleagues in the Romantic movement in Berlin; and (3) C. S. Lewis's "Joy"—the label he uses in his 1955 autobiography *Surprised by Joy* to describe those sporadic but transformative experiences of Transcendence that first occurred in his youth and became signposts to something more for him.

It is my contention that God's wider revelation is not something that is available to all humanity through the *imago Dei* based on our human capacity. Rather, with Barth, we must say, first, that revelation always needs the Spirit as Revealer—it is event. Secondly, with Schleiermacher, general revelation is not first of all accessible because of our rationality, but rather is rooted in that intuition of Something or Someone beyond us and our feeling that results

---

14. Kevin J. Vanhoozer, "What Is Everyday Theology?," in *Everyday Theology: How to Read Cultural Texts and Interpret Trends*," ed. Kevin J. Vanhoozer, Charles A. Anderson, and Michael J. Sleasman (Grand Rapids: Baker Academic, 2007), 42.

15. Leonard Cohen, "Anthem," *The Future* (Columbia, 1992).

from this encounter. And third, with Lewis (at least until the last chapter of his *Surprised By Joy*, where he undercuts his argument), general revelation is not merely a trace, something largely insignificant given Christ or incomprehensible because of our sin, but the experience of the wider Presence of God through his Spirit mediated through creation, conscience, and human culture.

Karl Barth's *Nein*

Alister McGrath, in his best-selling introduction *Christian Theology: An Introduction*, points out that "every now and then a theological debate takes place which is seen by both sides as representing a landmark."[16] McGrath gives two examples: the debate in 1524–25 between Luther and Erasmus over the freedom of the human will, and the dialogue between Karl Barth and Emil Brunner over natural theology. It was in 1934 that Brunner published *Nature and Grace* (German, *Natur und Gnade*), which prompted Barth's immediate and strong response, "Nein! Antwort an Emil Brunner" (English, "No! An Answer to Emil Brunner") in the journal *Theologische Existenz heute*, volume 5 (1934).[17] The exchange proved the final rupture in the relationship of two major Swiss theologians and has continued to define two mutually exclusive approaches to natural theology.

In *Nature and Grace*, Brunner argued that "the task of our theological generation is to find a way back to a legitimate natural theology." He suggested that this could be done by rooting it in a doctrine of creation, and more specifically in the fact that humans are created in the image of God, the *imago Dei*. Brunner understood this image as having two aspects: one *formal* and the other *material*. The formal *imago Dei* refers to humankind's unique relation to God, which is rooted in creation itself and which carries with it certain responsibilities. At its most basic, this image is what separates humanity from the animals. Even sin does not negate this formal image, the fact that we are the "central and culminating point of creation."[18] Rather, it is this formal image that makes men and women responsible for sin. (When a lion kills a deer, for example, this is not sinful. It is simply what lions are created to do. But given our relationship with God, when we do other than

16. Alister McGrath, *Christian Theology: An Introduction*, 5th ed. (Oxford: Wiley-Blackwell, 2011).

17. Both Brunner's essay and Barth's response were brought together and translated into English by the translator Peter Fraenkel in 1946, and that book is now republished as Emil Brunner and Karl Barth, *Natural Theology: Comprising "Nature and Grace" by Professor Dr. Emil Brunner and the Reply "No!" by Dr. Karl Barth*, trans. Peter Fraenkel (Eugene, OR: Wipf & Stock, 2002).

18. Ibid., 23.

God's intentions for our lives, when we murder another human being, for example, it is sin.) Materially, however—that is, in the actual course of our lives—Brunner believed that the *imago* is completely lost.[19] Because humankind is sinful, we are helpless and in need of rescue from beyond ourselves. Nevertheless, Brunner's point in *Nature and Grace* is that though we ignore it, there is still something within us as humans that causes us to be able to receive God's revelation to us.

Here, then, is Brunner's argument that there is within us all a "point of contact" with God. This point of contact is our formal *imago Dei*, the capacity for receiving God's revelation of himself. As with faith, this human capacity is completely passive; thus, Brunner believes, it does not compromise in any way the doctrine of *sola gratia*. Nevertheless, though humankind does not initiate any divine contact or even make independent steps toward it, men and women do have, as the writer of Ecclesiastes 3:11 states, eternity set in their hearts.[20] This is what gives humans the "possibility of being addressed." Brunner believes that this emphasis on a point of contact is important, for it explains the way in which the church's proclamation becomes understandable. Unless the church's proclamation is *"comprehensible* it is useless, however true it is."[21]

Put another way, Brunner argued that our human nature—that which constitutes our identity—finds its analogue in the Being of God. Although humankind is now sinful given the fall, we retain the ability to recognize God in nature, in the events of history, and in the reality of our guilt. Such knowledge that is "natural" to humankind becomes a "point of contact" for divine revelation. That is, to quote Brunner, "revelation thus addresses itself to a human nature which already has some idea of what that revelation is about."[22] When the gospel tells us to repent of sin, for example, we have some sense of what is being asked of us, for we already have some idea of what both "repentance" and "sin" mean. Revelation, to be sure, brings with it a fuller notion of what sin is, but it does this by building on these initial points of contact.

Brunner's argument rests in the belief that the Spirit of God is recognizable in his creation through words and pictures. After all, writes Brunner, "the artist is known by all his works."[23] God leaves an imprint of himself on whatever he does. For Brunner there are two revelations: one in creation, and one in

19. Ibid., 24.
20. I am appreciative of the fine work that one of my graduate students, David Johnson, did on the Barth-Brunner debate. I have benefited from his research.
21. Brunner and Barth, *Natural Theology,* 56.
22. Ibid.
23. Ibid., 24.

Christ. The knowledge of God that one can attain from the work of creation is limited; it is not enough for salvation. "From nature we know the hands and feet but not the heart of God," he says.[24] But humankind is without excuse in not recognizing the witness of God resident in creation. (Here, again, we find the traditional understanding of general revelation, one rooted in a particular reading of Rom. 1.) It is "only because mankind somehow knows the will of God are they able to sin."[25] Brunner cannot accept a creation devoid of God's imprint. It is, he thinks, too obvious in Scripture (Psalms, Rom. 1, etc.) and too obvious in the experience of humankind.

Barth's response to Brunner's theological essay, as we have said, was an emphatic and defiant *Nein!* (No!). When read today, the conversation between these two theological giants of the twentieth century seems too often to be that of speaking past each other. There is so much they agree on. But surely at the root of Barth's reply was his belief that Brunner's interest in a "natural revelation" was inevitably part of a closet "natural theology"—a belief in, to use the words of Francis Bacon, "that spark of the knowledge of God which may be had by the light of nature and the consideration of created things . . . divine in respect of its object and natural in respect of its source of information."[26] For Barth such a belief was simply a means of arrogantly inserting humankind into the revelatory equation. Brunner was suggesting that there was a source of revelation other than God himself in the person of Jesus Christ. Impossible, thought Barth. And as to Brunner's reason for this natural "point of contact," God simply did not need our assistance, our cooperation, if he were to become known. The Holy Spirit needed no point of contact other than that which the Spirit provides.

In Barth's understanding, any point of contact could never be a trait of humanity, an independent possession apart from the present work of God through the Spirit. Rather, revelation could only be the direct and immediate result of divine action. Any knowledge of God we might uncover could only be evoked by the Word of God. It was simply idolatry to suggest that humankind might permanently possess any knowledge of God rooted solely in our creatureliness. The living God who encounters us (not whom we encounter) in Jesus Christ cannot be known through some innate, human capacity, or from nature or even history. That is, Barth responds to Brunner, first of all, not by taking up and critiquing individual parts of his argument but by categorically rejecting the whole premise.

24. Ibid., 38.
25. Ibid., 25.
26. Francis Bacon, *De Augmentis Scientiarum* 3.2, quoted in Paul Avis, "Does Natural Theology Exist?," *Theology* 87 (Nov. 1984): 432.

That Brunner wanted to speak of a "capacity for revelation" was for Barth simply a violation of the principles of *sola scriptura* and *sola gratia*. Such a "natural theology," Barth believed, was based wrongly in the premise that we as humans can determine how and when we can know God. Barth's *raison d'être* for attacking Brunner was thus his determination within any theological formulation to safeguard the "Godness" of God, to grant God's revelation its full and independent integrity. Lurking behind such a commitment, surely, was the deep sense of betrayal that Barth had felt as a young pastor/theologian when he read a statement signed by many of his theological teachers supporting Kaiser Wilhelm II's imperialistic war. For Barth, this was sacrilege, a sociopolitical sellout of the gospel. Argued Barth, God cannot (or at least should not) be co-opted for the German, nationalistic cause. This sense of betrayal was again manifesting itself, thought Barth, as Hitler consolidated his power, often with the support of the German Lutheran church. And Brunner's "natural theology," thought Barth, could only aid their cause.

We cannot construct our own notions of God, thought Barth, but this will always be the inevitable result if one subverts revelation. Barth had already railed against such false religiosity in his landmark theological commentary on the Epistle to the Romans (1919). We simply do not whisper "God" by shouting "man." A theology that has its partial roots in nature has done just that; it is not theology at all, but rather humankind's false assertion of autonomy and self-justification. There can be, thought Barth, no second source of revelation apart from Jesus Christ. If we are to know God, it can only be the result of God's making himself known to us, which he has in Christ Jesus. *God's* revelation in Christ is both unique and necessary.

While Barth does not go so far as to claim that God is absent from creation, he does say that humankind's ability to attain any knowledge of God through creation is completely inadequate. If humankind cannot see God clearly in and through creation, as even Brunner suggests, then anything we do "see" apart from the present event of God's revelatory in-breaking is simply fantasy or the work of demons. If humanity can know something of God outside of the revelation of Christ, then we end up becoming part of the "salvation equation." We end up participating in our own salvation. Barth will have nothing of it. As for God's "preserving grace," Barth concedes that it is grace that allows the created world to continue to exist at all. But he rejects the idea that there is any grace apart from the saving grace of Jesus Christ. To what end would any other grace exist? And to claim, as Brunner did, that humankind has some "capacity of revelation" is simply heresy. Humankind does not supply, even "to some extent," any of the conditions for communion with God. To say that the formal image of God resident in humanity is "somehow" involved in the revelation of God is both to deny our utter helplessness as sinners and to undercut the doctrine of *sola gratia*. "Nein!"

The "landmark" status of this theological debate is, of course, based on the fact that there is truth in both Barth's and Brunner's arguments. On the surface, it would seem that Brunner's position might be more compatible with the biblical and experiential data that has so far surfaced in this book. The first four chapters have provided a number of occurrences, both contemporary and within the biblical record, where God has revealed himself to non-Christians/nonbelievers through the Spirit. These occurrences, moreover, are not connected in any explicit way with issues of soteriology (the focus is not on sin and salvation). Instead, the Spirit has been shown to address humanity in and through creation, in our human conscience, and through the vast array of human culture. It is creation/creature, not redemption, that is the locus of this revelation. Brunner is correct.

It is worth noting that in his recognition of this point of contact, Emil Brunner is, without doubt, closer to the theology of John Calvin than Karl Barth is, even though Barth understood himself to be a Reformed theologian in Calvin's tradition. Calvin wrote not of a "point of contact" but of a "sense of divinity" (*sensus divinitatis*) and a "seed of religion" (*semen religionis*) that was planted by God in each and every human being. The word pictures are analogous. Writing in his *Institutes* in the sixteenth century, Calvin argued that there was "no nation so barbarous, no people so savage, that they have not a deep-seated conviction that there is a God" (1.3.1).[27] "There is," he argued, "within the human mind, and indeed by natural instinct, an awareness of divinity. This we take to be beyond controversy. . . . God himself has implanted in all men a certain understanding of his divine majesty. . . . This is not a doctrine which is first learned at school, but one as to which every man is, from the womb, his own master; one which nature herself allows no individual to forget" (1.3.1). This is the case, thinks Calvin, for "God has sown a seed of religion in all men" (1.4.1). Calvin reasoned that although we may live as if there is no God, although we may become practical atheists, "the worm of conscience, sharper than any cauterizing iron, gnaws away within" (1.3.3). A few chapters later, Calvin extends his argument to include God's self-revelation in and through creation: "Men cannot open their eyes without being compelled to see him" (1.5.1). "Wherever you cast your eyes," wrote

27. John Calvin, *Institutes of the Christian Religion*, 2 vols., trans. F. L. Battles, ed. J. T. McNeil (Philadelphia: Westminster Press, 1960). Further references to the *Institutes* are given in the text (book, chapter, paragraph).

Calvin, "there is no spot in the universe wherein you cannot discern at least some sparks of his glory" (1.5.1).

It is the case that Calvin also believed that sin clouds our natural vision so that we cannot see God clearly. In this way, much as with our discussion of Romans 1 and congruent with Brunner's argument, general revelation, for Calvin, has rendered all of humankind without excuse. Moreover, this general revelation is incapable of giving us a saving knowledge of God. Writes Calvin, "God's likeness imprinted upon the most beautiful form of the universe [is] insufficiently effective" (1.6.3). Rather, to see the divine clearly, one needs Scripture's spectacles (see 1.6.1).[28]

With all this, Brunner would be in substantial agreement with Calvin. There is "an awareness of divinity," a "seed of religion," that is a point of contact between men/women and God, one implanted in us. "Beyond our reasoning and beyond our believing, there is," as Abraham Heschel reminds us, "a preconceptual faculty that senses the glory, the presence, of the Divine. We do not perceive it. We have no knowledge; we only have awareness." Heschel goes on to say: "We are asked to wonder, to revere, to think and to live in a way that is compatible with the grandeur and mystery of living." Such an awareness is easily repressed, for it is "an echo of the intimation that is small and still. It will not, however, remain forever subdued."[29] Here, from a Jewish biblical scholar, is a position similar both to Calvin's and to Brunner's. It is one that would seem to have widespread experiential, biblical, and theological support.

But Barth must also be listened to. His correction is fundamental. Barth might well have been wrong to isolate the act of human knowing developed on the basis of nature from the self-disclosure of the Triune God. He might also have been inadequately trinitarian, rooting his argument too singularly in Christology, and not recognizing the work of the Spirit in creation. Both of these positions were surely central to his strong negative reaction to Brunner's essay. But Barth was also right in his strident protection of the Godness of God, particularly as it relates to divine revelation. It is God's initiative, not ours, that is central to all theology. It is God and God alone who is the actor in revelation; it is God who speaks, not us. We should not accept any "natural

28. In his commentary on Psalm 19, Calvin writes, "While the heavens bear witness concerning God, their testimony does not lead men so far as that thereby they learn truly to fear him, and acquire a well-grounded knowledge of him; it serves only to render them inexcusable." John Calvin, *Commentary on the Book of Psalms*, trans. James Anderson (Grand Rapids: Eerdmans, 1948), 1:317.

29. Abraham Joshua Heschel, *God in Search of Man: A Philosophy of Judaism* (New York: Farrar, Straus & Giroux, 1955).

theology" that subtly turns itself into a syncretistic, if not an autonomous, exercise.

Barth opposed Brunner because he understood Brunner to be arguing that God's revelation was dependent in some way on a point of contact implanted within all humans and accessible to human reason by the fact of our existence. No in-breaking, God-empowered event was necessary; rather, revelation was the result of a human capacity. But such a faith, however "reasonable," strays from the singular revelation of the Word incarnate (Christ) and the Word inscripturated (the Bible), argued Barth. It wrongly makes God's revelation dependent somehow on our activity, our capacities, and our initiative. In attempting to describe a "bridge" between God and humanity that is resident in creation/creature/culture, Brunner seemed to have allowed revelation to be threatened by co-option by autonomous, human reason. This is exactly what had happened in Germany during World War I and was happening again, thought Barth, in the emergence of the "German Christian" support of the Aryan movement in Hitler's Germany. It is not human capacity, certainly not Aryan human capacity, that is foundational, but God's revelation in Christ. Any theology that strayed from the singular revelation of Christ should be strongly opposed in order to protect the Christian church from again having its theology preempted by a "nature" that had become almost deified. It must be God and God alone who remains our focus.

Here, not only did Barth prove prophetic (the German Christian church did, in fact, fall into this naturalistic trap with horrendous consequence for the whole world), but his words still carry with them a necessary caution that needs to be heard. To speak of general revelation, as many do, as the footprint of God in creation, or as an echo, the remainder after God has completed his creation (and departed? surely not), is to make revelation one step removed from the event of God's Presence. And this is one step too much. Barth is correct. It is not the footprint of God that reveals God to us, but the Spirit speaking in and through the footprint. After all, nature, when viewed independently, can be read tooth and claw. It is only, for Barth, the Spirit of Christ in creation who turns nature into revelation. (I would rather say "the Spirit of the Triune God in creation," but that is to get ahead of our argument. We will take this up in the next chapter.)

If by a "natural knowledge" of God (a "natural revelation") one means an independent, epistemological presupposition to a knowledge of God as Creator, Reconciler, and Redeemer (this is what Barth believed Brunner to have described), then Barth was right to reject this "natural theology." Barth called such an understanding a "sorry hypothesis." It is the claim that there is "a knowledge of God given in and with the natural force of reason, or to be attained through its exercise."[30] But if "natural theology" is instead to be understood as reflection on the relationship between such revelatory in-breaking and the whole of human knowledge and experience, then there might be a legitimate place for it, even in Barth's world. This is the position of Ray Anderson, my colleague in theology at Fuller for many years and a Barth scholar.[31] Anderson believed that what Barth came to reject was not "natural theology" itself as a valid component of a theology of the Word, but rather an autonomous natural theology that could stand alone as a basis for a theology of the Word. This is what Barth thought (perhaps wrongly?) Brunner was proposing.

Years after his controversy with Brunner, Barth did indeed write about signs of God's lordship, parables of the kingdom of heaven, that were evident not only in Scripture and the church but also in secular society. As God has dominion over the kingdoms of the earth as well, to deny that God could also speak through Balaam was "an unjustifiable excess of skepticism," thought Barth. Moreover, there were "other lights" in creation that are "not extinguished" by the light of Christ.[32] The creaturely world could indeed be a framework, a stage, a setting for the drama of salvation in Jesus Christ. God could be seen there as well. Creation (and by extension, conscience and culture) did in fact provide the backdrop—in Calvin's words, the *theatrum gloriae Dei*. Moreover, this creaturely world, argued Barth, "has also as such its own lights and truths, and therefore its own speech and words."[33] That is, besides the one Word of God there are other words that can be heard. And besides the one Light of life, there are other lights that can be seen. But these are lesser lights, and lights that shine only in the radiance of the one Light, and words that find their truth only in the one Word. (Imagine the difference between the light of the sun and the lesser and reflective light of the moon. Here is Barth's point.) Such lesser lights are "created lights." Barth writes:

These do not light up the world with the same brightness as God does in His Word or as the world has in His sight and knowledge. But they bring illumination . . . there is still a measure of brightness.[34]

Barth goes so far as to describe characteristics of these created lights: "the simple one of existence"; our being "for one another"; nature's rhythm—a

30. Karl Barth, *Church Dogmatics*, IV/3.1 (Edinburgh: T&T Clark, 1988), 117.
31. Ray Anderson, "Barth and a New Direction in Natural Theology," in *Theology Beyond Christendom: Essays on the Centenary of the Birth of Karl Barth, May 10, 1986*, ed. John Thompson (Pittsburgh: Pickwick, 1986), 241–66.
32. Barth, *Church Dogmatics*, IV/3.1, 122, 139.
33. Ibid., 137, 139.
34. Ibid.

certain "alternation of Yes and No, beginning and end, joy and pain, construction and destruction, life and death" (see my discussion of Mozart below); both natural and spiritual laws; a summons to the active shaping of things, a step into freedom; and, finally, a depth to the cosmos that remains an unfathomable mystery.[35] It is against this backdrop, or to slightly alter the metaphor substituting that of John Calvin, it is on this stage that God's great drama of salvation is played out. As the truth of God shines forth in history, argues Barth, the lesser lights of the created world also are lit up.

In his extended discussion in his *Church Dogmatics*, Barth purposely refuses to provide examples, wanting instead to frame his argument from above and not from below, from the perspective of God, not humanity. But in other writings, Barth presents a particularly telling example of such "lesser" light, the music of Mozart. When Barth listened to it, the event became almost revelatory. Barth never could integrate his experience of Mozart's music fully into his theological system, probably because he feared the result would be a natural theology. But Barth could nonetheless ask: "Why is it possible to hold that Mozart has a place in theology, especially in the doctrine of creation and also in eschatology, although he was not a father of the Church, does not even seem to have been a particularly active Christian . . . [who led] what might appear to us a rather frivolous existence when not occupied in his work?"[36] Barth spoke autobiographically of his first experience hearing Mozart.

> I must have been five or six years old at the time. . . . My father was musical and was fond of improvising at the piano. . . . One day, he was playing something by Mozart. I can still picture the scene. He began a couple of bars from *The Magic Flute*. . . . They went right through me and into me, I don't know how, and I thought, "That's it!"[37]

As with the testimonials we have noted of John Updike and Paul Tillich, C. S. Lewis and Albert Einstein, Barth recounts how art became "revelatory" for him, a joyful experience of heaven. Argued Barth, Mozart had heard, "and causes those who have ears to hear, even today, what we shall not see until the end of time—the whole context of providence."[38]

According to Barth,

35. Ibid., 143–50.
36. Karl Barth, *Church Dogmatics*, III/3 (Edinburgh: T&T Clark, 1976), 298.
37. Karl Barth, quoted in Colin Gunton, "Mozart the Theologian," *Theology* 94 (1991): 346.
38. Barth, *Church Dogmatics*, III/3, 298.

[Mozart] heard the harmony of creation to which the shadow also belongs but in which the shadow is not darkness, deficiency is not defeat, sadness cannot become despair. . . . Thus the cheerfulness in this harmony is not without its limits. But the light shines all the more brightly because it breaks forth from the shadow. The sweetness is also bitter and cannot therefore cloy. . . . Mozart saw this light no more than we do, but he heard the whole world of creation enveloped by this light. . . . Hearing creation unresentfully and impartially, he did not produce merely his own music but that of creation, its twofold and yet harmonious praise of God. . . . He himself was only an ear for this music, and its mediator to other ears.[39]

Barth seems to allow for the possibility that Mozart, a nonpracticing Catholic, might nonetheless have been the mediator of God's revelation to him and, by extension, all others who have ears to hear. Barth allowed Mozart's music to speak to his soul. Wrote Barth, "The golden sound and melodies of Mozart's music have from early times spoken to me not as gospel but as parables of the realm of God's free grace as revealed in the gospel—and they do so again with great spontaneity and directness."[40] As the novelist John Updike wrote in an introduction to Barth's writings about Mozart, "Mozart's music, for Barth, has the exact texture of God's world, of divine comedy."[41] Such "natural" revelation was always an event, a personal and contemporary gift from beyond us. It would never be our possession, our right. Nevertheless, the voiceless voice of God could be heard in and through Mozart's music.

According to Ray Anderson, "Barth, in his later years, was more open to the reality of God 'speaking' through creation (and by extension, conscience and culture), though the key word might be 'speaking.' In other words, Barth still viewed revelation as a form of proclamation, which involved an 'event' or an 'encounter.'" Thus, Mozart became, perhaps, "an 'unwitting' vehicle for God as Creator to 'speak' through his music as a 'voice' which can be 'heard' even by those who have not yet encountered the revelation of the divine Word in Christ as Reconciler and the Spirit as Redeemer."[42] Mozart, according to Barth, never used his music to communicate a message as Bach did, or to express a personal confession as Beethoven did. There was no moral to the

39. Ibid.

40. Karl Barth, quoted in Theodore A. Gill, "Barth and Mozart," *Theology Today* 43, no. 3 (October 1986): 404.

41. John Updike, foreword to Karl Barth, *Wolfgang Amadeus Mozart* (Grand Rapids: Eerdmans, 1986), 11.

42. Ray Anderson, private correspondence, June 21, 2002. George Hunsinger uses the phrase "unwitting witnesses" to speak of Barth's understanding of how cultural forms might be employed by the Word. See George Hunsinger, *How to Read Karl Barth: The Shape of His Theology* (Oxford: Oxford University Press, 1991).

story; rather, "he just sings and sounds."[43] And what sounded forth was the music of the spheres, in Barth's words, "a glorious upsetting of the balance, a *turning* in which the light rises and the shadows fall, though without disappearing, in which joy overtakes sorrow without extinguishing it, in which the Yea rings louder than the ever-present Nay."[44]

Barth asked, "How can I as an evangelical Christian and theologian proclaim Mozart? . . . He who has ears has certainly heard. May I ask all those others who may be shaking their heads in astonishment and anxiety to be content for the moment with the general reminder that the New Testament speaks not only of the kingdom of heaven but also of *parables* of the kingdom of heaven?"[45] Was Barth's experience of Mozart's music, something he listened to every day of his life, a description of Tillich's "revelational ecstasy" or Lewis's "surprise by Joy"? It seems so. Was Barth's experience all that different even from what Brunner was suggesting?[46] Perhaps not, though Brunner's language concerning an unmediated natural theology Barth rightly opposed. But wanting to proclaim the Godness of God at all points, Barth himself was never fully comfortable with admitting to a general revelation that found its staging in creation, conscience, and human culture. It remained a hypothesis, lacking any "final validity." He said that neither radical skepticism nor radical dogmatism would do. The danger of compromising the freedom of God remained an ever-present one for Barth.

Friedrich Schleiermacher: Feeling and Intuition (*Gefühl* and *Anschauung*)

Robert Jenson, in the first volume of his systematic theology, *The Triune God*, rails against "theological prolegomena of an epistemologically pretentious sort"—that is, those presuppositions that some bring to the theological task that control how one understands God.[47] He has in mind much the same fear that Barth expressed vis-à-vis Brunner's claim that there is resident within creature and creation a "point of contact" that functions "systematically to enable the rest of theology." Although he says such problems were not yet full

---

43. Barth, *Mozart*, 51.
44. Ibid., 55.
45. Ibid., 55, 57.
46. Brunner was simply amazed to read Barth's doctrine of lights when it came out. He called it "the new Barth." Emil Brunner, "Der neue Barth," in *Zeitschrift für Theologie und Kirche* 48 (1951): 89–100.
47. Robert W. Jenson, *Systematic Theology*, vol. 1, *The Triune God* (Oxford: Oxford University Press, 1997), 6.

blown in the early church, "the seeds of later trouble are present in classical theology." In particular, Jenson is concerned that "natural" knowledge was wrongly juxtaposed with "revealed" knowledge, as if there were "a body of knowledge about God and his intentions" that was not "intrinsically dependent on historically particular divine dispositions" and was "therefore properly the common property of humanity."[48] This, as we have seen, was the argument that many church fathers drew from Paul's discussion in Romans 1 and 2.

Jenson goes on to criticize how the "prolegomenal burden" of this theology developed still further during the eighteenth century. Accepting the culture's "hermeneutic of suspicion" with regard to all received wisdom, and needing a criterion by which to evaluate the church's teaching based on revelation, Enlightenment thinkers argued there was a knowledge of God natural to our being that could function as a norm for all theology. John Locke's *The Reasonableness of Christianity as Delivered in the Scriptures* (1695) might be taken as representative. When nineteenth-century theologians undertook the restoration of Christian theology by "overcoming the Enlightenment," they quite naturally, though unfortunately, took as the playing field on which they should fight that which had been laid out by earlier Enlightenment thinkers. That is, to quote Jenson again, they supposed they "had to find a functional replacement for the old natural theology" and accepted as a given the Enlightenment claim "that the church's specific theology was a problematic enterprise dependent on prior justification by more surely founded cognition."[49] Here, as we saw above, was Barth's criticism of Brunner as well.

Jenson goes on in this context to also criticize Friedrich Schleiermacher, who in his *The Christian Faith* (1830) replaced "reason" as the necessary beginning point for theology with "Christian religious experience." That is, he too was a child of the Enlightenment, living under its "prolegomenal burden." But though Jenson might rightly criticize Schleiermacher for making such experience the independent criterion for judging the intellectual respectability of all theology (he writes, "If theological prolegomena lay down conceptual conditions of Christian teaching that are not themselves Christian teaching . . . the prolegomena [will] sooner or later turn against the *legomena*"[50]), Jenson also realizes that Schleiermacher's analysis of "religion" is brilliant. In fact, he considers it vital for many theologians, including himself, when it is not used exclusively or foundationally. That is, in the language of this book, such experience has its rightful place in the doing of theology, but it must find its

48. Ibid., 7–8.
49. Ibid., 8.
50. Ibid., 9.

ultimate criterion in Scripture and its conversation with the theology of the church through the ages. But though Schleiermacher can be criticized for letting his *prolegomena* turn against the biblical *legomena* of the faith, rejecting important aspects of the gospel in the process, his critique of "reasonable" Christianity remains foundational for much theology, including this volume. Jenson is correct.

Schleiermacher rightly understood that general revelation is not first of all, as the received tradition argued, a reasoned deduction from creation, undercut by sin and of little help vis-à-vis redemption except to condemn the sinner. Instead, as he argued to his skeptical friends in *On Religion: Speeches to Its Cultured Despisers* (1799), revelation is the experience of "the Infinite in the finite" (36);[51] it is apprehending the living moment, having a sense and taste for the Infinite. Rooted in revelation, religion is to be sought "where the living contact of man with the world fashions itself as feeling" (63). It is to "bow before the gentle breath of the great Spirit" (81), the "Holy Spirit" (40). Such "feeling is piety," argued Schleiermacher, "in so far as it is the result of the operation of God in you by means of the world upon you" (45). Not any feeling is revelation. He cautioned:

> Remember in the first place that any feeling is not an emotion of piety because in it a single object as such affects us, but only in so far as in it and along with it, it affects us as revelation of God. It is, therefore, not an individual or finite thing, but God, in whom alone the particular thing is one and all, that enters our life. (93)

Religion, argued Schleiermacher, is based on such general revelation: "The sum total of religion is to feel that, in its highest unity, all that moves us in feeling is one . . . that is to say, that our being and living is a being and living in and through God" (49–50). As such, it is "immediate, raised above all error and misunderstanding"; it is "the holy wedlock of the Universe with the incarnated Reason for a creative, productive embrace" (43). Such a revelation "cannot be communicated scientifically, but can only be comprehended in the feeling of a religious disposition" (80). As feeling, it has "not yet passed through the stage of idea" (54). It is therefore not abstract thought; this is a "confusion between religion and that knowledge which belongs to theology" (56). Theology is necessary when "feeling is made the subject of reflection and comparison"; it is "absolutely unavoidable" (87–88). But such second-order abstraction is not

---

51. Friedrich Schleiermacher, *On Religion: Speeches to Its Cultured Despisers*, introduction by Rudolf Otto, trans. John Oman (New York: Harper & Row / Harper Torchbooks, 1958). Page citations, here and following, are noted in the text.

revelation, certainly not feeling; neither is feeling to be equated with fear. It is not joy, or amazement, or the consciousness of divine order, or the awareness of the sustaining care of nature (65–69). Rather, such feeling is of the "World-Spirit" (63): "The true nature of religion is neither this idea nor any other, but immediate consciousness of the Deity as He is found in ourselves [humanity/creature] and in the world [nature/creation]." True religion is to "feel all that moves us is one"; it is to sense "a unity permeated by the Divinity that fashions it" (70).

Schleiermacher believed,

> The whole religious life consists of two elements, that man surrender himself to the Universe and allow himself to be influenced by the side of it that is turned towards him is one part, and that he transplant this contact which is one definite feeling, within, and take it up into the inner unity of his life and being, is the other. (58)

Or again,

> Every original and new communication of the Universe to man is a revelation. . . . Every intuition and every original feeling proceeds from revelation. As revelation lies beyond consciousness, demonstration is not possible, yet we are not merely to assume it generally, but each one knows best himself what is repeated and learned elsewhere, and what is original and new. If nothing original has yet been generated in you, when it does come it will be a revelation for you also, and I will counsel you to weigh it well. (89)

Hopefully, such a pastiche of Schleiermacher's insights gives readers some sense of his understanding of revelation as an event of the Spirit (as well as a taste of his expansive, Romantic language). But to understand what Schleiermacher was driving at through his fecund prose, a consideration of his context and family is helpful. Friedrich Schleiermacher was born in Breslau, Germany, in 1768. His father was a Prussian army chaplain who retained his connections to the Reformed church and subscribed to their theology. But his father had also been influenced by the Moravian Pietists, so Friedrich started attending a Moravian school when he was fourteen and their seminary when he turned sixteen. From the Moravians, Schleiermacher would learn to value piety, friendship, and community. The well-reasoned doctrines of his Reformed heritage became less important than a life of faith lived deeply and in community. Despite his strong attraction toward the Moravians' radically personal experience of faith, given his increasing intellectual questions concerning certain doctrines and a growing skepticism regarding the historicity of the biblical text, Schleiermacher was expelled from the seminary. It was not that a theology of the Word could be ignored, but Schleiermacher came instead to value a theology of the Spirit, one that moved from Spirit to Word rather than vice versa. Enrolling at the University of Halle, he plunged into Kant and studied Greek philosophy (he would later translate Plato into German). In 1790, at age twenty-two, Schleiermacher became a minister in the Reformed church. And though Kantian idealism and rationalistic biblical criticism had become part of his toolbox as a minister, his concern with individual feeling and affection never wavered.

Added to these influences, however, must be his move to Berlin when he was twenty-five, after a brief small-town pastorate. There he became a pastor at Charita Hospital, where he preached, sang in the choir, and ministered to the needs of the patients. But Berlin also gave this young pastor exposure to something more. There Schleiermacher had access to the larger intellectual currents of the time, which in Berlin centered on the Romantic movement. Berlin had been the German headquarters of the Enlightenment, but its rationalism was wearing thin. Increasing numbers of those who were sensitive to other dimensions in life were revolting against its aridity. Labeled Romantics, these artists and scholars did not try so much to reject the "reason" of the Enlightenment as to broaden its vision. For perhaps fifty years (from 1780 to 1830) those like Blake, Wordsworth, Coleridge, Chopin, Schubert, Goethe, and Balzac embraced this new movement. In Berlin, Friedrich Schlegel became the leader of the Romantic circle, as well as Schleiermacher's close friend. It was Schlegel who introduced Schleiermacher to his friends in the movement.

With some reservations, Schleiermacher became an advocate of Romanticism in the field of religion. He saw it as a complement to his "Moravian" inclinations. Embracing its aim of inclusiveness (life's rich wholeness included both emotion and reason, experience and tradition, religion and science, the individual and the community, humanity and nature), its stress on personal experience (creativity, individuality, and freedom were seen as central), its valuing of diversity (all experiences were valuable, and thus the need for tolerance), and yet its belief in the existence of an overarching unity to life that was held together by a larger reality, Schleiermacher believed that Romanticism and Christianity could be mutually embraced. In the Romantics' language and commitments, Schleiermacher found his voice, even as he continued as an active pastor and theologian. As Kutter Callaway summarizes, "He was not 'simply' a romantic, nor was he 'simply' a Christian preacher; he inhabited both spheres simultaneously, and each one informed the other."[52] Thus,

52. Kutter Callaway, "Hearing Images: The Theological and Religious Significance of Music in Film" (PhD diss., Fuller Theological Seminary, 2010).

Schleiermacher agreed with the Romantics' deep appreciation for creativity and aesthetics; yet he remained dismayed that they saw their understanding of life as having no relationship with the Christian tradition.

Encouraged by his friend Schlegel to challenge the lack of interest and involvement in religion by those in their Berlin circle, Schleiermacher, while on temporary leave from his position in Berlin, wrote a series of addresses *On Religion* to those who were his friends and yet were "cultured despisers of religion." It is important to note the contours of Schleiermacher's audience, both for understanding *what* he said about revelation and for appreciating *how* he said it. Writing anonymously so as not to confuse what he was saying with his friendship (though the author was known immediately), he adopted the flowery style of his readers. His overall theme? Don't confuse a rationalized, second-order religion with its essence, which is experienced affectively; the one is dead, but the other is very much alive.

For the purposes of this book, the rest of Schleiermacher's life can be passed over quickly—his return to Halle in 1804 as a professor, then back to Berlin in 1809. He preached every Sunday (the conservative, American, Reformed theologian Charles Hodge wrote that when he attended Schleiermacher's church every Sunday during his graduate study in Berlin, the service was warm, faithful, evangelical, and stressing the gospel[53]), and he even prepared Otto von Bismarck for confirmation. Schleiermacher was a radical patriot, a translator of Plato, and an author. Never abandoning the skeptical biblical criticism of the day, Schleiermacher later wrote a two-volume work in systematic theology, *The Christian Faith*, which combined his experiential understanding of religion and his critical approach to Christianity. Questioning or rejecting historic doctrines of the church, Schleiermacher fell prey to Jenson's fear, *prolegomena* seeming to turn against the *legomena*.

But it would be wrong to jump too undialectically to this conclusion. Even an aging Barth was not too sure. For much of Barth's career, he believed Schleiermacher's "anthropological starting point" made "the Christianly pious person into the criterion and content of his theology"[54] (127). He therefore saw no way from Schleiermacher to the great tradition of the Christian church (127–28). Yet Barth remained uneasy with the critique, for he believed not only that Schleiermacher spoke of the "feeling of Absolute Dependence," but also that he "had that feeling—rather, it had him" (130). Thus, in his later years of life,

53. Charles Hodge, *Systematic Theology* (Grand Rapids: Eerdmans, 1940), 2:440n.

54. Karl Barth, "Concluding Unscientific Postscript on Schleiermacher," *Studies in Religion/Sciences Religieuse* 7, no. 2 (Spring 1978). Page citations here and following are noted in the text.

Barth became open to the possibility that his respected nemesis might be read differently. Barth asked,

> In Schleiermacher's theology or philosophy, do persons feel, think, and speak . . . in relationship to an indispensible [*unaufhebbar*] Other, in accordance with an *object* which is superior to their own being, feeling, perceiving, willing, and acting, an object toward which adoration, gratitude, repentance, and supplication are concretely possible and even imperative? Were that the case, then I would prick up my ears and be joyfully prepared to hear further things about this Other, in the hope of finding myself fundamentally at one with Schleiermacher. (131)

Barth is unable to answer the question, but it remained a possibility for him. Certainly the answer is a complex one. Schleiermacher does (wrongly, in my understanding) discard many of the historic doctrines of the faith, or at least reinterpret them beyond recognition. His movement from Spirit to Word was not without both friction and reduction.[55] The question is not, Is Schleiermacher orthodox in the tradition of the early church theologians and the Reformers? He is not. But that is not the important question for our concern here—God's general revelation to us. The question is, instead, does his starting point in the human spirit's experience of the Holy Spirit necessarily cause the *prolegomena* to cancel out the *legomena*? Was his reduction of Christian theology a necessary result of his methodology, his movement from Spirit to Word, or was it rather a result of his continuing critical approach to Christianity, his ongoing adherence to the dichotomous legacy of the Enlightenment (either objective or subjective), even as he reacted against it?

Let me attempt an answer to this fundamental question in two different ways: by noting first Schleiermacher's use not only of "feeling" but also of "intuition"; and second, by reflecting on his important, yet inconsistent, recognition of the human as a unity of thinking, feeling, and acting.

Feeling and Intuition

Perhaps the most common critique of Schleiermacher's theology is that his understanding of religion falls prey to a subjectivism that makes human consciousness the final arbiter of truth and loses God in the process. This was Ludwig Feuerbach's charge in *The Essence of Christianity* (1841). Having

55. Robert K. Johnston, "Of Tidy Doctrine and Truncated Experience," *Christianity Today* 21, no. 10 (February 18, 1977): 10–14.

studied under Schleiermacher for a brief time before finding philosophy a more congenial "home" for him, Feuerbach argued that "God" was just a human projection, a chimera. To shout "man" is not necessarily to even whisper "God." But such a critique, one surely that lies behind Barth's skepticism regarding Schleiermacher, fails both to take into account the apologetic nature of his writing and to take notice of his careful linkage of "intuition" with "feeling." Writing to his peers in Berlin's Romantic circle, Schleiermacher adopts their speech patterns. To the cultured despisers of religion, he does not often use the name "God," but rather is more apt to speak of "the Universe," "the One and Whole," "the World-Spirit," "the Holy Spirit," "the Spirit of the World," "the eternal World," "the Infinite," "the Genius of humanity," "the great Spirit," or "the Deity." Schleiermacher is certainly claiming for that revelation that undergirds religion more than simply the reality of the human subject; more, too, than a pantheism, which was sometimes the charge, given his nontraditional vocabulary.[56] We do not only feel when we are in this subjective state, but rather we find ourselves grasped by a self-revealed God who is beyond us and other than us. At times the language seems to equivocate, and God becomes World. From page to page the emphasis shifts, but this is in large part due to his audience. It is clear what he wants to say: feeling is a mode of objective apprehension of that which is other than us and beyond us. Precritical and prereflective, such revelation is mediated through our experiences of the world.

Rudolf Otto, in his introduction to an edition of *On Religion*, defends Schleiermacher's ambiguous speech by reminding readers that Schleiermacher was writing an apologetic to people who no longer took the existence of God for granted as being a natural or even necessary truth. Schleiermacher wrote to his contemporaries that there was a divine element in life, and he called on them to open themselves to this Reality. He was convinced that "if we first grasp the eternal, in due time we shall discern the Eternal One. If we

56. In 1801, Schleiermacher responded to the charge of pantheism in a letter to a pastor friend: "You say that I am a pantheist. Have I spoken of religion (in the sense in which you also take this word), have I spoken of faith in a personal god with scorn? Absolutely nowhere. I have only said that religion should not be dependent on whether one in abstract thought ascribes to the infinite transcendental Cause of the world a predicate of personality. This is why I adduced Spinoza as an example, though I am so little like a Spinozist, because throughout his ethics there dominates that way of thinking which one can only call piety. I have pointed out that the reason why certain people ascribe personality to God while others do not lies in differing orientations of the mind, and at the same time I have shown that neither of them is a hindrance to religion." Friedrich Schleiermacher, *Aus Schleiermachers Leben*, ed. L. Jonas and W. Dilthey (Berlin: Reimer, 1858), 3:283, quoted in Stephen Sykes, *Friedrich Schleiermacher* (Richmond: John Knox, 1971), 19.

awaken to the divine, our opened eyes will presently behold God."[57] Thus, Otto would conclude, I think rightly, that although what Schleiermacher did in the *Speeches* would have to be done over in the light of Jesus (and I would add, when Schleiermacher did this in his writing of a systematic theology, his Enlightenment training caused that translation to be a poor one), what he did as an apologist was a worthy first step (I might even say with Jenson, a brilliant first step.)

Schleiermacher's intention was to argue for the importance of one's experience of God. This is made particularly clear from his description of religion as the unity of "*Anschauung* ['intuition'] and *Gefühl* ['feeling']" (44). "Feeling" is that inner and immediate precritical awareness of ourselves as affected by the Infinite in and through the finite. "Intuition" is our immediate perception of the Spirit as it reveals itself through our lived experiences.[58] It is worth repeating Schleiermacher's description of the religious life: "The whole religious life consists of two elements, that man surrender himself to the Universe and allow himself to be influenced by the side of it that is turned towards him, is one part, and that he transplant this contact which is one definite feeling, within, and take it up into the inner unity of his life and being, is the other" (58). For Schleiermacher, "Every intuition and every original feeling proceeds from revelation" (89). In other words, while "feeling" describes our inner awareness of an "Other," "intuition" describes an outer self-disclosure by the "Other." And their perceived unity is revelation. Callaway is particularly helpful at this point. He writes,

> For Schleiermacher, these two concepts are inseparable. In the first edition of *Speeches*, he states: "Intuition without feeling is nothing and can have neither the proper origin nor the proper force; feeling without intuition is also nothing; both are therefore something only when and because they are originally one and unseparated."[59]

---

57. Quoted in Hugh Ross MacIntosh, *Types of Modern Theology: Schleiermacher to Barth* (New York: Charles Scribner's Sons, 1937), 52–53. An abbreviated translation of Otto's introduction to *On Religion* that does not contain this portion appears in the Harper Torchbooks edition of *On Religion* with a translation by John Oman (New York: Harper & Row / Harper Torchbooks, 1958), vii–xx.

58. In his translation of Schleiermacher's *Christmas Eve Celebration: A Dialogue*, Terrence Tice translates *Anschauung* as "concentrated vision." The focus is not on one's internal feelings, but on what one sees. Friedrich Schleiermacher, *Christmas Eve Celebration: A Dialogue*, ed. and trans. Terrence Tice (Eugene, OR: Cascade, 2010).

59. Callaway, "Hearing Images," 183. Interestingly, in the subsequent editions of *On Religion*, Schleiermacher removed many of his references to "feeling" *and* "intuition," choosing only the omnibus term "feeling." But though he gravitated toward the use of the simplified term "feeling" to describe the core religious experience, he makes it clear, even after these subsequent changes, that the feeling he speaks of is more than a human projection. That is, not any feeling will do.

The Unity of Thinking, Feeling, and Acting?

Trying to cleanse our false notions of religion, and needing to move beyond the arid theological soil both of Kant's autonomous moral law and Hume's objective skepticism, Schleiermacher ended up largely divorcing religion from both activity (he used a variety of terms: "practical knowledge," "ethics," "morals," "practice") and knowledge (i.e., "thinking," "perception," "theoretical knowledge," "science," "metaphysics"). Instead, Schleiermacher argued that religion should be understood as precritical and experiential, rooted in the immediacy of humankind's feelings and intuition. In *On Religion*, he began his second address, "The Nature of Religion," by contrasting his understanding with that of his Romantic colleagues who had too easily dismissed it: "Religion is for you at one time a way of thinking, a faith, a peculiar way of contemplating the world, and of combining what meets us in the world: at another, it is a way of acting, a peculiar desire and love, a special kind of conduct and character" (27). Though some tried to pass from "the laws to the Universal Lawgiver," and others allege that "nature cannot be comprehended without God," Schleiermacher maintained "that religion has nothing to do with this knowledge, and that, quite apart from it, its nature can be known" (35). Only when piety can take its place alongside science and practice as a third aspect of human nature will our understanding of humanity be complete. Schleiermacher wrote to his readers,

> Wherefore, as it has become so common to seek metaphysics and ethics chiefly, in the sacred writings, and to appraise them accordingly, it seems time to approach the matter from the other end, and to begin with the clear cut distinction between our faith and your ethics and metaphysics, between our piety and what you call morality. . . .
>
> In order to make quite clear to you what is the original and characteristic possession of religion, it [meaning "religion"] resigns . . . all claims on anything that belongs either to science or morality." (34, 35)

Rather than allowing religion to be subordinate to either science or ethics, or rather than religion being reduced simply to a mingling of theoretical and practical knowledge, Schleiermacher argued that religion must have its own identity as well. "Piety cannot be an instinct craving for a mess of metaphysical and ethical crumbs," was how Schleiermacher colorfully put it (31). As Schleiermacher developed his argument, though, he was at pains also to point out that religion, rooted in feeling and intuition, nevertheless remained related to both our thinking and doing. He said to his readers, "But pray hear me fairly. I do not mean that one could exist without the other, that, for example, a man might have religion and be pious, and at the same time be immoral" (38). To recognize the unity of the three, Schleiermacher believed that "you must apprehend a living moment" (41). Once you think about such unity, however, it has already been sundered. Such unity is real, but it is as "fleeting and transparent as the vapour which the dew breathes on blossom and fruit, it is bashful and tender as a maiden's kiss, it is holy and fruitful as a bridal embrace" (43). The imagery runs away with him! Yet Schleiermacher's intention is clear: he desires his readers to understand that perception, feeling, and activity—three aspects of the human—are "not identical and yet are inseparable" (45).

It is important to understand that Schleiermacher argued strongly for the precritical unity of the human as a "thinking," "feeling," and "doing" creature. But for all his talk, because this unity remained precritical for Schleiermacher, suffering an inevitable divorce whenever it came to consciousness, his argument ended in a false trifurcation of the human. As he spoke of religion, reason was relegated largely to the scrap heap. Ideas about God were necessary, but they remained second order. They were both contextually relative and expendable. Thus, in keeping with Enlightenment sentiment that continued to prevail even among his Romantic colleagues, Schleiermacher himself was quite willing to define away both immortality and any notion of God as personal (100, 97). While these were his opinions, he also was happy to say that one way or the other it was unimportant. He was indifferent. By the time Schleiermacher writes *The Christian Faith* thirty years after the first publication of his *Speeches*, his understanding of God is unfortunately one that is too often foreign to the pages of Scripture, and his understanding of the meaning of the Christ-event far from that of the early church. His movement theologically from Spirit to Word evidences both friction with and a reduction of the faith received, though this was more the result of his continued Enlightenment orientation than his pneumatological starting point.

What can we conclude? Schleiermacher's need to distance himself from the sterile understanding of much religion in his day—at least religion as understood by those outside the church in Berlin's Romantic movement—caused him to reject the place of traditional theology and ethics at the table of religion, even as he argued brilliantly that religion had been wrongly reduced to a subset of reason or ethics, surely nothing like the orienting experience of the Christian faith that he had experienced and that his Moravian upbringing had taught him to appreciate. But such distancing also caused Schleiermacher to rightly relocate the heart of religion in revelation—in the intuition of the Whole from which our feelings were generated, a feeling that he came later to describe as one of "absolute dependence." Thus, though his larger theological system might be found wanting, his understanding of the dynamics of our experience of revelation remains fundamental. It provides a second perspective as to why the received interpretation of Romans 1 cannot serve as the *locus classicus* for our understanding of general revelation. For those texts, as understood by the church through the centuries, and still interpreted by most in the Reformed and Roman Catholic traditions today, are interpreted as centering in humankind's (in)ability through reason to understand God's revelation in the divine footprint resident in creation. Schleiermacher would beg to differ, understanding revelation to be other and more, an act of the living Spirit speaking in and to us.

C. S. Lewis's "Joy"

In suggesting that the church in its theology needs to recraft its understanding of general revelation, an understanding informed by a particular interpretation of Romans 1 and 2, I have turned to what are on the surface two unlikely and at times opposing voices: Karl Barth and Friedrich Schleiermacher. In conclusion to this chapter, I want to turn to C. S. Lewis, someone who, though not a major theological voice, has had an immense influence on twentieth-century Christian thought. Lewis would seemingly be someone more amenable to our revelational project, and in many ways he is; though on closer inspection, he wrongly undercuts his understanding of God's revelatory Presence in and through everyday life in order to focus instead rationally on the full revelation of God in Jesus Christ.

When describing the debate between Barth and his nemesis Emil Brunner, I was sympathetic with Brunner's desire to ground revelation not only in Christology but also in creation. And certainly Barth comes close to conceding this point to Brunner when toward the end of his career he argued that there was not only the Light of Life, Jesus Christ, but also a number of lesser lights that nevertheless provided reflected illumination. But Barth's critique of Brunner also remains foundational to all else, his argument that revelation must always be understood as "event," as encounter with the living God through the Spirit. Revelation is never rooted somehow independent of God in creation's footprint. It is here that the voice of Barth remains necessary for us to hear again today. We do not possess a "point of contact" between us and God, but the Holy Spirit—the "go-between God"—is that point of contact speaking through Christ preeminently, but also through creation, conscience, and culture.[60] Revelation is never the result of creation independent of the Presence of the Spirit in and through it.

60. See John Taylor, *The Go-Between God: The Holy Spirit and the Christian Mission* (Philadelphia: Fortress, 1972).

To speak only of God's "footprint" resounding in creation or his "echo" heard through creation without recognizing it is the Spirit's Presence that we experience is to turn revelation into a simple epistemological exercise rooted in human reason. It is to fail to understand revelation as first of all a genuine event, an encounter with the living God. And here, Friedrich Schleiermacher has been a helpful conversation partner. Schleiermacher might rightly be viewed as the obverse of Barth—if Barth is too exclusively christocentric, Schleiermacher is too tied to the skeptical reasoning of his age. He is thus too willing to jettison as unimportant Christ's miracles, the church's traditional understanding of immortality, the virgin birth, and so on. But though Schleiermacher's under-standing of the Christian faith was compromised at its center, he nonetheless saw rightly the mistake in the church's overly rationalistic and/or moralistic approaches to revelation. With Schleiermacher, we have described "revelation" as an encounter with God through his Spirit, something that is both rooted in our "feeling" and concurrently the result of our "intuition" of the Presence of the Other (the Universe, the Whole, that which produces a feeling of "absolute dependence," God) to us and in us. Schleiermacher was unable to adequately tell his Romantic friends "what to believe," but he proved brilliant in sharing both with them and us "what it is to believe."[61]

Third and finally, we turn to C. S. Lewis for help in correcting the theological legacy we have inherited concerning the nature of general revelation. Here is someone whose whole life was shaped by a series of revelational experiences that occurred while he was still hostile to the Christian faith. Lewis's own experience might well be as good a witness to the theological importance of general revelation as one could discover. C. S. Lewis's life story is well known, and we already described it briefly in chapter 1. But a fuller discussion here is necessary, given the surprising turn at the end of his autobiography.

In his life story, *Surprised by Joy*, Lewis recounts a number of isolated aesthetic experiences where "beauty" ushered him into the Presence of God.[62] He did not know that the experiences were actually revelatory of God for a long time. But that is what they ultimately turned out to be for him. As a young child, Lewis had several experiences that he remembered as particularly significant for his life. They presented themselves to him as more real than reality, more fundamental than most of his everyday life. The first was the time when his older brother brought into the nursery "the lid of a biscuit tin which he had covered with moss and garnished with twigs and flowers so as

61. See Richard Crouter, introduction to Friedrich Schleiermacher, *On Religion*, ed. and trans. Richard Crouter (Cambridge: Cambridge University Press, 1996), xxix.

62. C. S. Lewis, *Surprised by Joy* (New York: Harcourt, Brace & World / Harvest Books, 1955). Page citations to this book will be noted in the text.

to make it a toy garden or a toy forest." Lewis recalled, "That was the first beauty I ever knew." Lewis commented, "What the real garden had failed to do, the toy garden did. It made me aware of nature . . . as something cool, dewy, fresh, exuberant." He says that throughout his life, his imagination of Paradise retained something of that toy garden (7). There was also the view of the "Green Hills" that he could see outside his nursery windows. He says they taught him "longing—*Sehnsucht*" (more on this below). So too did the Beatrix Potter books. Although Lewis was already writing stories about the imaginary world of Boxen by this time, he says that that use of his imagination was different. He was the creator, and so that imaginative world carried with it no charm for him, no longing for an "Other." But when his imagination was piqued by Beatrix Potter's *Squirrel Nutkin*, or later by Longfellow's *Saga of King Olaf*, it was a different kind of experience, one closer to "Milton's 'enormous bliss' of Eden (giving the full, ancient meaning of 'enormous')" (16). In these moments, he experienced something other—the "Idea of Autumn," "Northernness." What was common to these imaginative experiences was, for Lewis, "an unsatisfied desire which is itself more desirable than any other satisfaction." He called it "Joy" (18).

This Joy, thought Lewis, was neither Happiness nor Pleasure. These he could produce by his own power. But his experiences of Joy were different. It was always a surprise, something he received rather than produced, and something always experienced as of incalculable importance. "It was something quite different from ordinary life and even from ordinary pleasure; something, as they would now say, 'in another dimension'" (17). Moreover, it always had "the stab, the pang, the inconsolable longing" (72). After the death of his mother, Lewis did not experience such Joy again for a long time. But then he saw an illustration by Arthur Rackham of Siegfried and soon after heard Wagner's music anew. He did not know whether to call these experiences "pleasure," or "trouble, ecstasy, astonishment" (75). There was in him simply "a conflict of sensations without name" (75). As Lewis continued through his teenage years, he became a conflicted atheist—that is, he maintained that God didn't exist but confessed that he was angry at God because of that. There also continued those moments of ecstasy, that stab of Joy, when he was sick with desire, that sickness which was "better than health" (119). Lewis relates how he steeped himself in Wagnerian music and in Norse and Celtic mythology—all things "Northern." But though he added detail to detail, Joy could not be produced. His greedy impatience to snare it seemed to scare it away.

However, Lewis then happened upon the imaginative world of George Mac-Donald's *Phantastes*. I quote him:

> In one sense the new country was exactly like the old. I met there all that had already charmed me in Malory, Spenser, Morris, and Yeats. But in another sense all was changed. I did not yet know . . . the name of the new quality, the bright shadow that rested on the travels of Anodos. I do now. It was Holiness. . . . It was as though the voice which had called to me from the world's end were now speaking at my side. It was with me in the room, or in my body, or behind me. If it had once eluded me by its distance, it now eluded me by proximity—something too near to see, too plain to be understood, on this side of knowledge. (179–80)

This Joy, for Lewis, was inseparable from MacDonald's story. And while his previous experiences of Joy had seemed totally detached from his "ordinary" life, this time Joy's bright shadow came out of the book and into his real world, "transforming all common things and yet itself unchanged. Or more accurately, I saw the common things drawn into the bright shadow. . . . That night my imagination was, in a certain sense, baptized; the rest of me, not unnaturally, took longer" (181).

Lewis concludes, "The great Angler played His fish and I never dreamed that the hook was in my tongue" (211). It would take some years before Lewis would recognize this "great Angler" to be who he was—God. And it would take even longer before Lewis would believe that God had become incarnate in Jesus Christ. Along the way, Lewis would get help from a host of sources in understanding his experiences of Joy as the activity of "Spirit" (and eventually the Holy Spirit)—"Plato, Dante, MacDonald, Herbert, Barfield, Tolkien, Dyson, Joy itself" (225). But it was in reading MacDonald that Joy's bright shadow left its indelible mark. For a time still, Lewis continued to try to isolate what his "Joy" was, and to seek it directly. But he eventually came to the conclusion that focusing on his experiences of Joy could only lead him to find what had been left behind, the vapor that remained and not the true source. Wrote Lewis, "The great error is to mistake this mere sediment or track or byproduct for the activities themselves" (219). He had confused the track that Joy left behind with Joy itself. Rather than desire Joy, Lewis realized, "All the value lay in that of which Joy was the desiring." He wrote, "I had asked if Joy itself was what I wanted; and, labeling it 'aesthetic experience,' had pretended I could answer Yes. But that answer too had broken down. Inexorably Joy proclaimed, 'You want—I myself am your want of—something other, outside, not you nor any state of you" (221).

Finally, one night in 1929, Lewis gave in to that of which Joy is the desiring and admitted to himself that "God was God, and knelt and prayed." He describes himself memorably as "perhaps . . . the most dejected and reluctant convert in all England" (228–29). Though his imagination had been baptized much earlier and now perhaps his intellect, even here Lewis's conversion was not to Christianity but only to theism. It was still later that he accepted the incarnation as an act of his will—in the car one morning as he was driving to Whipsawed Zoo. "When we set out I did not believe that Jesus is the Son of God, and when we reached the zoo I did" (237). Lewis had "sought the Lord, and afterward he knew, he was found by Thee."[63]

Lewis thus shaped the whole of his autobiography around his revelatory encounters with God, around the surprising experience of that bright shadow that is Joy, something too near to be seen, on this side of his focal length. For him, "the central story of [his] life [was] about nothing else" (17). These experiences of Joy prior to his conversion at age thirty-one, though sporadic, were foundational, causing his imagination to be baptized and setting him off on a long search. And they had occurred outside the church and without direct reference to Jesus Christ.

In one of his better-known sermons, "The Weight of Glory," Lewis discusses such Joy once again, suggesting that all humans have a longing for Heaven, for this is what we ultimately were made for (for "our own far-off country") (4).[64] Such a desire is an "inconsolable secret" (11), one that hurts so much that skeptics call it "names like Nostalgia and Romanticism and Adolescence" (4). But though it is a desire for something beyond our experience, we cannot hide from it, for our experience is constantly suggesting it. Here was Lewis's own experience of Joy. Often, Lewis told his congregation of Oxford students and dons, we try to blunt the pangs by merely calling it "beauty." This is what Lewis himself had done. But, argues Lewis, the books, images, and music in which beauty is thought to be located will betray us if we give our trust to them; "it was not *in* them, it only came *through* them, and what came through them was longing [*Sehnsucht*]" (4). Again, Lewis's own autobiography is his sourcebook. Lewis cautions, "They are only the scent of a flower we have not found, the echo of a tune we have not heard, news from a country we have never yet visited" (5). But while beauty is fleeting, ephemeral, we notice its "glory." As the music ends or the landscape loses its light, there remains its illusion. Yet, says Lewis, "it is not the physical objects that I am speaking of, but that indescribable something of which they become for a moment the messengers" (11). It is the "promise of glory" (11) that the arts mediate—glory

63. See the anonymously written hymn, "I sought the Lord, and afterward I knew." The words of the first stanza are: "I sought the Lord, and afterward I knew / he moved my soul, to seek him, seeking me; / it was not I that found O savior true; / no, I was found of thee."
64. C. S. Lewis, "The Weight of Glory," in *The Weight of Glory and Other Addresses* (Grand Rapids: Eerdmans, 1949). Page citations to this book will be noted in the text.

in the sense of acceptance by God, of being "noticed" by God (12). Here, in sermonic form, was what Lewis understood to be his own experience of Joy.

As would be expected of something so fundamental to his own being, Lewis illustrated the importance of these revelatory experiences in his fiction as well—in his allegorical writings, his science fiction, and his children's literature.[65] Perhaps here were channels of communication where modernity still allowed room for the presentation of that which lay beyond the empirical and narrowly rationalistic. Thus, in *The Great Divorce*, Lewis writes: "When you painted because you caught glimpses of heaven in the earthly landscape . . . others got glimpses too."[66] Or again, in *The Screwtape Letters*, the junior devils are told by their boss that in their work of frustrating God's kingdom they must keep humans from "the incalculable winds of fantasy and music and poetry—the mere face of a girl, the song of a bird, the sight of a horizon."[67] And in *Till We Have Faces*, Orual says, "The nearest thing we have to a defense against [the gods] (but there is no real defense) is to be very wide awake and sober and hard at work, to hear no music, never to look at earth or sky, and (above all) to love no one."[68] Turning to his science fiction, at the end of *Out of the Silent Planet*, Lewis, as the author, in a wonderful turn of events, writes that his chief character in the novel, Elwin Ransom, suggested to Lewis that they "publish in the form of fiction what would certainly not be listened to as fact." "What we need for the moment," Ransom explained, "is not so much a body of belief as a body of people familiarized with certain ideas. If we could even effect in one per cent of our readers a change-over from the conception of Space to the conception of Heaven, we should have made a beginning."[69] Here are references to that thickness of experience that Lewis knew personally, that "baptism" of his imagination that he wanted others to experience as well.

And, of course, there is Lewis's children's fiction. Here, in particular, Lewis painted with words equivalent "experiences" to those he had had as a child, believing that through such fantasy others might receive glimpses of Joy as well. In *The Silver Chair*, for example, Puddleglum, the endearing Marshwiggle who befriends the children, is with them in the falsely empirical and bounded underworld of the Green Witch. Responding to her skeptical and belittling comments about Narnia, he tells her:

65. Cf. Adam Gopnik, "Prisoner of Narnia," *The New Yorker*, November 21, 2005, http://www.newyorker.com/printables/critics/051121crat_atlarge.
66. C. S. Lewis, *The Great Divorce* (New York: Macmillan, 1946), 80.
67. C. S. Lewis, *The Screwtape Letters* (New York: Macmillan, 1943), 144.
68. C. S. Lewis, *Till We Have Faces* (New York: Harcourt, Brace, 1957), 81.
69. C. S. Lewis, *Out of the Silent Planet* (New York: Macmillan, 1965), 153–54.

Suppose we have only dreamed, or made up, all those things—trees and grass and sun and moon and stars and Aslan himself. Suppose we have. Then all I can say is that, in that case, the made-up things seem a good deal more important than the real ones. Suppose this black pit of a kingdom of yours is the only world. Well, it strikes me as a pretty poor one. And that's a funny thing . . . four babies playing a game can make a play world which licks your real world hollow.[70]

Or again, in *The Voyage of the "Dawn Treader,"* as the story ends and the children are to return to England, Aslan (Lewis's reimagining of who Christ might be in the imaginary world of Narnia) tells the children that in their world "I have another name. You must learn to know me by that name. This was the very reason why you were brought to Narnia, that by knowing me here for a little, you may know me better there."[71]

As one might expect of an academic (!), Lewis not only wrote stories but also wrote about stories and their meaning. For Lewis, story should be more than mere plot; more even than any felt excitement by the reader. Rather, story can and should be a mediation of that which lies beyond the perception of the reader. Plot, wrote Lewis, is important, but only as "a net whereby to catch something else."[72] That something is more like a state or quality, not a process. Giantness in "Jack and the Beanstalk" or the desolation of space in H. G. Wells's *The First Men in the Moon* would be examples. So, too, would the "Autumn" Lewis encountered in Beatrix Potter, the "Northernness" he experienced reading Viking mythology, and the "Holiness" he encountered in George MacDonald.[73] This "something more" that readers encountered was not an escape from reality, though it was a reality baffling to the intellect. "It may not be 'like real life' in the superficial sense," he argued, "but it sets before us an image of what reality may well be like at some more central region."[74] Story, as one example of those aesthetic experiences that had surprised Lewis by Joy, not only allowed readers to reach outward, but also could become the occasion to hear that voice "from the world's end speaking at our side." (One can perhaps find similarities in Schleiermacher's description of "feeling and intuition.") Returning to this theme in an essay on writing for children,

---

70. C. S. Lewis, *The Silver Chair* (New York: Macmillan / Collier Books, 1953), 159.

71. C. S. Lewis, *The Voyage of the "Dawn Treader"* (New York: Macmillan / Collier Books, 1952), 216.

72. C. S. Lewis, "On Stories," in *Essays Presented to Charles Williams*, ed. C. S. Lewis (Grand Rapids: Eerdmans, 1966), 103. See also Robert K. Johnston, "Image and Content: The Tension in C. S. Lewis' Chronicles of Narnia," *Journal of the Evangelical Theological Society* 20, no. 3 (September 1977): 253–64.

73. Lewis, *Surprised by Joy*, 16, 73, 168, 179.

74. Ibid., 101.

Lewis argued that when young boys read of enchanted woods, they do not end up despising the real woods. Rather, "the reading makes all real woods a little enchanted."[75]

Lewis's hope, in much of his fictional and imaginative writing, was twofold. First, it was to retool the imagination of his readers, who had become through their predominant education "half-hearted creatures, fooling about with drink and sex and ambition when infinite joy is offered us, like the ignorant child who wants to go on making mudpies . . . because he cannot imagine what is meant by the offer of a holiday at the sea."[76] In his *The Abolition of Man*, a series of lectures on his philosophy of education that he presented at the University of Durham in 1947, Lewis was particularly caustic about modern education that attempted both to undercut the importance of emotion—to starve the sensibility—and to deny all belief in any Reality that might lie behind all predicates—Lewis labeled this a belief in the "Tao." "As far back as Plato, it was recognized that reason rules the mere appetites in man by means of the 'spirited element.'" That is, the head rules the belly through the chest. It was this middle element—the heart—that makes us human, for by our intellect we are but spirit, and by our appetite we are but animal. Unfortunately, thought Lewis, modern education had produced "men without chests": "It is not excess of thought but defect of fertile and generous emotion that marks [such people] out. For their heads are no bigger than ordinary; it is the atrophy of the chest beneath that makes them seem so."[77] One hears in the background the importance of Lewis's own experiences of Joy.

Second, Lewis's intention through his fiction was to invite the process of "transposition."[78] His stories were intended as invitations to open one's self to Eternity's in-breaking—to understand the conception of "space" as actually the conception of "heaven." Certainly, for Lewis, the incarnation was the primary expression of God's revelation to us, Eternity entering into time, the Infinite becoming finite. But Lewis believed that there were also other, more incomplete forms of God's revelational Presence—general revelation, that is. Like other Platonists, Lewis believed that humankind could only understand the world through its relationship with a higher spiritual power. As we have seen in his autobiography, this is what he had experienced in his repeated pangs of Joy. That sense of longing that Lewis described as so

75. C. S. Lewis, "On Three Ways of Writing for Children," reprinted in C. S. Lewis, *Of Other Worlds* (London: Geoffrey Bles, 1968), 30.

76. Lewis, *Weight of Glory*, 2.

77. C. S. Lewis, *The Abolition of Man* (New York: Macmillan, 1947), 34–35.

78. See C. S. Lewis, "Transposition," in *Transposition and Other Addresses* (London: Geoffrey Bles, 1949), 9–20.

overpowering—*Sehnsucht*—was a longing for that which was both beyond us and yet partially visible to us.

Such experiences of the Numinous might connect us with Eternity, thought Lewis; they might be a seed of religious experience. But lacking any specific content, Lewis saw them as more typically being interpreted simply as a special form of aesthetic experience rather than an encounter with Eternity.[79] Surely, this had been his own experience at one point in time. He had needed help in understanding his experiences of Joy for what they were. That the natural world was more than nature, that it was the Creation, was another such insight from beyond us, yet again needing religion to come along and retrospectively transpose our experiences before nature could yield its secret of a Creator. Whether "Joy," the "Numinous," or "Creation," such experiences offered glimpses of that which was beyond us, that which was transcendent to us, though we might misinterpret their meaning. Writing on Lewis's doctrine of transposition, P. H. Brazier comments that for Lewis,

> Revelation proceeds eschatologically, from eternity and into our reality; this is primarily in the form of the Incarnation, but secondarily in the modes of general and incomplete revelation. Reality, for Lewis, was simply a veil through which we might glimpse the source of this greater reality: eternity, heaven.[80]

All of this is to say that though the experiences of Joy that surprised Lewis were foundational and revelatory, they functioned more like signposts pointing him in the direction of a fuller understanding of God than something with their own value and meaning. Though Joy might move one Godward, Lewis believed that Joy imparted little explicit knowledge itself and thus, apart from God's full revelation in the incarnation, was of limited value. Thus, though he spent the whole of his autobiography extolling the wonder of Joy, and though he says the experience of Joy is "the central story of my life,"[81] he can nonetheless end his autobiography by largely taking back most of what he had previously offered. He writes (and here perhaps is the real surprise of the book):

> But what, in conclusion, of Joy? for that, after all, is what the story has mainly been about. To tell you the truth, the subject has lost nearly all interest for me since I became a Christian. I cannot, indeed, complain, like Wordsworth, that the visionary gleam has passed away. I believe (if the thing were at all worth

79. C. S. Lewis, *God in the Dock: Essays on Theology and Ethics*, ed. Walter Hooper (Grand Rapids: Eerdmans, 1970), 175.

80. P. H. Brazier, "C. S. Lewis: A Doctrine of Transposition," *The Heythrop Journal* 50 (2009): 679.

81. Lewis, *Surprised by Joy*, 17.

recording) that the old stab, the old bittersweet, has come to me as often and as sharply since my conversion as at any time of my life whatever. But I now know that the experience, considered as a state of mind, had never the kind of importance I once gave it. It was valuable only as a pointer to something other and outer. While that other was in doubt, the pointer naturally loomed large in my thoughts. When we are lost in the woods the sight of a signpost is a great matter. He who first sees it cries, "Look!" The whole party gathers round and stares. But when we have found the road and are passing signposts every few miles, we shall not stop and stare. They will encourage us and we shall be grateful to the authority who set them up. But we shall not stop and stare, or not much; not on this road, though their pillars are of silver and their lettering of gold. "We would be at Jerusalem."[82]

Lewis thus is functionally the obverse of Schleiermacher in his theology of general revelation. Schleiermacher was "romantic about theology," ultimately and wrongly judging aspects of the received tradition concerning the nature of God's revelation in Christ as unimportant and even expendable if judged as conflicting with what his culture deemed "reasonable." Lewis, on the other hand, was "theological about romance," ultimately and wrongly reducing his experiences of Joy to mere signposts, pointers to theological truth and goodness that have no intrinsic meaning but that find their only significance in the Christ event. Though Lewis brilliantly describes the feeling of Joy he repeatedly experiences, he wrongly finds it to be contentless apart from the incarnation. Having subsequently met Jesus, Lewis then finds little to interest him in God's continued aesthetic interventions in his life through his Spirit. Though these might even be of silver with gold lettering, he would eschatologically and proleptically see "Jerusalem." Though he continues to have revelatory experiences of divine Presence, he says he is not sure they are even worth recording!

Different from most of the early commentators on Romans 1 and 2, Lewis would rightly understand that general revelation functions more than simply as a means of condemnation—it also points. But though it points, such revelation is of marginal value, thinks Lewis, without the knowledge that God's revelation in Christ can bring. Where Schleiermacher keeps Christian "feeling" but compromises Christian "thought," Lewis ends up compromising Christian "feeling" while embracing Christian "thought." When all is said and done, Lewis ends up at much the same point as Barth: fearful, as Robert Jenson expresses it, of humankind's propensity to pretentiously claim to know God by our own efforts as we interact with human conscience, creation, and culture.

82. Ibid., 238.

But though Lewis thus proves as complex as both Barth and Schleiermacher in our search to learn from the tradition of the church about general revelation, Lewis is nonetheless helpful to us, even as a negative example. For he provides us a warning not to undercut that general revelation he so perceptively describes, even as one embraces God's special revelation in Christ.

And thus we end this extended theological conversation with the received tradition concerning general revelation. Though one could interpret Romans 1 to include the witness of the Holy Spirit in and through the "things [God] has made," and though it could be implied that God's "eternal power and divine nature" are understood from God's creation only through the Spirit's work—something Paul seems to suggest with regard to human conscience in Romans 2—certainly this is not what the preponderance of early exegetes of the church concluded. And Paul surely is ambiguous as to his intended meaning in this passage vis-à-vis general revelation, for his intention, his concern, is elsewhere—on sin and salvation. Given both the uncertainty of the text's revelational gaze and the absence of the Spirit's role in most traditional interpretation of the text, we must conclude that Romans 1 has mistakenly been used as the biblical *locus classicus* for the church's constructive theology of general revelation. Romans 1 simply fails to make clear (1) that general revelation is always event and not possession; (2) that it is primarily not a rational deduction but an experience of our imagination that has as its referent Something (Someone?) beyond us; and (3) that this revelation is foundational and directional, providing precritical knowledge of the Divine that not only proves "prevenient" but also continues to illumine even those who have experienced the Light of Life—Jesus Christ.

It is this third conclusion that needs more unpacking, however. How does this precritical experience actually add insight, and how might it be seen as connected to a personal God? In the next chapter we will consider the theologies of John V. Taylor, Jürgen Moltmann, and Elizabeth Johnson as we look for help in moving beyond our christocentric, soteriological impasse. Can they be of help to us in understanding how our experiences of the Spirit of God, whether through conscience, creation, or culture, might fit into a larger trinitarian theology? These theologians will help us move our investigation forward through a broader discussion of the role of the Holy Spirit in general revelation, for here is where these more contemporary "doctors of the church" would lead us.

7

Moved by the Spirit

John V. Taylor, in his classic text *The Go-Between God: The Holy Spirit and the Christian Mission* (1972), understands the mission of the church to be that of discerning what the creative Spirit is doing in the world and then coming alongside him. He begins his study by speaking of the Spirit's work of "annunciation," asking, what is it that the Spirit is doing and saying? He asks, "What sort of power are we to expect beyond that of ordinary men and by what kind of communication does he point out the way?"[1] In seeking an answer, Taylor, similar to the first four chapters of this book, turns both to firsthand descriptions of encounters with the Spirit of Life (what he labels "annunciations") and also to the biblical record, particularly to the ancient images of "the breath of life, the hovering wings, the unpredictable winds, the fire in the mouth."[2]

The Spirit Encountered

As with C. S. Lewis, Taylor begins his reflection on the Spirit and the church's mission by recounting what he learned from his own childhood experiences. He relates that when he was quarantined with the measles at around ten years

1. John V. Taylor, *The Go-Between God: The Holy Spirit and the Christian Mission* (Philadelphia: Fortress, 1972), 5.
2. Ibid., 7.

of age, he ended up listening to a wooden box gramophone for hours on end in order to amuse himself. Taylor says he was surprised to discover that music could "speak"; he had not known that such a language existed. But a short musical passage, one later judged trivial by Taylor as an adult, nonetheless affected him with "a shock of excitement." Making use of Martin Buber's categories, Taylor reflected that what had been up to that time an "I-It" experience became for him an "I-Thou" encounter. Later in his life the same type of personal encounter happened as Taylor glimpsed Mount Kilimanjaro shining above the cloud line in Tanzania. He says, "The fact that something, or someone, [was] *there* suddenly became important." The mountain was no longer simply part of the landscape, but it presented itself, became present, commanded attention. Such an experience, he reflected, happens as well when one falls in love—think of Romeo catching Juliet's eye—but it also happens in the ordinariness of everyday life. "In a manner of speaking, we are falling in love at every turn of the road, with a fold in the hills, the mist over the lake, the stars tangled in the bare branches, the yellow chair in the sunlight, an old song at the peasant's fireside, a new thought flashing from the pages of a book, a lined face on a hospital pillow, a hair-ribbon from Ur of the Chaldees." Taylor illustrates his thesis by quoting from the poets Edwin Muir and Wordsworth, as well as from a prisoner of war who described his joy in seeing larks rise into the air and sing their joyous song: "There was no one to be seen for miles around; there was nothing but the wide earth and sky and the lark's jubilation and the freedom of space. I stopped, looked around, and up to the sky—and then I went down on my knees."[3]

Taylor says the best description he can give to such experiences—encounters similar to those we have referenced in the previous chapters of this book—is to call them "annunciations." In using this term, he says he is not trying to limit, or narrow, himself to specifically "religious" experiences, though that might be the impression. Rather, he wants also to include, just as I do, quite unreligious, commonplace events as well. His interest is in what can be said about those experiences when a mountain or a tree ceases to become an object and instead becomes a subject "nodding to me in a private conspiracy." Here is, in fact, the meaning of the word "numinous"—from the Latin *nuo*, meaning to nod. Such annunciations, such nods, force us to recognize the real otherness (Otherness?) of what one is looking at, something we have already encountered in the writings of Tillich and Schleiermacher, Lewis and Hay. Something real is being communicated as the ordinary becomes extraordinary. There is a cause for wonder. What has been simply an object meets the beholder

3. Ibid., 8–10.

in his or her own authenticity. Says Taylor, "I am face to face with the truth *of* it, not merely the truth *about* it."[4] Here surely is what my students who saw *It's a Wonderful Life* and *Easy Rider* experienced.

As was the case with C. S. Lewis, Taylor found that the repetition of such experiences caused him to realize that the source of such joy and wonder was not himself but a P/presence to which he was responding. Quoting Martin Buber, Taylor writes about this annunciation, "Through the graciousness of its comings and the solemn sadness of its goings it leads you away to the *Thou* in which the parallel lines of relations meet. It . . . helps you to glimpse eternity."[5] What we might be prone to call the object of our response is actually its subject, its activator, thinks Taylor. But, he realizes, perhaps that is not entirely accurate either. For what makes a landscape or person come to life for another and become a presence toward which one surrenders (when I recognize, respond, worship, fall in love) is more accurately "an anonymous third party who makes the introduction, acts as a go-between, makes two beings aware of each other, sets up a current of communication between them. What is more, this invisible go-between does not simply stand between us but is activating each of us from the inside." To speak of the "go-between" in these terms, concludes Taylor, is to speak in "very personal terms." This is inevitable, for the effect of the P/power experienced is always to bring about a personal relationship. Taylor concludes, "So Christians find it quite natural to give a personal name to this current of communication, this invisible go-between. They call him the Holy Spirit, the Spirit of God."[6]

The Spirit as the "Go-Between God" is behind Paul's benediction at the end of 2 Corinthians when he speaks of "the communion of [the "sharing in"] the Holy Spirit" (2 Cor. 13:13). It is the Spirit who rivets our attention, opening eyes that are closed and hearts that are unaware (cf. Acts 9:17). Taylor concludes, "The spirit of man is that facility which enables each of us to be truly present to another. The Spirit of God is that power of communion which enables every other reality, and the God who is within and behind all realities, to be present to us."[7] Moreover, such communion is not simply private or individualistic. For just as the Spirit opens our own eyes, both to the cosmos and our own inner self, so the Go-Between God fosters communion between peoples. Posits Taylor, when you are speaking of the Spirit, there are no differences of scale.

Taylor realizes that, by framing the discussion of the Spirit's mission in this way, he risks, just as I have in this book, being too inclusive. Can we really

4. Ibid., 11–13.
5. Ibid., 14–15.
6. Ibid., 17.
7. Ibid., 19.

say that every "I-Thou" experience is an encounter with God? Taylor leaves the question open, but believes a passionate concern for all things human is nevertheless the right starting point. So too is the belief, rooted in experience and Scripture, that the Spirit of Life is present in the ordinary, not just the extraordinary. But if this is so, how, then, do you recognize the Spirit's Presence—the Spirit's communion? We will return to this question in the next chapter, but Taylor is insightful in suggesting that a key is our "attention" to the matter—our attending (from the Latin, meaning "to stretch out") totally to something or someone, our outside or extraneous thoughts being temporarily arrested. Such attention happens spontaneously and is an involuntary surrender. But paradoxically, it is always with the sense as well that we are freely choosing it. And the result is significant—the encounter makes a difference, proves to be a turning point, as our old ideas are challenged and we are forced to take a new direction.

Taylor quotes Robert Browning's poem where Bishop Blougram speaks of the sad skeptic Gigadibs and his buttoned-up philosophy.

> Just when we are safest there's a sunset touch,
> A fancy from a flower bell, someone's death,
> A chorus-ending from Euripides,
> And that's enough for fifty hopes and fears,
> As old and new at once as nature's self,
> To rap and knock and enter in our soul.[8]

Such a poetic description brings to mind the reflection of C. S. Lewis, someone whom we have already considered. God is present in all things; as Lewis writes, "All ground is holy and every bush (could we but perceive it) a Burning Bush." But although the world may be crowded with the divine Presence, Lewis also believes that the Spirit walks everywhere "incognito." And though this incognito is not always hard to penetrate, it does take "attention." We must remain awake. When we do, however, the Spirit's communion proves a turning point.[9] Here is an almost identical description to that of Taylor.

For both Taylor and Lewis, there is an obvious paradox that is present with regard to our needed "attention." In one sense the Go-Between God commands our attention. His compelling power is absolute. It is the Spirit that keeps the stars on track and energizes life's flourishing. But in humankind, the all-powerful

8. Robert Browning, "Bishop Blougram's Apology," quoted in Taylor, *The Go-Between God*, 16.
9. C. S. Lewis, *God in the Dock: Essays on Theology and Ethics*, ed. Walter Hooper (Grand Rapids: Eerdmans, 1970), 75.

God who is present for us chooses also to be with us and in us in a way that allows for relationship—allows, that is, human freedom and choice. Reflecting on this seeming contradiction, Lewis writes: "The higher the creature, the more, and also the less, God is in it: the more present by grace, and the less present (by a sort of abdication) as mere power. By grace He gives the higher creatures power to will His will ('and wield their little tridents'): the lower ones simply execute it automatically."[10] But though we must remain awake, though we must seek, though we must choose, though we must "attend," it is also the case that the Spirit's Presence is compelling, seeking us out, opening our eyes, redirecting our evasions and turning them into our freely chosen prayers. We seek the divine Presence, only to discover as the hymn writer wrote, "We were found by Thee." Though we choose to attend, it is also the case that our attention is riveted by an Other—by the Spirit, the Go-Between God.

In the book of Acts, Luke describes Paul's trip to Philippi. He writes, "A certain woman named Lydia, a worshiper of God, was listening to us. . . . The Lord opened her heart to listen eagerly [that is, to "attend"] to what was said by Paul," and she was converted, becoming "faithful to the Lord" (Acts 16:14–15). Here is the Spirit's work of annunciation—a work that has at its center a paradox, even a contradiction. The Spirit's "annunciation," his revelation, is an invitation that is powerful, yet is received spontaneously. It comes through words and acts, sight and sound, creation and culture; yet it is also always the case that the "Spirit [bears] witness [together] with our spirit" (Rom. 8:16).

Taylor identifies three questions that we might ask as we seek to discern the Spirit's revelatory Presence in our lives.

> Which factors in this situation are giving people the more intense awareness of some "other" who claims their attention or of some greater "whole"? Which factors are compelling people to make personal and responsible choices? Which factors are calling out from people self-oblation and sacrifice?[11]

These questions recall the three components of a definition of religion that my friend and teacher in graduate school, Wesley Kort, offered: for there to be a religion, there must be a sense of the Transcendent, which is somehow made available to us, and which, at least potentially, makes some difference in our lives. Here also is what Taylor is suggesting with regard to the "Go-Between God." The Spirit is an Other, a Presence, who compels free choice, leading to commitment and even transformation as we give the Spirit our "attention."

10. Ibid., 74–75.
11. Taylor, *The Go-Between God*, 39.

The Spirit Described Biblically

In Scripture, no definition of the Spirit is given; rather, the Spirit is "*narrated as an event—as happening.*"[12] Here perhaps is the basic difficulty one has in attempting a definition of revelation, which is an encounter with the Spirit. The Spirit becomes known as God reveals his personal Presence in creation and re-creation, in quickening and sustaining power and wisdom, and in in-breaking expectation. Understood as such, the Spirit is to be identified with the divine Presence in all of life. In the Spirit's activity as our creator, sustainer, redeemer, and finisher, we *encounter* God drawing us beyond ourselves. It is the Spirit who quickens creation, conscience, and culture, making them alive in and through God's wider Presence. In *The Go-Between God* Taylor is right to stress that this experience of the Spirit is an encounter with the Triune God, not just with an aspect of God. The three are one; the one, three. To speak of the Spirit present with us is, thus, to speak of God in the world. It is not that God needs the world in some way, but rather that God—for the sake of a community that he has freely chosen—creates, sustains, redeems, and completes the world by his Spirit.

Perhaps indirectly referencing the Presence of God in that mighty wind (*ruach*) that parted the sea making possible Israel's exodus from Egypt, Scripture speaks in Genesis 1:2 of the "spirit [*ruach*] of God" (NRSV, a "wind from God") hovering over the surface of the waters. Exegetes have argued as to the appropriate translation of *ruach*—"spirit" or "wind." But must one choose? The Hebrew listener would have heard both. The God who accomplished the redemption of his people through a blast of "wind" (Exod. 15)—by "his holy spirit" (Isa. 63:10–14)—is the same God who creates and sustains the earth and all that is within through his Spirit. Thus writes the songwriter in Psalm 33:6: "By the word [*dabar*] of the LORD the heavens were made, and all their host by the breath [*ruach*] of his mouth." Or consider Psalm 147:18: "He sends out his word [*dabar*], and melts them [the snow]; he makes his wind [*ruach*, "spirit"] blow, and the waters flow." The writer of Psalm 104 also had Genesis in mind as he offered praise to God for his manifold works in creation (v. 24). "When you send forth your spirit, they are created; and you renew the face of the ground" (v. 30). The voice that speaks to Job out of a whirlwind speaks similarly of the divine wisdom that creates, directs, and sustains all creation (Job 38:4, 36–37; 39:26). Here, surely, is an indirect reference to the Spirit's work.

Scripture portrays the Spirit of God to be in and through the whole of the cosmos, creating and sustaining. Yet, when this universal perspective is

12. Eduard Schweizer, *The Holy Spirit* (Philadelphia: Fortress, 1980), 47.

applied to humankind generally, too often the Spirit's work among and in all people is wrongly reduced to the Spirit's work in the Christian community. Often the Holy Spirit's role is limited to the Spirit of redemption and sanctification. And this has a certain logic to it, for the New Testament almost exclusively portrays the work of the Spirit in humankind as that of the Spirit of Christ with reference specifically to God's people. But such a focusing on the Spirit's role in Christ's mission, though central to the New Testament, is not exhaustive of the Bible's perspective. This is particularly the case if the more general references to God's wisdom, power, and Presence in the Old Testament are understood to pertain also to the Spirit in his role as the Go-Between God.

The Spirit and Wisdom

Confronted with the spirits of other gods as Israel interacted with her neighbors, Israel expanded the way she spoke of God to include "the Spirit of wisdom." Pharaoh had said there was "no one so discerning and wise" as Joseph, for in him "is the spirit of God" (Gen. 41:38–39). So, too, Nebuchadnezzar said of Daniel that he was "endowed with a spirit of the holy gods" (Dan. 4:8; cf. 5:11, 14). Both of these judgments are made by foreign rulers who compare their wise counselors to God's chosen. Here is the context for Yahweh's also being described as "the Spirit of wisdom."

We observe this same international perspective as lying behind the book of Job. The story is set in the distant past in a far-off land. Job needs to discern in his spirit whether and in whom God is speaking. Though young in years, Elihu confronts the elder Job, saying: "I said, 'Let days speak, and many years teach wisdom.' But truly it is the spirit in a mortal, the breath of the Almighty, that makes for understanding" (Job 32:7–8). Elihu is adopting an experiential argument here. It is not the wisdom of age but the experience of the Spirit (breath) of God that brings understanding. And Job, when confronted with the voice of the Lord out of the whirlwind (note again the symbolic "wind"), finally comes to the same conclusion. He confesses that he has darkened "counsel by words without knowledge" (Job 38:2; cf. 42:3). "But now my eye sees you" (Job 42:5).

In Isaiah, when Israel is in need of comfort as it is confronted by the specter of foreign invaders, it is "a shoot from the stump of Jesse" who is promised as bringing hope. "The spirit of the LORD shall rest on him, the spirit of wisdom and understanding, the spirit of counsel and might, the spirit of knowledge and the fear of the LORD" (Isa. 11:2; cf. 40:13). This Spirit-filled individual can be contrasted with the rebellious Israelites who the Lord says "carry out a plan, but not mine; who make an alliance, but against my will [spirit, *ruach*], adding sin to sin" (Isa. 30:1). Israel is acting without Yahweh's "counsel" (Isa. 30:2).

In the intertestamental period, as the Israelites came in contact with Hellenistic culture and its concern for *Sophia*, they described the Spirit as personified Wisdom and, as such, a mediator between humankind and God. It is Wisdom that worked in the history of God's people against the Egyptians (Wis. 10:1–12:27; cf. Isa. 63:11, where it is "his holy spirit" who is said to have been at work in the exodus). But Wisdom's involvement is broader than this. As "a kindly spirit" (Wis. 1:6), she is everywhere; "the spirit of the Lord has filled the world" (Wis. 1:7).

> Wisdom, the fashioner of all things, taught me. There is in her a spirit that is intelligent, holy . . . all-powerful, overseeing all, and penetrating through all spirits that are intelligent, pure, and altogether subtle. . . . For she is a breath of the power of God, and a pure emanation of the glory of the Almighty; . . . in every generation she passes into holy souls and makes them friends of God, and prophets; for God loves nothing so much as the person who lives with wisdom. . . . She reaches mightily from one end of the earth to the other, and she orders all things well. (Wis. 7:22–25, 27–28; 8:1)

One is immediately reminded of the personification of Wisdom that had occurred in Proverbs 1–9. There, again, one finds many affinities between Lady Wisdom and the Spirit's work in creation, though there is no direct mention of Wisdom being a/the Spirit.

There is considerable debate as to the influence of the Wisdom of Solomon on Paul's thought, particularly in his First Epistle to the Corinthians. Gordon Fee is no doubt correct in arguing for an experiential basis for Paul's argument, not a theoretical one. It is the experience of the eschatological Spirit of Christ that controls this larger discourse, not a phenomenology of wisdom. Given this theological starting point, it is telling to note Fee's comment that because "wisdom is not a Pauline word," Paul's use of it in 1 Corinthians 2:6–16 must be dictated "by the Corinthians' fascination with it."[13] In other words, as Paul focused his attention on the Spirit of Christ as experienced in the life of the believer and in the church, he would not have been expected to turn to wisdom as a category. Yet Paul, as we have already observed, was not beyond reshaping his argument to speak to the challenges and insights of the wider culture (see Acts 14 and 17). In a similar way, the description of the Spirit as seen in 1 Corinthians 2 picks up some of the *Sophia* imagery of the day, seeing the Spirit as having a more general mediatorial role, revealing "even the depths of God" (1 Cor. 2:10): "And

---

13. Gordon D. Fee, *God's Empowering Presence* (Peabody, MA: Hendrickson, 1994), 912–13.

we speak of these things in words not taught by human wisdom but taught by the Spirit, interpreting spiritual things to those who are spiritual" (1 Cor. 2:13).[14]

Confronted with the claim of divine "wisdom" in the cultures around them, God's people expanded their description of the Spirit's involvement with our spirits. The Spirit is to be understood as the human spirit's source of true wisdom. Over against this Spirit, who would presume to "darken counsel by words without knowledge?" (Job 38:2).

The Spirit and Power

As has been noted above, the original images of the Spirit relate to God's power. Miriam sings, "At the blast [*ruach*] of your nostrils, the water piled up. . . . You blew with your wind [*ruach*], the sea covered them" (Exod. 15:8, 10). The psalmist sings, "By the word of the LORD the heavens were made, and all their host by the breath [*ruach*] of his mouth" (Ps. 33:6). And Isaiah proclaims, "The grass withers, the flower fades, when the breath [*ruach*] of the LORD blows upon it" (Isa. 40:7). The Spirit (*ruach*) is to be identified with God's power. It is God through his Spirit, not just the wind, that moved the water. As we are told in Isaiah 31:3, "The Egyptians are human, and not God; their horses are flesh, and not spirit [*ruach*]."

It is this same powerful Spirit who takes possession not only of Gideon (Judg. 6:34) and David (1 Sam. 16:13) but also of those who are far, or stray far, from God. One thinks of Balaam (Num. 24:2), Samson (Judg. 13:25), and Saul (1 Sam. 10:6). Balaam goes back to his home in Mesopotamia, presumably to again work as a diviner. Samson's character is portrayed as seriously flawed, and the Old Testament says, "the LORD was sorry that he had made Saul king over Israel" (1 Sam. 15:35). But whether among the godly or the wayward, the testimony is the same regarding those on whom the Spirit descends: "I am filled with power, with the spirit of the LORD" (Mic. 3:8).

The use of the term "Spirit" is rare among the prophets. But we do find Isaiah speaking of the Spirit of the Lord who will come to judge and restore (Isa. 4:4; 11:2; 30:28). It is the power of the Spirit that is needed, not only in the house of Israel (Ezek. 39:29), but also in creation itself (Isa. 32:15) and among all nations (Isa. 42:1).

The Spirit as power over all creation and humankind is in evidence throughout the Old Testament. But it is helpful to return to Genesis 1:2, the Bible's first

14. It is interesting to note a certain circularity in Paul's argument. Paul has described Christ in chapter 1 as "the power of God and the wisdom of God" (1 Cor. 1:24). Here, he turns to two central attributes of the Spirit, wisdom and power, for Paul understands Christ in terms of his experience of Christ's Spirit.

reference to *ruach*, or spirit, to capture an important nuance concerning this power. I began this chapter by suggesting that the association of God's *ruach* with the Red Sea allows a certain ambiguity to often remain in the biblical text as to whether the term should be translated "wind" or "Spirit." The Israelite listener would have heard both together. But where the *ruach* is described in the Exodus account as a God-given "strong east wind," violent enough to push back the waters of the sea, the power of the *ruach* described in Genesis 1 seems best understood in other ways. Although the text can be debated, I believe a preferred translation might read, "The spirit/wind of God was hovering over the surface of the waters."[15] The verb "hovering" (*rakhaph*) is not often used in Scripture in any of its forms. But in Deuteronomy 32:11, the verb refers to a bird of prey (an eagle?) that stirs up its nest and then hovers (*rakhaph*) over its young. Just as the mother teaches her young to fly by the presence and force of her wings above the nest, so the Spirit's Presence empowers the young cosmos.

The Spirit as Co-Relational

To speak of the Presence of the Spirit in humankind as wisdom and power, while true to the biblical witness, is also to risk misunderstanding the biblical witness. For one can easily fall into abstraction. The modern propensity to divide knowledge into the objective and the subjective is a real and present danger. To gain certainty, we have often attempted to remove the personal quotient from wisdom. Even when we realized that the more critical, or personal, the knowledge is, the less adequate our empirical thinking becomes, we have not improved our situation by fleeing to the subjective. For then we are not sure how to escape our own human "subject." The depersonalization of wisdom is not redressed by an all-encompassing mysticism. In a similar way, to speak of power is to risk misunderstanding, for power is often correlated with an impersonal force or energy (e.g., "May the Force be with you!"). But the Spirit is personal.

What must be recognized is this: the biblical encounter of humankind with the Spirit, which takes place in wisdom and power, is constitutive of a new relation, a "co-relation" if you will, between our spirits and the Spirit.[16] To experience the Spirit is to be in relation with God. Our understanding of the

15. For a discussion of the various possibilities, see Victor P. Hamilton, *The Book of Genesis, Chapters 1–17* (Grand Rapids: Eerdmans, 1990), 111–15; cf. Lloyd Neve, *The Spirit of God in the Old Testament* (Tokyo: Seibunsha, 1972), 64–71; and Wilf Hildebrandt, *An Old Testament Theology of the Spirit of God* (Peabody, MA: Hendrickson, 1995), 30–37. Understanding *ruach* in the violent terms of the Exodus text, but now as a chaotic rather than redemptive force, the NRSV translation reads, "A wind from God swept over the face of the waters."

16. I am indebted to Tom Langford for this term's use with regard to the Holy Spirit. See also Robert K. Johnston, "Rethinking Common Grace: Toward a Theology of Co-relation," in

Spirit is neither objective nor subjective but personal. Here is the clear biblical perspective. Thus the psalmist can plead with God, using a typical poetic parallelism of two synonymous phrases: "Do not cast me away from your presence, and do not take your holy spirit from me" (Ps. 51:11). Or again in a more positive vein, the psalmist can plead, "Teach me to do your will, for you are my God. Let your good spirit lead me on a level path" (Ps. 143:10). Jesus as he begins his ministry similarly appeals to a personal Spirit, speaking of the Spirit of the Lord as anointing him to preach good news and sending him to proclaim release to the captives (Luke 4:18). In John, as Jesus draws his ministry to a close, he speaks to his disciples of a Counselor/Comforter (*paraclete*) whom the Father will send to teach them all things and to bear witness of Jesus (John 14:16–17; 14:26; 15:26). This Spirit will "guide you into all the truth; for he will not speak on his own, but will speak whatever he hears, and he will declare to you the things that are to come" (John 16:13; see vv. 7–15).

In the book of Acts, the Holy Spirit not only comes with the sound of wind and the appearance of fire, but also speaks (Acts 1:16; 10:19), sends (Acts 13:4), forbids (Acts 16:6), appoints (Acts 20:28), and is resisted (Acts 7:51), among other personal turns of phrase. Such personal descriptions of the Spirit continue in Paul's epistles as, for example, in Romans 8: the Spirit leads, bears witness, and makes intercession (Rom. 8:14, 16, 26). The Spirit is more than, and other than, the power of God, or even the wisdom of God, according to the Bible. The Spirit's personal nature needs also to be recognized, as the developing doctrine of the Trinity in the early church bears witness.

Yet having said this, Christians have continued to struggle with how best to understand the personal dimension of the Spirit. George Hendry, the former Princeton Seminary theologian, observed that with regard to the human spirit and the Holy Spirit, there has existed a theology of correlation going back to the early church theologians: "Thou has made us for thyself, and our hearts are restless till they find their rest in thee" (Augustine). Here the aspiration of the human spirit (an *eros* motif) is met relationally in the gift of the Spirit. Hendry thus emphasized the human spirit's potential for personal relationship, a potential that becomes actual as the Spirit of Christ changes our "false freedom from God into that true freedom for God, which is 'the glorious liberty of the children of God.'"[17]

Ray Anderson, my former colleague at Fuller Seminary, also operated out of a Reformed christological grid, but saw the need to speak of the human

---

Grace upon Grace: Essays in Honor of Thomas A. Langford, ed. Robert K. Johnston, L. Gregory Jones, and Jonathan R. Wilson (Nashville: Abingdon, 1999), 153–68.

17. George Hendry, *The Holy Spirit in Christian Theology* (Philadelphia: Westminster, 1956), 96–117.

spirit in order to navigate between passivity on the one hand (Barth "positing spirit as an immortal dimension to human existence") and an independent potential for the divine resident in humankind on the other (Brunner positing "spirit as a potentiality of will"). Spirit, he concluded, "might be considered the life of the soul [the person] as an orientation toward God, summoned forth by the divine Word and enabled by the divine Spirit." Anderson's focus, as might be expected of someone writing from out of a Barthian perspective, was on our differentiation through the Word of God. But the enablement of the Spirit is noted and the basic shape of human life (our spirit) is recognized to be that of "response-ability."[18]

Or to give a third example, Arnold Come argues that our knowledge of God (including that of the Spirit) cannot be developed in isolation from our knowledge of ourselves (our spirits). Furthermore, our knowledge of ourselves in Christ must not be isolated from our knowledge of ourselves apart from Christ. Thus, although any Christian understanding of God will be developed fully only in light of the Spirit of God in Christ, this need not, and should not, be our starting point. Come would have us shift our perspective away from "Spirit to spirit" to "spirit to Spirit."[19] Having said this, Come confesses that a Christian understanding of man/woman as spirit is hard to come by. We so easily slip into abstraction. Whether in reference to ourselves or to God, we often equate the Spirit with power in a way that depersonalizes. Think of how often we refer to the Holy Spirit as "It." Instead, we must view God as Person and ourselves as person. Only "on the level of interpersonal relationship" are the two fully "present" with each other. Come, like John Taylor, quotes Martin Buber, "He who is not present perceives no Presence." According to Come, the human spirit can be understood as an inner capacity or power to realize one's self, but only as this is attained in relationship.[20]

Common to these studies is a desire to show relationality as being at the core of reality—the Spirit is God working in our spirit to make us who we are. Such a dynamic, interactive unity does not slide into an identity; nor is the relationship one of equality. There is always an asymmetrical character to the Presence of the Spirit with our spirit. Our spirit reaches out, but we are transformed by the Spirit. As the hymn writer penned, "I sought the Lord, and afterward I knew he moved my soul to seek him, seeking me." Such a relationship finds its full realization as the human spirit unites with the Spirit

---

18. Ray Anderson, *On Being Human* (Grand Rapids: Eerdmans, 1982), 212.
19. Arnold Come, *Human Spirit and Holy Spirit* (Philadelphia: Westminster, 1959), 7–9.
20. Ibid., 70–74.

of Christ. But this in no way diminishes the Spirit's personal "Presencing," which is experienced by all humankind.

Common to these studies, as well, however, is their Reformed, epistemological focus, which centers on Christology, not pneumatology. And when pneumatology is discussed, it is the Spirit of Christ that takes precedence, not the Spirit in and through creation. Or perhaps to speak more accurately, the Spirit of creation is present, but accessed mainly through the Spirit of Christ. The result of this marginalization of the Spirit of creation is an inability both to integrate adequately the biblical insights of the Spirit as wisdom and power with that of Christology and to take into account our phenomenological witness to the Spirit in life. What is needed as an antidote is to treat the pneumatological as a parallel and helpful perspective to the christological as we seek a fuller understanding of God. And here the theologies of Elizabeth Johnson and Jürgen Moltmann can prove helpful to us as we construct a pneumatological theology of God's wider revelatory Presence.

A Cosmic Pneumatology: Elizabeth Johnson

Elizabeth Johnson is a former president of the Catholic Theological Society of America and winner, for her book *She Who Is* (1993), of the Louisville Grawemeyer Award in Religion honoring creative and constructive insights into the relationship between human beings and the divine.[21] In that book, Johnson seeks to reimage the Triune God of classical Christian theology using both female terms discovered in Scripture and the experience of women's flourishing. While some critics have, not unexpectedly, found such an experientially grounded theology to be just the latest in a long series of discredited "liberal" agendas for constructive theology in which experience functions as authorizing agent, and though more recently the United States Conference of Catholic Bishops declared her book *Quest for the Living God: Mapping Frontiers in the Theology of God* (2007) unfit for use in the classrooms of Catholic schools because of alleged errors concerning the nature and experience of God, these criticisms seem hardly a fair description of her work.[22] For Johnson has not only focused in her theology on the experience of the living God, but also rooted her insights strongly and effectively in the biblical text, while also putting her constructive theology into conversation with the Christian tradition.

---

21. Elizabeth A. Johnson, *She Who Is: The Mystery of God in Feminist Theological Discourse* (New York: Crossroad / Herder & Herder, 1992).

22. Elizabeth A. Johnson, *Quest for the Living God: Mapping Frontiers in the Theology of God* (New York: Continuum, 2007).

Johnson's inductive approach—her theology of the Triune God "from below," one that begins with the experience of the Spirit in/of life—is not in itself particularly controversial, though it will be challenged by those doing theology from out of a christocentric paradigm. A fully trinitarian theology should be able to move as freely from "Spirit to Word" as from "Word to Spirit." One should be able to say, as the New Testament does, "Spirit-Son-Father" (Eph. 4:4–6), just as one can say "Son-Father-Spirit" (2 Cor. 13:14). What is controversial about Johnson's theology is her desire to redress the Western theological tradition's embrace of a patriarchal image of God (thus her critics' discomfort with female images and concepts about God). Take, for example, her theological comments on the environment.

> Our eyes have been blinded to the sacredness of the earth, which is linked to the exclusion of women from the sphere of the sacred, which is tied to a focus on the monarchical, patriarchal ideas of God and a consequent forgetting of the Creator Spirit, the Lifegiver who is intimately related to the earth.[23]

But Johnson's theology cannot so easily be dismissed as simply the latest cultural fad. It is always done, like all Christian theology, with the "Bible" in one hand and the "newspaper" in the other, with an ear open to the wisdom of the Christian community through the ages. Johnson's constructive theology can be a help as we seek to reinvigorate a theology of God's wider revelation for the twenty-first century, even if, like all theology, it is not without the need for emendation.

As Johnson has taken her experience as a woman to Scripture, she has found in its pages three symbols that stand out as promising, not only for her task of reconceiving a theology of God from her vantage point as a woman, but also for our own present agenda of reconsidering God's wider revelation. These three are "spirit," "wisdom," and "mother."[24] For the purposes of this book, we will focus chiefly on the first of these, but all are important. That there is a proliferation of images and a variety of names for God in Scripture, including these three, should not surprise us, Johnson reasons, given that God remains a mystery, beyond and other than us, even as God chooses to reveal himself to us. Thus, rather than judge such multiplicity of descriptions a weakness, it is better to see them as a strength, with such plurality acting as a corrective against any tendency to make overly literal any single image or understanding of God. (Johnson says there is a "revelry of symbols for the divine that nourish

23. Elizabeth A. Johnson, *Women, Earth, and Creator Spirit* (Mahwah, NJ: Paulist Press, 1993), 21.

24. Johnson, *She Who Is*, 82–103.

the mind and expand the spirit."[25]) For Johnson, God's mystery is based not in a divine absence (though the bishops who criticized her thought as such) but in

> a divine overabundance that fills the world to its depths and then overflows. [Readers might recall our discussion of both Rollins and Lewis.] There is no end to the being and fullness of God, who creates heaven and earth and is continuously present and active throughout the world, in all ages and all cultures. Throughout history this gracious mystery approaches us with little theophanies, signs and revelations and events that invite us into relationship.[26]

Spirit

Instead of taking as her starting point God's self-disclosure in Jesus Christ, Johnson turns first to consider the experience of the Spirit as "God's livingness subtly and powerfully abroad in the world."[27] Trinitarian, that is, in her theology, Johnson moves from Spirit to Word. Spirit, "the creative and freeing power of God let loose in the world," is experienced, writes Johnson, "wherever we encounter the world and ourselves as held by, open to, gifted by, mourning for the absence of, or yearning for something ineffably more than immediately appears, whether that 'more' be mediated by beauty and joy or in contrast to the powers that crush."[28] If we ask which moments and experiences these are, Johnson responds that

> the answer can only be potentially *all* experience, the whole world. There is no exclusive zone, no special realm, which alone may be called religious. Rather, since Spirit is the creator and giver of life, life itself with all its complexities, abundance, threat, misery, and joy becomes a primary mediation of the dialectic of presence and absence of divine mystery. The historical world becomes a sacrament of divine presence and activity, even if only as a fragile possibility. The complexities of the experience of Spirit are cogiven in and through the world's history: negative, positive, and ambiguous; orderly and chaotic; solitary and communal; successful and disastrous; personal and political; dark and luminous; ordinary and extraordinary; cosmic, social, and individual.[29]

Since the middle of the twentieth century, Johnson believes, a burgeoning renaissance of insight concerning the living God—or better, the living Spirit—has been taking place as people have discovered God through the divine

25. Ibid., 118.
26. Johnson, *Quest for the Living God*, 161.
27. Johnson, *She Who Is*, 161.
28. Ibid., 83, 124–25.
29. Ibid., 124.

Spirit, not in abstract reasoning and deduction but in the everyday experiences of life, both ordinary and extraordinary.[30] Forgetting the Spirit, then, is far from ignoring "a faceless, shadowy, third hypostasis, but the mystery of God vivifying the world."[31] For Johnson, a pneumatological theology of everyday life, one born out of a deep sacramentality toward life, recognizes that the natural world is the dwelling place of God. This life-giving God is closer to us than we are to ourselves. Immanent in the world, and yet transcendent over the world, the Spirit's indwelling Presence circles around to concurrently embrace the whole world. Theologically, this is known by the technical term "panentheism," or the existence of all things in God. Unlike "theism," which separates God and world, paying little attention to divine nearness, and unlike "pantheism," which merges God and world, erasing all difference between Creator and creation, Johnson argues that

> panentheism holds that the universe, both matter and spirit, is encompassed by the Matrix of the living God in an encircling that generates freedom, self-transcendence, and the future, all in the context of the interconnected whole. The relationship created by this mutual indwelling, while non-hierarchical and reciprocal, is not strictly symmetrical, for the world is dependent on God in a way that God is not on the world. Yet the Spirit's encircling indwelling weaves a genuine solidarity among all creatures and between God and the world.[32]

Johnson understands the Spirit relationally as "a partner in the divine dance of life."[33] The Spirit is a person of the Trinity. But the Spirit is also "the creative power who dwells at the heart of the world sustaining every moment of its evolution."[34] "What results," suggests Johnson evocatively, "is a mutual abiding for which the pregnant female body provides a good metaphor." It is the Spirit who "pervades the material world with graceful vigor."[35] Or, put conversely, it is the natural world that is indwelt by God. In her presidential address to the American Theological Society in 2007, Johnson suggested:

> Seen in the light of continuous divine presence, nature, instead of being divorced from what is sacred, takes on a sacramental character. Sacramental theology has always taught that simple material things—bread and wine, water, oil—can be

30. Johnson, *Quest for the Living God*, 13–14.
31. Johnson, *Women, Earth, and Creator Spirit*, 20.
32. Ibid., 42–43.
33. Johnson, *She Who Is*, 222.
34. Elizabeth A. Johnson, "Pneumatology Revisited: Creator Spirit in Ecological Theology" (Presidential Address, American Theological Society, Princeton, NJ, April 13, 2007), 4 (manuscript).
35. Ibid., 4.

bearers of divine grace. This is so, it now becomes clear, only because to begin with, the whole physical world itself is the matrix of God's gracious indwelling. Matter bears the mark of the sacred and has itself a spiritual radiance. In turn, divine presence is sacramentally mediated in and through the world's embodiment, not necessarily nor absolutely, but graciously and really.[36]

Using the same logic, Johnson expands her pneumatology beyond creation in other of her writings to also include all of culture: "Every personal encounter of God with human beings occurs in the Spirit, and it is in the Spirit that people make their response."[37] Quoting John Paul II, she argues, "'The Spirit's presence and activity affect not only individuals but also society and history, peoples, cultures,' and [Johnson adds] religions."[38] Quoting from Roman Catholic conciliar teaching, Johnson argues that a bountiful God has distributed treasures among the nations of the earth, even including other religions. Johnson narrates how her faith has been enriched through her dialogue with other religious stories. In the religions of the world, there has been manifest for Johnson "a sense of the sacred, a thirst for wholeness, an openness to renunciation, compassion over suffering, an urge to goodness, a commitment to service, a total surrender of the self, and an attachment to the transcendent in their symbols and rituals."[39] Assuming the presence of grace and truth in human culture to have divine origin, Johnson believes "the religions can thus be seen as God's handiwork. In them we catch a glimpse of the overflowing generosity of the living God who has left no people abandoned but has bestowed divine love on every culture."[40] Given the evidence of the fruit of the Spirit in other religions, she wonders, might that not be understood as "wisdom"?

Wisdom

Johnson points out that "wisdom" is "the most developed personification of God's presence and activity in the Hebrew Scriptures."[41] Here is a second metaphor Johnson holds up as she attempts a reconfiguring of our understanding of God. The Bible makes use in Scripture not only of nature images for the Spirit of God but also the image of Woman Wisdom. Not only are the biblical words for wisdom grammatically feminine (*hokhmah* in Hebrew,

36. Ibid., 5.
37. Johnson, *Quest for the Living God*, 162.
38. John Paul II, *Redemptoris Missio*, quoted in Johnson, *Quest for the Living God*, 157–58.
39. Johnson, *Quest for the Living God.*, 162.
40. Ibid., 162–63.
41. Johnson, *She Who Is*, 86–87.

sophia in Greek), but, writes Johnson, "the biblical portrait of Wisdom is consistently female, casting her as sister, mother, female beloved, chef and hostess, teacher, preacher, maker of justice, and a host of other women's roles. In every instance," writes Johnson, "Wisdom symbolizes transcendent power pervading and ordering the world, both nature and human beings, interacting with them all to lure them onto the path of life."[42]

Particularly important, thinks Johnson, is the image of Woman Wisdom who dominates the pages of Proverbs 1–9. She is the personification of God's Presence and activity. In Proverbs, Woman Wisdom is the giver of life, a tree of life; in fact, "she is your life" (Prov. 4:13). She delights in all creation (Prov. 8:22–31). So intimately is she tied to life that she can even proclaim, "Whoever finds me finds life" (Prov. 8:35). But important for Johnson as well is the description of divine Wisdom in the apocryphal Wisdom of Solomon, where she is described as a people-loving spirit, "a kindly spirit" (Wis. 1:6), and where the giving of wisdom is put in synonymous parallelism with the sending of the Holy Spirit (Wis. 9:17). From her comes all creation (Wis. 7). Pervading and penetrating all things, she fashions all things and "renews all things," "for she is a breath of the power of God" (Wis. 7:22–27). Even Solomon is surprised to learn the scope of Wisdom's influence, admitting, "but I did not know that she was their mother" (Wis. 7:12).

Quoting text after Wisdom text Johnson seeks to demonstrate the biblical importance of Woman Wisdom as a symbol for the divine Spirit.[43] Writes Johnson, "This is the same divine presence spoken about in the Jewish rabbinic tradition of the *shekinah*, the female symbol of God's indwelling, the weighty radiance that flashes out in unexpected ways in the midst of the broken world."[44] What Johnson finds of particular interest vis-à-vis Woman Wisdom is the fact that she is described both in Proverbs 1–9 and in Wisdom 7 as the functional equivalent of Yahweh. Here is a powerful female symbol of Israel's one God, a female counterpoint to the dominant male images of Father-Son.

Mother

Important biblically, as well, are the references to the Spirit as mother. Johnson mentions Jesus's conversation with Nicodemus, for example, where the maternal image is clear. When Jesus tells Nicodemus he must be born again to enter the reign of God, Nicodemus responds quizzically, "How

42. Johnson, *Women, Earth, and Creator Spirit*, 52.
43. Ibid., 51–57.
44. Ibid., 54.

can anyone be born after having grown old?" (John 3:4). Johnson explains Jesus's response:

> Jesus' reply keeps the metaphor of physical birth and amplifies it to speak of the Spirit: "No one can enter the reign of God without being born of water and the Spirit. What is born of the flesh is flesh, and what is born of the Spirit is spirit" (3:5–6). Creator Spirit is here likened to a woman giving birth to offspring who are henceforth truly identified as "born of God."[45]

Johnson finds other imagery of the Spirit of God as mother (or at least maternal) in the Old Testament. Like a woman at work with her knitting needles, the Spirit knits together new life in a mother's womb (Ps. 139:13); like a woman in childbirth, she gasps and pants to bring about the birth of justice (Isa. 42:14); like a midwife, the Spirit worked deftly to deliver the new creation (Ps. 22:9–10); and like a washerwoman, the Spirit will scrub away all bloody stains (Isa. 4:4; Ps. 51:7). Though the symbol of the maternity of the Spirit, like the feminine images of Wisdom and Shekinah, have been largely forgotten, Johnson understands their resonances to still abide in Scripture and tradition, and thus they are capable once again of evoking divine Presence. Rather than women's fertility being seen as dangerous or polluted, its use as a symbol for the Spirit's fecundity and Presence helps us to recover something of the cosmic community that links Creator, creation, and creature. Writes Johnson, "Enfolding and unfolding the universe, the Spirit is holy mystery 'over all and through all and in all' (Eph. 4:6)."[46]

The Spirit's Paradoxical Presence: Jürgen Moltmann

Exploding onto the theological scene with his *Theology of Hope* (1964), followed by *The Crucified God* (1972) and *The Church in the Power of the Spirit* (1975), Jürgen Moltmann began his career by centering his trinitarian theology on a strong Christology. Positing a radical discontinuity in the dialectic of Jesus's cross and resurrection, death and life, the absence of God and the Presence of God, what reality is now and what God promises to make it, he found hope both in the risen Christ's promise of a new creation and in the crucified Christ's solidarity with the suffering of the world. Moltmann proclaimed that "from first to last, and not merely in the epilogue, Christianity is eschatology, is hope."[47] The Spirit, in

45. Ibid., 55.
46. Ibid., 57.
47. Jürgen Moltmann, *Theology of Hope: On the Ground and the Implications of a Christian Eschatology* (New York: Harper & Row, 1967), 16.

this trinitarian scheme, derived his mission from the dialectic event of cross and resurrection, moving creature and creation toward his resolution as the godforsaken world is filled with God's Presence and the coming kingdom is anticipated.

Refocusing on the Spirit

But as Moltmann has continued on his theological pilgrimage, he has become more and more critical of Western Christianity's subordination of pneumatology to Christology and has, instead, developed a theology in which there is a social Trinity of equals—all three persons of the Godhead being a community of divine, perichoretic love that enfolds the world within it. This change in focus with regard to the Holy Spirit—now seen as an equal partner in a "Trinitarian communion with the Father and the Son"[48]—has evidenced itself in a series of monographs and other writings. Moltmann has written about the Spirit as the power and life of the whole creation (*God in Creation*, 1985), about Spirit Christology as a necessary complement to a Logos Christology (*The Way of Jesus Christ*, 1989), and about eschatology as including the cosmic Shekinah of God—his very indwelling in and through the Spirit (*The Coming of God*, 1996). But in particular, Moltmann's book about our personal and shared experience of the Spirit (*The Spirit of Life*, 1991) has sought to spell out his refocused pneumatology.

Moltmann begins his book *The Spirit of Life* not with Scripture, philosophical theology, or even reflection on tradition, but "with the personal and shared *experience of the Spirit*." Writes Moltmann: "To begin with experience may sound subjective, arbitrary and fortuitous, but I hope to show that it is none of those things. By experience of the Spirit I mean an awareness of God in, with and beneath the experience of life, which gives us assurance of God's fellowship, friendship and love." To speak first of experience is important for Moltmann, for it recognizes "the intermediate state of every *historical experience* between remembered past and expected future"—between, that is, "when Christ is made present and when the new creation of all things is anticipated."[49]

Having recognized the role experience played in his theology, Moltmann ended his series of systematic contributions to theology with a reflection on his method, which he titled *Experiences in Theology* (2000). Not interested in simply defending doctrine or dogma, but seeking to do constructive theology in light of contemporary issues and experiences, biblical truth, and

---

48. Jürgen Moltmann, *The Spirit of Life: A Universal Affirmation* (Philadelphia: Fortress, 1992), 17; cf. Jürgen Moltmann, *The Trinity and the Kingdom of God* (London: SCM, 1981).
49. Moltmann, *Spirit of Life*, 17.

ecumenical dialogue with Catholics, Orthodox Christians, Protestants, and Jews throughout the world, Moltmann has continued to emphasize the role of the Spirit in both theology and life.[50] Rather than subsume pneumatology under Christology—the Spirit under the Word—Moltmann in his later theology has sought to embrace both the personalism of a Christic model and the panentheism of a pneumatologically charged creation theology. Developing a robust pneumatology that moves beyond our tendency to view the Holy Spirit solely as the Spirit of redemption, Moltmann has argued for the Spirit's "relative independence." In his preface to *The Spirit of Life*, Moltmann writes:

> My starting point is that the efficacy of Christ is not without the efficacy of the Spirit, which is its goal; but that the efficacy of the Spirit is nevertheless distinguishable from the efficacy of Christ, and is not congruent with that or absorbed by it. As the Old Testament shows, the operations of God's spirit precede the workings of Christ; and the New Testament tells us that they go beyond the workings of Christ. . . . The operations of God's life-giving and life-affirming Spirit are universal and can be recognized in everything which ministers to life and resists its destruction. This efficacy of the Spirit does not replace Christ's efficacy, but makes it universally relevant.[51]

Such a theology of the Spirit implies for Moltmann a rethinking of traditional understandings of the Trinity, particularly the need for the removal of the *filioque* clause from the Western creed. The insertion of this word in the creed placed the Spirit as subordinate to the Son—"in third place" is how Moltmann describes it.[52] It is true, thinks Moltmann, that one can find this trinitarian structure in salvation history, but that is only because when it was written, the Christian community had already received the Spirit as the Spirit of the exalted Lord. But if one were instead to consider Jesus's experience of the Spirit, the order would reverse itself, "the operation of the divine Spirit [being] the precondition or premise for the history of Jesus of Nazareth."[53] And if one were to consider the interactions of Son and Spirit, Spirit and Son, one would surely stress unity, not hierarchy. Better, thinks Moltmann, to say that both the Son and the Spirit proceed from the Father alone.[54] For the Spirit is not only

---

50. Besides Moltmann's *Experiences in Theology: Ways and Forms of Christian Theology* (Minneapolis: Fortress, 2000) and *The Spirit of Life*, of particular interest for our purposes here is *The Source of Life: The Holy Spirit and the Theology of Life* (Minneapolis: Fortress, 1997), a compilation of lectures and talks he gave following the publication of his larger monograph.
    51. Moltmann, *Spirit of Life*, xi.
    52. Ibid., 293.
    53. Ibid., 60.
    54. Ibid., 71–73; see also Moltmann, *Experiences in Theology*, 307–12.

the Spirit of Christ the Redeemer but also the Spirit of the Father the Creator. To remain with the status quo risks stifling the Spirit. Moltmann is correct.

Immanent Transcendence

Rejecting any antitheses between revelation and our experience of the Spirit, between theological transcendentalism and theological immanentism, between divinity and humanity, Moltmann instead has understood the Spirit's Presence among us as an "immanent transcendence," uniting polarities that too often have competed. After all, Moltmann argues, there are not two different theologies: "There is only one, because God is one."[55] For Moltmann, "immanent transcendence" declares that God is *"in, with and beneath"* each everyday experience of the world. "If experiences of God embrace experiences of life (and every existential interpretation says that they do), then—seen in reverse—experiences of life can also embrace experiences of God."[56] Suggests Moltmann,

> To experience God in all things presupposes that there is a transcendence which is immanent in things and which can be inductively discovered. . . . To experience all things in God means moving in the opposite direction. . . . We sense that in everything God is waiting for us. . . . For this, the term *immanent transcendence* offers itself.[57]

It is simply false, thinks Moltmann, to set divine revelation over against the human experience of the Holy Spirit as some do. If revelation remains external—"the Wholly Other"—to the human spirit, then there is permanent discontinuity between God's Spirit and ours, and "the Holy Spirit is not a modality of our experience of God."[58] To set experience against revelation in this way is to create a double bind for theology: either revelation as totally other becomes ineffective, or when correlated with human feelings and aspirations becomes an experience devoid of revelation. Moltmann recognizes that his theology rooted in the experience of the Spirit might sound subjective, and surely there have been abuses in the experiential paradigm. But, thinks Moltmann, "The possibility of perceiving God in all things, and all things in God, is grounded theologically on an understanding of the Spirit of God as the power of creation and the wellspring of life."[59]

55. Jürgen Moltmann, *God in Creation: A New Theology of Creation and the Spirit of God* (New York: Harper & Row, 1985), 59.
56. Moltmann, *Spirit of Life*, 34.
57. Ibid., 34–36.
58. Ibid., 5.
59. Ibid., 35.

Given the Spirit of Life, every experience that we have can have an inward, transcendent side. But, argues Moltmann, this should not be understood as somehow limited to our experience of ourselves. No, that transcendent side may also be encountered "in the experience of the 'Thou,' in the experience of sociality, and in the experience of nature."[60] Transcendence, that is, can be experienced throughout the whole world and the whole of life. In saying this, Moltmann believes one need not flatten out all such possible experiences, turning them into the same thing and pantheistically reducing them to a matter of indifference. "Given the premise that God is experienced in experience of the world and life, it once again becomes possible to talk about special experiences of God in the contingent and exceptional phenomena which are called 'holy,' without having to declare everything else profane."[61] Here is a theological rationale for positing God's wider revelation.

It was Calvin who called the Spirit the "well of life." If this is correct, then for Moltmann, every experience of life can and should be a discovery of this living source as well. Biblical texts such as Job 33:4; 34:13–15; and Psalm 104:29–30 have provided Moltmann his grounding. "We carry experiences of the world into the experience of God. 'Reverence for life' is absorbed into reverence for God, and the veneration of nature becomes part of the adoration of God. We sense that in everything God is waiting for us."[62] Some have concluded that Moltmann has in this way embraced divine immanence at the expense of God's transcendence. But to be open to the possibility of experiencing God in all things presupposes a Transcendent which/who is immanent and can be discovered inductively. Moltmann is arguing for the *Eternal* in the temporal, the *Infinite* in the finite.

One might find a helpful analogy to Moltmann's "immanent transcendence" in the principle of "complementarity" put forward first by the Danish Nobel Prize–winning physicist Nils Bohr. Bohr argued for the need to accept multiple and even contradictory models to explain a reality that was larger than any individual scientific theory. Light, for example, could be studied with profit using both wave and particle theories. Both seemed valid in their explanatory utility. Yet these two models were utterly distinct. Moreover, whatever light is, it may even have other properties that escape detection using either of these models. All one can say is that the particle model reveals certain aspects/properties of light, while the wave model reveals other aspects/properties. As Richard Doyle rightly concludes, "Complementarity has epistemological,

60. Ibid., 34.
61. Ibid., 35.
62. Ibid., 36.

not just ontological implications."[63] In an analogous manner, Moltmann has proposed the need to speak of God as being both "immanent" and "transcendent," while recognizing that even here, mystery remains.

Using Spatial Metaphors

In setting out his understanding of the Presence of God in the world, Moltmann has also chosen to use both temporal and spatial metaphors. His "new and specifically Christian vision of reality . . . is stamped by faith in the incarnation of the Son of God [a temporal notion]," as well as "the experience of the indwelling of the Spirit of God [a spatial concept]."[64] Moltmann recounts that his early "theology of hope" was dominated by prophetic, temporal concepts—promise and protest, liberation and exodus. All were drenched in time. But there were other aspects of the Christian life, experiences such as our "play" and our respect for creation, as well as the indwelling of the Spirit, that didn't fit well into this model. These Moltmann had trouble understanding theologically, given his focus on time, for they had to do more with space and "home," with "being" more than "doing."[65]

Again, an analogy from science can be helpful. Richard Doyle comments on another of Bohr's group of Danish scientists: Heisenberg, who formulated the famous and related Uncertainty Principle. "There are two usual applications: position/momentum, and energy/time. The Uncertainty Principle says that these parameters are deeply coupled, in that the more precisely one measures the one of the pair, the more uncertain is your knowledge of the other. There is a basic uncertainty that is irreducible." Doyle continues: "It's not actually all that mysterious. If you pin down a particle's position exactly, then you've lost all knowledge of where it was coming from/where it is going. But if your knowledge of a particle's position is a bit 'smeared,' that actually gives a good hint about where it was coming from/where it is going."[66] Thus, in addition to his prophetic, temporal models of hope-centered christologically, Moltmann has turned to more spatial models, those that focused on "being" over "doing." And here, Moltmann's developing pneumatology has been of help to him, particularly his reflection on the "Shekinah" glory, the descent or indwelling of God's Spirit.

63. I am indebted to Richard Doyle, a computer scientist at Cal Tech's Jet Propulsion Lab, for helping me clarify my description of Bohr's work.

64. Jürgen Moltmann, "Theology of Mystical Experience," *Scottish Journal of Theology* 32, no. 6 (1979): 518.

65. See Jürgen Moltmann, *Theology of Play* (New York: Harper & Row, 1971). Also see Robert K. Johnston, *The Christian at Play* (Grand Rapids: Eerdmans, 1983) for a critique of Moltmann's inability in this book to understand play as a "time out" from our work.

66. Richard Doyle, private correspondence, July 9, 2013.

In the Old Testament, this Shekinah is not an attribute of God; rather, it is the very Presence of God among us. Moltmann turns to Ezekiel 37, for example. There we read of the Lord speaking to Ezekiel, after leading him into the valley of dry bones: "I will put my Spirit within you, and you shall live, and I will place you on your own soil. . . . My dwelling place shall be with them; and I will be their God, and they shall be my people" (vv. 14, 27). Moltmann comments: "When God puts his Spirit 'into' a people, his 'dwelling place' will be among them. To be filled with the Spirit is God's Shekinah."[67]

Described as originally present in the ark of the covenant and later in the temple's holy of holies, the Shekinah became for Israel, after the destruction of the temple and their deportation to Babylon, a way of speaking of God's continuing dwelling place with them. The Shekinah became, Moltmann suggested, *"the God who suffers with us."*[68] According to Moltmann, the Shekinah's indwelling Presence had both an immanent side and a transcendent one. As present, "God's Spirit-immanence in the soul" "draws people to him." The experience is thus not only subjective, but intersubjective.[69] But as the Spirit of God, the Shekinah remained the transcendent Other—in Moltmann's words, "the terrible which makes us shudder and which fills us with fathomless amazement—the tremendous before which we human beings sink into the dust; and not least, that which fascinates us, holding us spellbound and never letting us go again."[70] To describe the Shekinah's Presence, Moltmann thus uses the language of Rudolf Otto's "Wholly Other," the *"mysterium tremendum et fascinans"* we have already considered.[71]

For Moltmann, we live *in* as well as *through* God's Spirit. Key to Moltmann's double perspective has been his increasing experiential turn to the Spirit, yet without turning his back on the Son. We should recall that the divine Spirit (*ruach*) and the divine Word (*dabar*)—God's breath and God's voice—are both found in the opening verses of Genesis. They complement each other (see Ps. 33:6—"By the word of the Lord the heavens were made, and all their host by the breath [*ruach*] of his mouth"). In Protestant thought, the divine Word has taken precedent. But Yahweh's *ruach* is also foundational to life. Failing to understand the Spirit's role in creation, Christians have too often severed the divine *ruach*, seen only as the Spirit of redemption, from both the natural world and our bodily life, and the results—a "Holy *Ghost*"—have

67. Moltmann, *Spirit of Life*, 55.
68. Ibid., 49 (italics mine); see also Moltmann, *Experiences in Theology*, 315.
69. I am indebted here and in what follows to my student Kutter Callaway for his insightful discussion of Moltmann.
70. Moltmann, *Spirit of Life*, 43–44.
71. Rudolf Otto, *The Idea of the Holy* (New York: Oxford University Press, 1971), 1–40.

proven disastrous. Any such notion needs to be abandoned, whether the Greek *pneuma*, the Latin *spiritus*, or the German *geist*. We need, rather, to recognize once again the divine Spirit, the *ruach*, as both transcendent and immanent, spiritual and sensual.

> The *ruach* as Yahweh's *ruach* is of course transcendent in origin; but it is equally true to say that as the power of life in all the living it is immanently efficacious. The creative power of God is the transcendent side of *ruach*. The power to live enjoyed by everything that is alive is its immanent side.[72]

As *ruach*, the Spirit is for Moltmann "the divine wellspring of life—the source of life created, life preserved and life daily renewed, and finally the source of the eternal life of all created being."[73] Here the transcendent Spirit is experienced in and through immanence.

A Paradoxical Theology

What might Moltmann's paradoxical theology have to do with God's wider revelation? In his final volume of his series of theological monographs, *Experiences in Theology* (2000), Moltmann understands there to be both a "natural" and a "Christian" theology (that is, both a theology rooted in the Spirit of creation and a theology rooted in the Spirit of redemption). In the language of this book, we might say there is both God's wider revelation that is experienced creationally, through our conscience, and in culture; and there is God's saving revelation culminating in the birth, life, death, and resurrection of Jesus. Both are important, both are grounded in biblical truth, and both are intertwined. But natural revelation—that arising from out of God's immanent transcendence—has too often been wrongly ignored or misunderstood as simply a naturalism, given that its focus is on the cosmic, not the Christic. What has been misunderstood is that even a knowledge of God through nature (conscience, creation, culture) is still revelation, if it is to be knowledge of the One God at all. Moltmann is crystal clear at this point. He writes:

> It is intrinsic to the strict concept of God's self-revelation that God himself is alone the criterion for his revelation. Revelation does not prove itself to be God's revelation because it accords with the conscience, or with a natural religious, already-given understanding, but only because it accords with God himself.[74]

72. Moltmann, *Spirit of Life*, 42.
73. Ibid., 82.
74. Moltmann, *Experiences in Theology*, 74.

The problem with natural revelation, argues Moltmann, is not its nature, but the use of it by self-deifying men and women. Says Moltmann, "Luther was right when he pointed to this essential point in his Heidelberg Disputation of 1518. He called natural theology [*theologia naturalis*] the theology of glory [*theologia gloriae*], which is what it really is."[75]

In *Experiences in Theology*, Moltmann goes on to say that it is not the natural person, not the "sinner," who can fully comprehend God's revelation through the creaturely world, but only those who have been redeemed. "*After* the analogy of faith comes the analogy of essence, *after* the theology of the cross comes the theology of glory, *after* the theology of grace the theology of nature, and *after* the theology of nature natural theology."[76] Nevertheless, natural theology has a universality, "a kind of advanced radiance, projected and perceived in advance from all things and in the conscience of human beings." It is a "fore-*shining* of revealed theology's eschatological horizon, the theology of glory." It is both "the real presence and advance radiance of the coming kingdom." Because the world is transparent to God's invisible presence, the Spirit's immanent transcendence becomes "the promise of the kingdom of glory."[77]

Humankind's experiences of God in and through creation, conscience, and human culture's creativity are a reflection of the coming new creation, a parable of God's coming kingdom made possible in Christ, an encounter with the immanent transcendence of the Spirit of Life. This Spirit can be fully known only by the Christ-one, the Christian, for the Spirit of Life is also the Spirit of Christ. But while "Christian theology" is the presupposition of a full "natural theology," the world also functions sacramentally. The truth of God also shines out in history, lighting up the created world. Moltmann concludes his reflection on natural theology (we might alternately say, on "natural revelation") by suggesting, "It is through a natural theology that others can be brought to the mystery of God's presence in all things and in all the complexities of life, and that Christians can gain an interest in the perceptions and wisdom of others."[78]

Like Johnson, Moltmann ends his reflection on creation's core sacramentality by suggesting that here is a real ground for interfaith coexistence and dialogue. Thinks Moltmann, what natural theology/natural revelation suggests is a shared territory with other religions, something that "after all, is already presupposed in the concept of religion to which all lay claim."[79] Here

75. Ibid., 78.
76. Ibid., 79.
77. Ibid., 68–73.
78. Ibid., 80.
79. Ibid., 82.

also, as we have seen, is the basis for the neo-Romantic claim to the arts as also functioning today as a resource spiritually. We have already dealt with the arts in some detail, but as we conclude our reflection on God's wider revelatory Presence, it is to the Christian's dialogue with those of other faiths that we turn. How might our constructive theology of God's wider revelational Presence play out concretely vis-à-vis this central spiritual opportunity and challenge of our age?

8

God's Wider Revelation Reconsidered

In the preceding chapters, we have sought to construct a theology of God's wider revelatory Presence. Beginning with the experiences of a broad range of people, we then turned to the Bible and its witness, finding throughout its pages evidence of God's revelation extending outside both Israel and the church. Although there has been relatively scant theological attention paid to the topic throughout the history of the church, and though much of what has been written has been singularly centered on issues of salvation, not revelation, the interlacing of Bible and experience with the church's tradition nonetheless has added depth and insight to our discussion. Particularly important has been the growing theological discussion concerning the Trinity, in which the Spirit has found her place at the divine table as a full partner.

Such interlacing of experiential reports with biblical narrative and the church's theology has highlighted the importance of God's revelatory Presence outside the walls of the church, both for Christians and for non-Christians alike. God's self-revelation extends beyond word and sacrament—beyond, that is, what has been traditionally understood as the Presence of Christ both in the individual and in the collective life of Christian believers. In the language of traditional theology, revelation includes not only "special revelation" but "general revelation" as well. But as we have seen, here the discussion has often become stilted and lifeless, as what has been considered "general" has been at one and the same time both overly narrowed (to include only that knowledge of God now resident in creation and creature) and too expansive (to that which is available to all people at all times and in all places). If a theology of God's wider revelational Presence is to be true to biblical description and representative of human experience, traditional definitions of what general revelation is must be amended.

The experiences we have sought to understand theologically in the preceding pages are not those available to all people, everywhere, at all times—the Spirit blows where she wills. Rather, they are those occasional encounters with God's Spirit experienced by many—Updike's "supernatural mail"; Lewis's "Joy" that surprises; Dulles's epiphany upon seeing new buds on a tree in winter; the numinous stillness of the ocean for Louis Zamperini; Gerard Manley Hopkins's "inscape"; my student's viewing of *Easy Rider*—experiences that break into our world from time to time and transform our beings. Such experiences not only fill our world, but are replete throughout the pages of Scripture as well. We have considered many of the narratives that reveal God's wider revelatory Presence—stories of Neco and Cyrus, Melchizedek and Abimelech, Elijah and Balaam, to name only a partial list. Though occasional, these experiences are far from elitist. It is not just the scholar or the artist who reports them. Rather, they are described both in Scripture and in everyday life by old and young, male and female, educated and uneducated, east and west, artist and scientist.

As both the witness of experience and the narrative of Scripture reveal, it is the God who surprisingly and mysteriously meets us that is the basis of general revelation, not the simple extrapolation or deduction arising from creation or creature that is generally available to all. And rather than being the possible experience of every person, at all times, everywhere, God's wider revelatory Presence is instead the specific experience of people sometimes and on some occasions. Watching the movie *Becket*, for example, was one such occasion for me to hear God speak, as I understood the need to obediently respond to God's call into the Christian ministry, but it was not that revelatory event for the hundreds of other viewers who also saw a screening of that film in the theater that night. Although Einstein thanked Yehudi Menuhin after hearing his concert, saying that Menuhin had again proved to him "that there is a God in heaven," this was not the experience of others who heard the same music.[1] "Rose is a rose, is a rose, is a rose," wrote Gertrude Stein. But we all know the experience of a rose is simply not the same for all who gaze upon it. For those whom the Spirit chooses to indwell, it becomes an epiphany.

The problem with traditional notions of general revelation that have been based in God's past revelatory action, not his present revelatory Presence, is

1. Albert Einstein, quoted in Richard Viladesau, *Theological Aesthetics* (New York: Oxford University Press, 1999), 104.

that nothing fresh is seemingly "communicated"; rather, the knowledge that is garnered is simply "derived." But that is to say that such knowledge is not really revelation at all. It is rather the recollection of or human projection from God's past actions—God's past revelation—whether rooted in culture, creation, or conscience. However, revelation is never derivative; it does not exist independent of the Revealer. Rather than merely flowing from the *cultural* memory of God's past Presence, or being an inference from God's past *creational* activity, or being understood as the outworking of humankind's *conscience*, general revelation should be understood as referring to present, particular experience(s) of the Transcendent in life. General revelation is not a universal, second-order reflection derived from the human capacity for transcending one's self (conscience)—the image of God (*imago Dei*) in men and women—nor is it a human inference from creation's "glory" that there is something greater than humankind. General revelation is not to be confused with human culture's residual memory of God's prior relationship with humankind. For each of these common descriptors fails the test of revelation, remaining rooted in creature and not Creator. Creature does not compel Creator. Only the Spirit of God—the Go-Between-God—can mediate God's Presence to us.

Misunderstandings of God's Revelatory Presence

As we conclude, it will be useful to pause at this point to reflect in some detail on the danger that traditional theology represents for a constructive theology of God's wider revelation, for a misunderstanding of God's revelatory Presence as narrowly resident in creation, culture, or conscience has been typical of most traditional theology. It is the default position that continues to relegate to the theological sidelines conversations about God's revelation outside the church.

Creation

The danger of confusing creation (as itself revelatory of God) with the revealing Presence of God speaking in and through creation has been a perennial one. The First Vatican Council, for example, wrongly declared: "God, the source and goal of all things, can be certainly known from created things, by the light of natural human reason."[2] Most typically, as we have seen, it is a surface reading of Romans 1:19–20 that has been used to support such confusion. "For what can be known about God is plain to them, because God

---

2. Dogmatic Constitution, caput ii, quoted in Robert W. Jenson, *Systematic Theology*, vol. 2, *The Works of God* (New York: Oxford University Press, 1999), 153.

has shown it to them. Ever since the creation of the world his eternal power and divine nature, invisible though they are, have been understood and seen through the things he has made." Here, Paul seems to speak of creation as revealing God's nature and power. But is it creation that speaks, or is it God's revelatory Presence speaking in and through his creation? Creation's evidence of God's past activity should not be equated with God's present revelation. The issue has to do with how we are to understand verse 19, where it says, "God has shown it to them." Are these words simply a poetic description to be taken metaphorically? Do they refer only to past creational activity? Or do they also include God's present providential care and revelational Presence?

The text in Romans admits to these possible interpretations, but as Robert Jenson argues, there is no collateral support anywhere in the New Testament for Paul arguing for "a knowledge of God that human agents derive by intellectual operations on observed phenomena." Jenson writes:

> Paul has nothing to say for or against what modernity usually means by "natural theology" or about what fathers of the council [Vatican I] may have conceived under some such label. If God is manifest among the gentiles, this is because God has *made* himself manifest; just as the knowledge of God in Israel is the result of what he did at Sinai and by his prophets.[3]

As fellow theologian Colin Gunton states in his *A Brief Theology of Revelation*, in reading Paul we must not be led astray by "intellectual trends of our era [that] have replaced a concept of revelation with a concept of truth as something lying within the control of the human rational agent."[4] Romans 1 states that there is in creation a clear and compelling revelation—that is, in and through it, God speaks.

The same surface ambiguity in a text's meaning is found in Psalm 19, where commentators have again sometimes wrongly suggested that creation itself is to be understood as a source of revelation. One might recall, in this regard, the words of Isaac Watts's hymn based on that psalm, "The heavens declare your glory, Lord" (1719). In that hymn, God's power and praise that the cosmos *silently* conveys is contrasted with the distinct *words* of grace and truth found in God's Word. The one is meager, thinks Watts; the other, profound. But is this the psalmist's intentions for his hymn of praise? Does the psalmist intend to make a contrast between these two forms of revelation with creation's silent revelation being negatively contrasted with the revelation from God's

---

3. Ibid., 2:154.
4. Colin Gunton, *A Brief Theology of Revelation* (Edinburgh: T&T Clark, 1995), 21, quoted in Jenson, *Systematic Theology*, 2:154.

Word? Or, as we have argued, are the two forms of revelation more to be seen in parallel—two means by which God himself declares his glory?

If humans are left only with our projections from nature's "silent speech," independent of God's contemporary, illumining Presence, then humankind would not only marvel at creation's beauty and design but also become terrified, since nature is also written "tooth and claw." But the psalmist marvels at creation because he has heard God's Spirit silently speaking into it. Within and yet beyond creation, the Creator chooses in his good pleasure to reveal himself to us. How else can one explain that occasional epiphany while looking at a sunset or gazing at the moon hanging low on the horizon?[5] Admittedly and gloriously, what is known heuristically in nature's speechless speech becomes more fully known through the law where language adds another layer of understanding to our experience and wonder. But it is not only "words" that are important for this psalmist; important as well are the precritical "murmurings" of our hearts. As the psalmist closes his song of praise, verse 14 makes this clear: "Let the words of my mouth and the murmurings of my heart be acceptable to you, O Lord, my rock and my redeemer."

In describing creation's revelatory possibility in this way, I am reminded of that scene in the movie *American Beauty* (d. Mendes, 1999) where Ricky Fitts shows his friend Janie a video he has taken of the wind playing games with a paper bag one pregnant fall day. He tells her, "That's the day I realized there was this entire life behind things and this incredibly benevolent force that wanted me to know there was no reason to be afraid . . . ever." Ricky admits that the video he is showing Janie of the windblown bag is "a poor excuse . . . but it helps me remember. I need to remember. . . . Sometimes, there's so much beauty in the world I feel like I can't take it . . . and my heart, she's going to cave in." Significantly, the screenwriter, Alan Ball, says he inserted this scene into the movie because it was an experience he actually had had.[6] Such an experience does not need words in order for meaning to be communicated. In fact, words can even reduce its significance and impact, as anyone who has had such experiences knows. Creation on its own terms is an important arena of God's wider revelatory Presence.

But not all agree. Consider, for example, the confusion of creation with the Creator's revelatory Presence that is found in Jonathan Edwards's sermon based on Psalm 48:10: "Your name, O God, like your praise, reaches to the end of the earth." Edwards notes how God himself appealed to creation to rebuke Job

5. See Robert K. Johnston and J. Walker Smith, *Life Is Not Work, Work Is Not Life* (Berkeley: Wildcat Canyon Press, 2001).

6. Alan Ball, quoted in Bob Longino, "'Beauty' Maker," *Atlanta Journal-Constitution*, March 26, 2000, sec. L, p. 4.

for his lack of faith and to call him back to a proper trust in divine providence and grace. According to Edwards, God did not need any special revelation to convince Job. Instead, God gave Job a tour of his creation, pointing out the vast array of his creatures, as well as his own role in their creation and nurture. For Edwards, such a look at creation was enough to return Job to faith.[7]

According to T. M. Moore, creation was for Edwards "clear and compelling, giving us insight into the wisdom, power, and holiness of God. Sinful men will not receive it: they are thus under His wrath. Yet the elect of God will be drawn by the light of general revelation, in the context of the preaching of the gospel."[8] But again, the ambiguity concerning what "creation's" speech might mean needs clarification. In the book of Job, it is not creation that speaks to Job, but God's revelatory Presence in and through the whirlwind—that is, in and through creation. For some, the distinction might seem a minor one, but as Barth cautions us, it is fundamental. We do not create God in our image; neither does creation apart from the Spirit of its Creator declare God's praise. Rather, the wonder, awe, dependence, and gratitude that we experience in and through creation are a response to the Creator God who reaches out to us through the Spirit. Here is the perspective of Job.

The writer of Proverbs can be helpful in clarifying "creation's" revelatory core. Chapters 1 through 9 of Proverbs provide readers a theological introduction to the wise sayings that follow. How are we to understand the observations on creation and creature that the sages provide? Is their wisdom simply their experiential knowledge of how things happen in the world, their careful observation of what is? Something available to us as rational human agents? No. It is more than this. The proverbs that follow are introduced, as Elizabeth Johnson reminds us, by Lady (Woman) Wisdom, who calls us to follow her. It is Lady Wisdom who grants life and allows us to find favor with the Lord (Prov. 8:35). But Lady Wisdom is not to be equated with creation or creature. She was there "at the first, before the beginning of the earth. When there were no depths. . . . Before the mountains had been shaped, . . . or the world's first bits of soil" (Prov. 8:23–26). Wisdom concerning creation is certainly not humankind's possession; instead, the call of Lady Wisdom needs to be heard from beyond us (Prov. 8:1–3), for she was with God from the beginning ("I was beside him, like a master worker; and I was daily his delight, rejoicing before him always, rejoicing in his inhabited world and delighting in the human race" [Prov. 8:30–31]).

7. Jonathan Edwards, "Sermon on Psalm 48:10," in *The Works of Jonathan Edwards*, ed. Edward Hickman (Edinburgh: Banner of Truth, 1974), 2:108, referenced by T. M. Moore, *Consider the Lilies: A Plea for Creational Theology* (Phillipsburg, NJ: P&R, 2005), 146.

8. Moore, *Consider the Lilies*, 140.

Some biblical scholars suggest that wisdom has here been apotheosized by the author of Proverbs, Lady Wisdom perhaps representing what Christians would later recognize as the second person of the Trinity. But more likely, we are to understand the use of Lady Wisdom in Proverbs as a literary device, a means of speaking of God himself and one of his attributes. But regardless of the outcome of this debate among Old Testament wisdom scholars, in either case Lady Wisdom is not to be understood as our possession. Humankind does not learn of God through an independent creation or by the independent use of human reason; rather, readers are instructed in Proverbs to listen for God who speaks to us through creation—who stands at the gate crying out, who raises her voice beside the way, at the crossroads. It is Lady Wisdom, not creation itself, who instructs us in and through her creation.

Conscience

As with creation, there is a similar danger of misunderstanding human-kind's conscience as somehow independently revealing God, rather than our conscience being the locus of the revealing Presence of God's Spirit speaking in and through his creatures. And the result is also similar—a confusion over the meaning of revelation. This theological mistake is easily illustrated by turning to Lewis's apologetic writings. Lewis develops his understanding in *The Abolition of Man*, an extended essay on the mistaken philosophical underpinnings of the British educational system of his day, and, in particular, in *Mere Christianity*, a collection of radio talks where Lewis spelled out the essentials of the Christian faith. Underlying all existence, Lewis believes, there is some kind of Law or rule of fair play, some morality, or Law of Human Nature, if you like—some evidence that there is "a Something that is directing the universe."[9]

In *The Abolition of Man*, Lewis calls this universal, unchangeable moral code the *Tao*: "This thing which I have called for convenience the Tao and which others may call Natural Law or traditional morality or the First Principles of Practical Reason or the First Platitudes is not one among a series of possible systems of value. It is the sole source of all value judgments."[10] If this Tao is rejected—if all statements of value are thought to be mere statements of subjective feeling—then all value is rejected. The result of such a turn to the relative, thinks Lewis, would be "Men without Chests" (the title of the best of the book's three chapters) and the end of civilized culture. There is,

9. C. S. Lewis, *Mere Christianity* (New York: Macmillan, 1960), 34.
10. C. S. Lewis, *The Abolition of Man* (New York: Macmillan, 1947), 28.

according to Lewis, an objective, transcendent value; certain attitudes really are true. It is simply erroneous to claim, as some moderns are prone to do, that the historic moral principles of Western civilization are different from the norms of other cultures and thus nonbinding. In a lengthy appendix to *The Abolition of Man*, Lewis provides example after example that the central moral principles that have guided us in the West have also been accepted through the ages by all civilized societies. In *Mere Christianity*, Lewis again summarizes his claim: "If anyone will take the trouble to compare the moral teaching of, say, the ancient Egyptians, Babylonians, Hindus, Chinese, Greeks, and Romans, what will really strike him will be how very like they are to each other and to our own. . . . Human beings, all over the earth, have this curious idea that they ought to behave in a certain way, and cannot really get rid of it."[11]

What Lewis is here arguing is the presence of "God's" moral footprint within men and women, a divinely given moral compass internal to humankind that guides and directs us, though we often fail to practice what it is we expect from other people. And Lewis seems correct in such an assessment. One example will need to suffice. During the World Series in 2010, a Liberty Mutual ad showed a woman pedestrian kicking a basketball back to a child and his dad playing basketball. Then we continue to watch silently as an African American man helps a small, older, white man get his large suitcase off the carousel at an airport. Finally, a voice comes on saying, "When individuals do this, it's called 'doing the right thing.' When a company does this it's called 'Liberty Mutual.'"[12] The assumption of the company is that we all would agree about the two vignettes we see: here is moral action. In making his argument based on such a conscience, Lewis is not arguing for a natural theology that moves directly from our conscience to a full understanding of the Christian God. The evidence from conscience is much more meager. Here are Lewis's words: "We have not yet got as far as the God of any actual religion, still less the God of that particular religion called Christianity. We have only got as far as a Somebody or Something behind the Moral Law."[13]

Lewis is arguing based in his understanding of general revelation that there is a Lawgiver behind what he perceives to be a natural law. He writes:

My reason was that Christianity simply doesn't make sense until you have faced the sort of facts I have been describing. Christianity tells people to repent and promises them forgiveness. It therefore has nothing (as far as I know) to say to people who do not know they have done anything to repent of and who do not

11. Lewis, *Mere Christianity*, 19–21.
12. Fox Network, World Series Game One, October 27, 2010.
13. Lewis, *Mere Christianity*, 37.

feel that they need any forgiveness. It is after you have realized that there is a real Moral Law, and a Power behind the law, and that you have broken that law and put yourself wrong with that Power—it is after all this, and not a moment sooner, that Christianity begins to talk.[14]

But of course, such an argument, while important, is not an argument for or against revelation. Such a "point of contact," if that is what it is, is not to be confused with revelation. Perhaps the human recognition of morality is, rather, an aspect of humankind's "capacity for relationship," the *imago Dei* given all humanity at creation, our relational possibility to love others and the Other. But as Barth emphatically responded to Brunner, a creation/creature-based "point of contact," however present, should not be confused with revelation; it is incapable of bridging the chasm between the finite and the infinite, between time and eternity.

Basic to such misunderstandings of the role of conscience in revelation is a confusion over the meaning of Paul's argument in Romans 2, a confusion already discussed at length in chapter 5. With regard to Romans 2:15 ("They show that what the law requires is written on their hearts, . . . and their conflicting thoughts will accuse or perhaps excuse them"), many commentators have spent more time trying to explain it away than seeking to understand what it is saying. Some have posited that Paul is here speaking only hypothetically; others, that he has only gentile Christians in mind or that the passage is simply an anomaly in Pauline thought. G. C. Berkouwer believes that the statements of general revelation in Romans 1 and 2 do teach that there is in fact some form of divine revelation in creation and conscience, but because of sin it cannot result in any real knowledge. Such general revelation, he concludes, "issues in no true knowledge of God which reveals itself in true service of God." Rather, such revelation "is changed, rendered vain, and distorted, as it is encountered by the natural man."[15] For Berkouwer, there might be a natural morality common to humanity, but it is darkened. Though the natural mind can occasionally line up with God's orderings—with God's law—humanity is incapable of true obedience. According to Berkouwer, God reveals himself truly, but our perceptions only distort it.

But as we have seen, the text in Romans 2 fails to support such contentions. Paul writes, "For he [God] will repay according to each one's deeds" (Rom. 2:6). This judgment applies both to Jew and gentile, though both are judged according to the light they have received (Rom. 2:12–16). Ultimately, as the larger

14. Ibid., 38–39.
15. G. C. Berkouwer, *General Revelation*, Studies in Dogmatics (Grand Rapids: Eerdmans, 1955), 150.

argument of Romans 1–8 makes clear, it is the work of Christ, his death and resurrection, that will provide forgiveness of our sins. It is his work that will save. But as Paul develops his argument, it is also the case that he recognizes that at times some gentiles are sensitive to the law of God and actually do it, even though they are without knowledge of the Jewish faith. Paul writes:

> When Gentiles, who do not possess the law, do instinctively what the law requires, these, though not having the law, are a law to themselves. They show that what the law requires is written on their hearts, to which their own conscience also bears witness; and their conflicting thoughts will accuse or perhaps excuse them on the day when, according to my gospel, God, through Jesus Christ, will judge the secret thought of all. (Rom. 2:14–16)

That gentiles do at times follow the law written on their hearts to which their conscience bears witness is not because of their own efforts or because of some natural law of the universe. Rather, their obedience is said to be the result of the activity of God in them. They are obedient to the law because it is "written on their hearts" by the Spirit in them.

Again, as with creation, it is necessary to distinguish between an intellectual knowledge of God attained by consideration of right and wrong and a revelatory knowledge of God given by his self-revelation through the Spirit. The former can be obtained in a number of ways but is impotent; the other enlightens our understanding by God's Spirit. One is not revelation, but human projection. The other is real enlightenment based in God's wider revelatory Presence, one that will bear fruit in our actions. Such revelation is much more than a meager trace, an echo that simply serves to condemn us for not responding. As Jerome wrote long ago: "For the law is spiritual, and a revelation is needed to enable us to comprehend it."[16]

Culture

As we have noted, George Steiner, in his provocative and prophetic book *Real Presences*, writes about the creative process. In our modern world, Steiner believes, our creativity has too often been wrongly reduced to the words, sounds, or images we produce, signifying themselves and nothing more. With Gertrude Stein, some moderns say, "there is no there there." But this is fallacious, Steiner thinks. There is a "there" there. Arguing for God's revelatory Presence in and

---

16. Jerome, *Epistles of Paul* 53, in *The Nicene and Post-Nicene Fathers 2*, ed. Phillip Schaff and Henry Wace (New York: T&T Clark, 1893), 6:98. Also in Robert Barclay, *An Apology for the True Christian Divinity, Proposition II*, first published in 1648, www.qhpress.org/texts /barclay/apology/index.html.

through culture, Steiner asks, "Why art? Why poetic creation?" And Steiner answers, "I can only put it this way (and every true poem, piece of music or painting says it better): there is aesthetic creation because there is *creation*." While there will always be mystery that surrounds us on all sides, and though we can never know fully about that which lies behind what we create, that is exactly the point. Why there is painting or poetry or music at all is precisely because through them we are at times ushered into the Presence of something "More." As George Steiner argues, humankind's creative endeavors—particularly its art, music, and poetry—"relate us most directly to that in being which is not ours."[17]

Some will counter that in arguing this way, Steiner does not get beyond a notion of the sublime—something beyond our broken world to be sure, but not necessarily something revelatory. Brian Horne, for one, believes that Steiner's argument remains within the realm of anthropology, or that he perhaps speaks as a Unitarian, even while often using Christian theological categories. Horne believes Steiner to be "unwilling to recognize the possibility of the divine mystery as radically immanent, the Holy Spirit, as well as ultimately transcendent, the Father, and the union of these two modes of Being in the expressive form of the Incarnate Son." Instead, argues Horne, Steiner "posits an absolute freedom [embodied in the work of art] that denies the possibility of 'real presence.'" Horne says that his own position is quite different: "The human being possesses only relative freedom, and the boundaries or shape of that freedom are determined by the gift of the Spirit." What the artist receives is "the Spirit of God who, alone, moves in total freedom." For Horne, "What enables the human artwork—poem, symphony, dance, statue—to become the expressive form of divine radiance is the human will responding freely to the movement of the Holy Spirit."[18]

As should be clear from my discussion in chapter 6, I am sympathetic with the direction of Horne's remarks. It is in the movement of the Holy Spirit that the artist experiences true freedom. I will return to this point below. But Horne need not disparage Steiner's recognition that there is a real Presence at art's center, even if Steiner is insufficiently trinitarian. Take for example these words from Steiner:

> All good art and literature begin in immanence. But they do not stop there. Which is to say, very plainly, that it is the enterprise and privilege of the aesthetic to quicken into lit presence the continuum between temporality and eternity, between matter and spirit, between man and "the other."[19]

17. George Steiner, *Real Presences* (Chicago: University of Chicago Press, 1989), 201, 226.
18. Brian Horne, "Art: A Trinitarian Imperative?" in *Trinitarian Theology Today*, ed. Christoph Schwöbel (Edinburgh: T&T Clark, 1995), 87–91.
19. Steiner, *Real Presences*, 227.

Though our creativity flows for Steiner "out of human questioning, solitude, inventiveness, apprehension of time and of death," Steiner argues that the epistemological act of reception of such creativity within us is also

> a metaphysical and, in the last analysis, a theological one. . . . It is theology, explicit or suppressed, masked or avowed, substantive or imaged, which underwrites the presumption of creativity, of signification in our encounters with text, with music, with art. The meaning of meaning is a transcendent postulate.[20]

Despite his Romantic tendency to move from human creativity to Creator, Steiner nonetheless is clear about that divine locus through which God continues to reveal himself: in the creativity of God's finest creation—humankind—the Creator also speaks.

How then are we to understand God's wider revelatory Presence? Our words often fail us. For C. S. Lewis it is as mysterious as a "bright shadow." With Otto, it is a *mysterium: tremendum et fascinans.*" Peter Berger believes it a rumor of angels. Brunner believes that it is rooted in creature and creation; Barth, that God and God alone is the actor in revelation. And both Brunner and Barth are right. Rollins provocatively writes, "That which we cannot speak of is the one thing about whom and to whom we must never stop speaking."[21] Though we in the West have been tempted during the Enlightenment by "the distraction of clarity," we also know that God's revelatory Presence both raises questions and clarifies. But though such revelation cannot be contained, or its experience adequately communicated, what is revealed is more than a trace; it resounds, not sounds as a mere echo. Christian revelation is not to be captured by Plato's analogy of the cave. Such anemic language is a far cry from the witness of countless people to the experience of the numinous in their lives, including those within the pages of Scripture. God is not a second-order deduction, but something/someone/a mystery too close to be seen clearly, who meets us personally in the Spirit. It is the Spirit who is present in and through creation, conscience, and culture.

A Theology of Religions: A Closing Case Study

As we bring together our thoughts about God's wider revelatory Presence in and through creation, conscience, and culture, a brief case study can serve to both illustrate our contentions and integrate praxeologically the interlacing

20. Ibid., 215–16.
21. Peter Rollins, *How (Not) to Speak of God* (Brewster, MA: Paraclete, 2006), xii.

of our various theological probings—experiential, biblical, and theological. In chapter 1 of this book, I mentioned the increased interest today in a theology of religions as one compelling reason for attempting a constructive theology of general revelation. Let us look at what a renewed focus on God's wider revelatory Presence might mean for this increasingly vital theological topic.

As is evident to all, our world's shrinking borders have created in us a new awareness of our neighbors, including their religions. Do you recall the visually stunning movie *Life of Pi* (d. Lee), which came out in 2012 and captured eleven Academy Award nominations and four Oscars?[22] Based on Yann Martel's bestselling novel, the film mixes the sacred mythologies of Islam and Hinduism together, sprinkling with it a mixture of Catholic guilt. Immersed in an enchanted universe where gods are his superheroes, the young Pi is called "Swami Jesus" by his friends as they make fun of his religious syncretism. Even his father tells him, "Believing in everything equals nothing." The story is thus set up to chronicle how Pi's naive faith will respond to the ultimate test. After a ferocious storm kills the rest of his family and most of a zoo that is traveling on the same ship, Pi survives on a makeshift life raft, only to find his only companion to be a ravenous tiger. And as the adventure unfolds, the young boy grows into a man before our eyes.

Though visually magnificent with flying fish, enchanted islands, and seamless computer graphics, the movie proved to some of us largely a disappointment, as the director Ang Lee chose not to deal in any serious way with the religious issues he had used to set up his story. Is the movie an argument for God? We are not sure. More likely, it is simply an example of how a growing number in our postmodern world believe they can simply construct their own faith from a pastiche of others. But as Pi's father suggests, surely interfaith dialogue must be more than the casual sampling of conflicting belief systems. Nonetheless, whether the filmmakers proved to be adequate theologians or not, what is clear amid the lush scenery and adrenalin-producing plot line is the givenness of our multifaith world. India is but a rich microcosm of the world as a whole. Living today with what Veli-Matti Kärkkäinen, my colleague at Fuller, has labeled "persistent plurality," the question of how to account theologically for the spiritual insights, values, and beliefs of those from other religious traditions has taken on for everyone a new urgency.[23]

Perhaps a personal reference to two general assemblies of the World Council of Churches (WCC) can further highlight the issue for us. I attended the WCC

---

22. The four Oscars included Best Director for Ang Lee.
23. Veli-Matti Kärkkäinen, "Theologies of Religions," *Evangelical Interfaith Dialogue* 1, no. 2 (Spring 2010): 3.

sixth assembly in Vancouver, Canada, in 1983. In one of the draft reports that was presented to all the delegates for adoption, there was a section on the relationship of Christians to people with other religious convictions. It read in part, "While affirming the uniqueness of the birth, life, death and resurrection of Jesus to which we bear witness, we recognize God's creative work in the religious experience of people of other faiths." After a heated debate on the floor that suggested no possible compromise, the matter was finally referred to the WCC central committee, which meets between assemblies for deliberation and decision. But when the central committee met, it, too, was unable to reach unanimity with regard to a position. Rather, in a split decision, they watered down the sentence to read, "While affirming the uniqueness of the birth, life, death and resurrection of Jesus to which we bear witness, we recognize God's creative work in the seeking for religious truth among people of other faiths."[24] Unable to confidently affirm God's actual, creative work in the religious experience of peoples with other faith traditions, but challenged by its real possibility given the increased dialogue and interaction between Christians and those of other religions that was then going on, the WCC chose only to affirm the Spirit of God's preliminary work in causing people to want to seek after the truth.

But eight years later, in 1991, with debate over a theology of religions in full flower, I heard at the WCC seventh assembly in Canberra, Australia, what proved to be one of the most controversial plenary speeches ever delivered at a WCC world assembly. A Korean feminist theologian who had been trained at Union Seminary in New York, Chung Hyun-Kyung, spoke on the chosen theme of the gathering: "Come Holy Spirit—Renew the Whole Creation." Entering a darkened but spotlighted assembly hall with fifteen young Korean and aboriginal dancers, and dressed herself in a traditional Korean gown, the speech was as much an enactment as a pronouncement. Chung read a litany of death for the spirits of all who have been oppressed throughout history—women like Hagar and Joan of Arc, children, the indigenous, the earth and its air and water, the victims of war, even Jesus himself. The paper on which the litany was written was then lit on fire and disintegrated into smoke while the Korean theologian held it in her hands. Identifying these spirits of anger, resentment, and grief as the spirits of Han, Chung said, "These Han-ridden spirits . . . have been agents through whom the Holy Spirit has spoken her compassion and wisdom for life. Without hearing the cries of these spirits, we cannot hear the voice of the Holy Spirit." In this way, Chung referenced

---

24. Quoted in Emilio Castro, "Mission in a Pluralistic Age," *International Review of Mission* 75 (1986): 200.

the suffering Han-ridden spirits of her ancestors, calling them "icons of the Holy Spirit."[25]

As delegates listened to the speech, many felt scandalized. Afterward, most evangelicals and many mainline Protestants joined the Orthodox in protest—certainly the Han-ridden spirits of her ancestors had no connection with the Spirit of Christ who would lead believers into all truth. The Orthodox participants wrote:

> Some people tend to affirm with very great ease the presence of the Holy Spirit in many movements and developments without discernment. . . . We must guard against a tendency to substitute a "private" spirit, the spirit of the world or other spirits for the Holy Spirit. . . . Pneumatology is inseparable from Christology or from the doctrine of the Holy Trinity.[26]

Evangelicals also wrote: "As the assembly discussed the process of listening to the Spirit at work in every culture, we cautioned, with others, that discernment is required to identify the Spirit as the Spirit of Jesus Christ and thus to develop criteria for and the limits to theological diversity."[27]

Certainly the wind of the Spirit blows where it might. But if so, how are Christians to know? The very fact that Chung gave such a speech at a WCC assembly together with the strong negative responses generated by it illustrates well the rising importance of a theology of religions that took place during the 1980s. It also highlights the stated need for developing criteria of discernment for the Spirit's present work among us. How might the church "test the spirits to see whether they are from God" (1 John 4:1)? And what might Jesus's statement mean, "Whoever is not against us is for us" (Mark 9:40)? If religion was viewed also as a cultural expression (and it is), then could the Holy Spirit be present in the religious expressions of other faiths, just as the Spirit's Presence might be recognized in the arts? Must the Spirit's Presence in these Han-ridden spirits be seen as a denial of the Trinity or of the Spirit as also the Spirit of Christ? Is God to be removed from the anger and grief of those who have suffered? The questions spill forth.

For the first time in its history, at the Canberra world assembly, the WCC both chose for its theme a prayer, "Come Holy Spirit—Renew the Whole Creation," and focused its attention on the third article of the creed. Both decisions

---

25. Chung Hyun-Kyung, "Come Holy Spirit—Renew the Whole Creation," in *Signs of the Spirit*, ed. Michael Kinnamon (Geneva: WCC, 1991), 39. The Korean word *Han* is sometimes translated as "sorrow"—a sorrow caused by suffering and injustice that is endured with bitter acceptance, even while one yearns for vengeance. *Han* permeates the whole of Korean culture.

26. "Reflections of Orthodox Participants," in Kinnamon, *Signs of the Spirit*, 281.

27. "Evangelical Perspectives from Canberra," in Kinnamon, *Signs of the Spirit*, 282–86.

were of significance. The debate that followed was evidence that theologians had much more work to do on Christian pneumatology. Here would be the window into a more developed theology of religions. Chung was correct, at least with regard to this. And given the pluralistic and contentious world in which we lived at that time, it seemed appropriate for statements by the WCC to give way to prayers and liturgical enactments, as pneumatology was given its rightful place alongside Christology. The reality of Canberra included the recognition that as Christians moved forward together into the twenty-first century, a theology of religions would be near the center of Christian reflection, and theology would be both rooted in a developing understanding of the Spirit and humbly spoken as a prayer.

In asserting a central place for a theology of religions, one must realize how radically new this turn in Christian theology was. Oh, the biblical narrative is set against the backdrop of other religions to be sure—Melchizedek, the high priest of Salem, was the one who "ordained" Abraham to his calling; Balaam, a seer from a neighboring tribe, nevertheless blessed Israel; Josiah cleansed the temple of offerings to other gods; and Paul spoke to those on Mars Hill about the "unknown God" of their altars. But the church rarely if ever has viewed the insights and experiences of those of other religions as important, let alone has seen them in a positive light as they constructed their own theologies. Paganism was simply judged or ignored, as a brief summary of church history indicates. In the immediate centuries after the birth, life, death, and resurrection of Jesus, the early apologists needed to make an "apologia" for the faith. They had little interest in incorporating non-Christian insight into their theologies, believing that Christ came into the world to judge paganism, even in its best expressions. Similarly, though Augustine could make clear use of Plato, he was not looking for truth in other belief systems, and his hierarchy was clear: Christ was the standard, and all other religious thought was referred to only as it matched up with this truth. Though Aquinas made similar use of Aristotle, whom he learned of from the Arabs, he had little patience with nonbelievers, infidels. They were either to be converted or eliminated (!), so as not to contaminate believers. In the Reformation era, Luther gave little to no mention in his writings of either Buddhism or Hinduism, and one is embarrassed today by his vitriol against both Jews and Muslims (whom he called Turks). But again, Luther's concern was elsewhere, in purifying the church by carrying forward his reform against Rome. Throughout these long centuries, a theology of religions was simply nowhere on the radar screen.

With Calvin, there begins to be more thought directed toward those of other religions, for as a theological systematizer, his reflections on other matters caused him to reflect as well on those outside the church. For Calvin, though, as with many who reacted strongly to Chung's presentation at Canberra centuries later, his comments on other religions centered christologically and were rooted soteriologically. Turks (Muslims), for example, might proclaim the Creator to be their God, but their rejection of Christ meant they had substituted an idol in his place. Though pagan culture owes much to God, given that the divine glory is reflected in the very fabric of the world, such knowledge is for Calvin diffused and blocked by sin; it is surely unable to lead one to Christ. As with those shapers of the Christian faith who had preceded him, Calvin had little to no real interest in engaging those of other faiths in dialogue; nor did he have any desire to learn from them. Calvin's agenda was elsewhere.

It is two centuries later, with the Enlightenment in full flower, that with John Wesley things begin to be different. Though Wesley had little knowledge of Islam and no direct engagement (his term was Mohametans), in two of Wesley's late sermons, "On Faith" (1788) and "On Living without God" (1790), he chose, according to Wesley scholar Randy Maddox, to "1) forbid a summary damnation of Muslims, 2) praise the sincerity of their response to the limited revelation they have received (in explicit contrast to the English Deists!), and 3) argue that we have great reason to hope that some Muslims have indeed come into experience of true religion through their sensitivity to God's inward voice."[28] Wesley had long believed that all people could infer from God's creation that there was a powerful, wise, just, and merciful Creator. Here was for Wesley "initial revelation," what this book has critiqued as inadequate, but which theology has traditionally labeled "general revelation"— that which is available to all people at all times and in all places. But by the 1780s Wesley too was dissatisfied with this formulation and began to develop his ideas further. He came to believe that God may also have taught some heathens a measure of true religion by an "inward voice." That is, prevenient grace might do more than simply testify about creation; its "initial revelation" might also address our "spiritual senses," inviting our free response. Given such an understanding, and consistent with the claims of some Quakers in his day, Wesley came to believe that God would judge heathens who had never heard of Christ only in terms of the revelation (light) that they had received, including God's inward voice.

But though Wesley presaged a new interest in a theology of religions, a robust discussion of the religions did not follow. It was not until the second half of the twentieth century that a theology of religions came to be of real interest among Christians more generally. No doubt this can be understood

---

28. Randy L. Maddox, "Wesley and the Question of Truth or Salvation through Other Religions," *Wesleyan Theological Journal* 27, nos. 1–2 (Spring–Fall 1992): 11.

as part of that change in our culture, as breakthroughs in transportation and communication radically transformed our world, turning it into a global village. Roman Catholics were in the vanguard of this contemporary theological reflection on other religions, given in particular the deliberations of Vatican II (1962–65). As Elizabeth Johnson notes, "Virtually every church pronouncement [within Roman Catholicism] since Vatican II . . . has acknowledged the presence and activity of the Spirit in the religions themselves."[29] But it was, in particular, Pope John Paul II, who, beginning with his first encyclical, *Redemptor Hominis*, in 1979, repeatedly expressed the desire of the Catholic Church to engage in respectful dialogue with members of other religions. As Clark Pinnock summarizes, "This encyclical sounded the note that would characterize his approach to the dialogue: namely, respect for the presence and activity of the Holy Spirit among non-Christians, a presence and activity discernible even in their religious life, in their practice of virtue, their spirituality, and their prayers."[30] Without compromising the unique role of Jesus Christ for salvation, John Paul understood the universal activity of the Spirit as offering grace to every person. Thus, he argued that we should look for signs of the Spirit's gifts in non-Christians as well as Christians. Moreover, where the initial conciliar texts from Vatican II (e.g., *Gaudium et Spes* 22 and *Lumen Gentium* 16) spoke of the Spirit's work only in individual terms, John Paul spoke also of the activity of the Spirit in collective terms, in terms of non-Christian religions themselves, seeing the Spirit as seeking to bear fruit in them all.

It was during this same time period, when John Paul was advancing an agenda among Roman Catholics vis-à-vis the Spirit and the religions, that Protestants and the Orthodox churches also began to wrestle with how best to understand the insights and faith of their neighbors of other religions. Thus, by the 1980s, what had been for over nineteen hundred years a largely neglected discussion with little relevance for the larger theological agenda was pushed to the forefront, as Christians increasingly came to know personally adherents of other faith traditions. It was in this changing and theologically charged context that three theological positions with regard to a theology of religions took shape. Unfortunately, they did not follow the trajectory that Pope John Paul II had laid down by focusing on the universal activity of the Spirit, but instead concerned themselves soteriologically. In this way, the WCC debate, both at Vancouver and at Canberra, can be seen as indicative of the wider church's conversation. Leaving any discussion of general revelation and

29. Elizabeth Johnson, *Quest for the Living God: Mapping Frontiers in the Theology of God* (New York: Continuum, 2007), 177–78.

30. Clark H. Pinnock, "Religious Pluralism: A Turn to the Holy Spirit," *McMaster Journal of Theology and Ministry* 5 (2002), www.mcmaster.ca/mjtm/5-4.htm.

the work of the Spirit in creation in the background, Christ's atoning work on the cross dominated this first round of theological reflection.

To the question of who might be saved, *exclusivists* held that salvation was available only in Jesus Christ through a personal response to faith; *inclusivists* held that salvation was only through Christ's atoning work, but its benefits had been made more universally available to those who had not heard the Christian gospel through the salvific richness of other faiths; and *pluralists* believed that though Christianity was their path to salvation, to insist on the superiority or finality of Christ and Christianity was wrong, for other religions also had their legitimate means of salvation. Representative of these conflicting positions are Ajith Fernando's *Sharing the Truth in Love: How to Relate to People of Other Faiths* or Harold Netland's *Encountering Religious Pluralism: The Challenge to Christian Faith and Mission* (exclusivist); Karl Rahner's notion of the "anonymous Christian" appearing in several of his volumes of *Theological Investigations*, or Clark Pinnock's *A Wideness in God's Mercy: The Finality of Jesus Christ in a World of Religions* (inclusivist); and Paul Knitter and John Hick's book, *The Myth of Christian Uniqueness—Toward a Pluralistic Theology of Religions* (pluralist).[31]

It is an interesting exercise to compare and contrast these three positions, as well as a host of permutations within each general category, as discussion of a theology of religions has proliferated over the last thirty years. But for our purposes here, it is unnecessary. It is enough to note that the controversy between these first-generation theologians of religions has largely centered on issues of soteriology. While for the exclusivists salvation is unavailable to the unevangelized, for the pluralists each religious tradition has its own path leading to salvation, and for the inclusivists, salvation is through Christ by the Holy Spirit, but it is mediated through a variety of religions outside Christianity. Behind such differences, of course, is the appeal to different emphases within Christian theology and different strands of biblical discussion. On the

31. Ajith Fernando, *Sharing the Truth in Love: How to Relate to People of Other Faiths* (Grand Rapids: Discovery House, 2001); Harold Netland, *Encountering Religious Pluralism: The Challenge to Christian Faith and Mission* (Downers Grove, IL: InterVarsity, 2001); Karl Rahner, "Anonymous Christians," *Theological Investigations*, vol. 6 (London: Darton, Longmann & Todd, 1966), and "Anonymous and Explicit Faith," *Theological Investigations*, vol. 16 (London: Darton, Longmann & Todd, 1979); Clark H. Pinnock, *A Wideness in God's Mercy: The Finality of Jesus Christ in a World of Religions* (Grand Rapids: Eerdmans, 1992); Paul Knitter and John Hick, *The Myth of Christian Uniqueness—Toward a Pluralistic Theology of Religions* (Maryknoll, NY: Orbis, 1987). See also the excellent compilation of essays, chiefly from an inclusivist position, in Gavin D'Costa, ed., *Christian Uniqueness Reconsidered: The Myth of a Pluralistic Theology of Religions* (Maryknoll, NY: Orbis, 1990), with chapters by Rowan Williams, Christoph Schwöbel, Francis Clooney, Wolfhart Pannenberg, John Cobb, Lesslie Newbigin, Jürgen Moltmann, and John Milbank, among others.

one hand, Scripture speaks of God's light as enlightening everyone (John 1:9), his love extending across the whole world (John 3:16–17), and his desire being for "everyone to be saved and to come to the knowledge of truth" (1 Tim. 2:4). This has indeed taken place, for Jesus Christ "is the Savior of all people, especially of those who believe" (1 Tim. 4:10). On the other hand, Peter is recorded in Acts as proclaiming, "There is salvation in no one else, for there is no other name under heaven given among mortals by which we must be saved" (Acts 4:12). Perhaps behind Peter's assertion are texts like Isaiah 45:22: "Turn to me and be saved, all the ends of the earth! For I am God, and there is no other." Jesus himself said, "I am the way, and the truth, and the life. No one comes to the Father except through me" (John 14:6). And he commissioned his disciples as he left them, saying, "Go therefore and make disciples of all nations" (Matt. 28:19). While each of the three positions makes sense out of some of these texts, other texts are unfortunately too often ignored or given unlikely interpretations. Discussion, it seems, has, in the words of Amos Yong, largely come to an impasse. The dialogue has grown stale.

Amos Yong

In his book *Beyond the Impasse: Toward a Pneumatological Theology of Religions*,[32] Yong therefore proposes a new direction for a constructive theology of religions. Here is where a second generation of theologians of religions needs to concentrate. It consists of two parts, both of which have strong resonances with our discussion of God's wider revelation in this book. First, recognizing that most exclusivist and inclusivist theologies of religions have too rarely consulted the religions themselves, not venturing beyond data garnered from Christian theology, Yong proposes that a theology of religions be rooted in the particular experiences of each religious tradition. Finding the model of Pentecost to be suggestive, where Christians encountered a diversity of language and culture (of which religion is an integral part) that God had embraced, Yong develops an inductive paradigm rooted in the religions themselves.

And second, in contradistinction to the pluralists, who discard the normativity of the Christian tradition as they reach out to the diversity of religious expression beyond them, Yong, like John Paul II, grounded his theology in pneumatology, in a Christian understanding of the Spirit. Rather than risk being unduly optimistic by focusing on the first article of the creed with its emphasis on the Creator's common grace, and rather than risk being unduly

---

32. Amos Yong, *Beyond the Impasse: Toward a Pneumatological Theology of Religions* (Grand Rapids: Baker Academic, 2003).

pessimistic by focusing on the second article of the creed with its emphasis on Christ the Redeemer, Yong argued that he had chosen to ground his theology of religions in the third article of the creed, where the Spirit is at work. In order for this locus to prove productive, however, Yong believed that the church in the West must reject the *filioque* clause (that the Spirit is from the Father *and the Son*). We have already encountered this same conclusion in our discussion of Moltmann in chapter 7, and it seems a necessary one. This clause, Yong believes, is "an intrusion into the creed outside the recognized conciliar process." If the clause is removed, thinks Yong, a pneumatological approach to the theology of religions would be possible, one that would "allow for more neutral categories to emerge when attempting to discern the presence and activity of the Spirit in other traditions."[33]

No longer portraying the Spirit as simply subordinate to the Son, Yong instead makes use of the helpful patristic metaphor of Logos (Word) and Pneuma (Spirit) as the two hands of the Father, an image first offered by Irenaeus in the second century. To be thoroughly trinitarian, he argues, we must recognize Word and Spirit as coequal. In this way, any contradiction between particularity (of the Son) and universality (of the Spirit) is taken up and transcended in the life of the Trinity itself. Rather than connecting the Spirit first of all to Christology, Yong suggests that "God's Spirit is the life-breath of the *imago Dei* in every human being and the presupposition of all human relationships and communities."[34] It is by the Spirit that people receive understanding (wisdom) about life in all its dimensions—rational, volitional, moral, interpersonal, and relational. Seen in this light, the religions of the world, like all else, are rooted in general revelation, though Yong does not use the term in this way. Rather he speaks of non-Christian religions as providentially upheld by the Spirit of God for divine purposes. Quoting Clark Pinnock, Yong reasons, "It would seem strange if the Spirit excused himself from the very arena of culture where people search for meaning."[35]

For Yong, then, a theology of religions must (1) be rooted in the religious experiences and understanding people have, and (2) be grounded in a Christian understanding of the Holy Spirit. As Yong understands, a theology of religions "needs to navigate between the Scylla of a monologistic . . . imperialistic . . . defining of religious others . . . and the Charybdis of a syncretistic, (simply) empiricistic, and relativistic attitude toward the other."[36] The result of such open yet committed relationships with other faiths, Yong believes, will be an

33. Ibid., 186.
34. Ibid., 45.
35. Ibid., 131.
36. Ibid., 20.

opportunity for both mutual engagement and mutual transformation: "If all truth is God's truth," he argues, "we can be open to learning from and being transformed by others even while being committed to the God of Jesus Christ to transform others in our interactions with them by the power of the Holy Spirit."[37] Rooting religion in the revelatory Presence of the Spirit that produces wisdom about life, Yong can then move on to recognize the importance of also addressing the soteriological question, understanding full well that a trinitarian theology must deal with the interrelatedness of pneumatology and Christology. But each also must have its own integrity.

Clark Pinnock

A second theologian of religions that can prove helpful to us as we seek to understand God's wider revelatory Presence is Clark Pinnock. In his books *A Wideness in God's Mercy* and *Flame of Love: A Theology of the Holy Spirit*, Pinnock sets forth an inclusivist position with regard to a theology of religions, stressing both "the finality of Jesus Christ in a world of religions" (the subtitle of his book on God's mercy) and "genuine openness to the truth and the goodness found in other religions."[38] In arguing his case, Pinnock, as we have done in this book, considers a wide range of relevant data, but particularly scriptural and phenomenal sources. "Both Scripture and experience tell us there are pagan saints outside the church due to the work of the triune God in the world," writes Pinnock. "God's being revealed definitively in Jesus Christ does not imply that he is not working in the wider world. His working in the wider world is rooted in a covenant with the race through Noah. All nations are blessed with revelation. God's grace is given in every context."[39]

Pinnock believes such a claim has been largely undisputed in Christian theology, until, that is, it is applied to the religious life of non-Christians. But Pinnock is convinced that "world religions [also] reflect to some degree general revelation and prevenient grace. Just as God himself is present in the world," writes Pinnock, "so too is God's reality and revelation. Since God never leaves himself without witness (Acts 14:16–17), people always have divine light to respond to."[40] Though some critics will say as we have seen that such general, or cosmic, revelation functions only negatively to reveal human culpability,

37. Amos Yong, "Significant Turns in Contemporary Theology of Religions," *Theology News & Notes* 52, no. 1 (Winter 2005): 22.

38. Pinnock, *Wideness in God's Mercy* and *Flame of Love: A Theology of the Holy Spirit* (Downers Grove, IL: InterVarsity, 1996), 83.

39. Pinnock, *Wideness in God's Mercy*, 93.

40. Ibid., 104.

with no one able, or at least willing, to respond favorably to the revelation that is offered, Pinnock rejects such reasoning, turning to Paul's statements in Romans 2 that speak of the possibility of some being "excused" on the day of judgment for the actions they have done.

The building blocks of Pinnock's argument should be familiar by this time to readers of this book. They include not only the finality of Jesus Christ but also the positive value of what he labels "general revelation" through the Spirit's work in the wider world. Writes Pinnock,

> Spirit is present in the farthest reaches of this wonderful, ambiguous world . . . present everywhere, both transcending and enfolding all that is, present and at work in the vast range of happenings in the universe. . . . No nook or cranny is untouched by the finger of God. His warm breath streams toward humanity with energy and life. . . . If history is thought of as a stage play, Spirit is its director, touching the world and directing the economy of salvation by subtle influences.[41]

Building as well upon the Bible's holy pagan tradition of those like Abimelech and Cornelius, Pinnock provides biblical example after biblical example to suggest that God's revealing Presence extends beyond the walls of the church. Rather than see Melchizedek or Jethro—both pagan priests outside the covenant community, but also God-fearers—as the rare exception, Pinnock sees them as signs of hope within the context of a larger hermeneutic of hopefulness.

Neither Karl Barth's insistence that all religions are unbelief nor Karl Rahner's claim that non-Christian religions are vehicles of salvation are adequate theological conclusions, reasons Pinnock. The nations' religions neither must be unbelief nor must they be valid. There are degrees of truth and falsehood in every religion. A middle way is called for, one that "allows us to be positive as well as discerning." Concludes Pinnock, "On the one hand, it is possible to appreciate positive elements in other faiths, recognizing that God has been at work among them. On the other hand, it is not necessary to be blind to oppression and bondage in religion, Christ being our norm and criterion for measuring."[42] Though religions can be life-sustaining and spiritually enriching, they can also be delusory and destructive. For Pinnock, it remains true that God's revelatory Presence, his light, shines everywhere in the darkness, and his grace precedes people everywhere (John 1:5). How then can we know "false" religion from "true"? Pinnock lets the experience of Scripture's holy pagans suggest criteria for discernment: "Does the person fear God?" "Do people pursue righteousness in their behavior?" Here are criteria that allow

41. Pinnock, *Flame of Love*, 187–94.
42. Pinnock, *Wideness in God's Mercy*, 109.

us to test the spirits, particularly in community, to see if they are indeed the Holy Spirit at work (1 John 4:1). Here are criteria that point to those people who worship rightly.

Theological Reflections

Certainly, such a cursory overview of a burgeoning field does not do it justice, but that is not my real intention here. Rather, my intention is simply to suggest that as a theology of religions enters into its second stage of development and reflection, a recognition of God's wider revelatory Presence, rooted in the Spirit in and through creation, needs to become increasingly central. Here the work of Yong and Pinnock might provide a starting point. Our discussion also has suggested several preliminary conclusions as to what a theology of religions might include.

First, such a revelatory perspective will need to root itself in God's Spirit, not merely in creation's "footprint." Such traces, or echoes, of God's past revelation minus the Spirit's energizing and illumining power will prove stillborn. It is not just our common grounding in the *imago Dei* (whether understood as our capacity for relationship, for reason, for morality, or for spirituality) that provides theological guidance and understanding for non-Christian religions; in fact, it is just the opposite. It is not "religion as human possibility" that will provide the context for dialogue. Instead, an adequate context for Christian learning, critique, and witness with regard to the religions can only be the recognition that God's Spirit is at work throughout humankind revealing the grace of God and his desire for his creation also in and through the religions. Here is one concrete locus of God's wider revelatory Presence.

Second, a recognition of God's wider revelatory Presence will challenge those theologians of religions who, based on other theological a prioris, have adopted a cautious and predominantly negative assessment of God's activity outside the walls of the church. It will not be enough to say that the evidence of general revelation in non-Christian religions is only enough to convict adherents of their sin; the Spirit's revelatory Presence will also need to be seen as convincing religious followers both to will and to do God's good pleasure. It is not enough to say that general revelation helps preserve the world from destruction; the Spirit's revelatory Presence must also be seen as providing humankind, including adherents of other faiths, all that is good. Christians will need to act on the belief that all truth, goodness, beauty, and holiness in human culture (including in religion) comes from the free grace of God through the Spirit. It was John Wesley who spoke of the Spirit's "preventing grace" (prevenient grace) as "all that 'light' wherewith the Son of God 'enlighteneth everyone that cometh into the world,' showing every man 'to do justly, to love mercy, and to walk humbly with his God'; all the convictions which his Spirit from time to time works in every child of man."[43] For Wesley, to separate anything from God was a form of "practical atheism." Instead, we must affirm God's universal, life-giving Presence also in the religions. (Again, because misunderstanding is so easy, I must reiterate that I am not speaking here of salvation, though since the Spirit is one, that is the Spirit's ultimate trajectory. But as the Spirit of Life, such Presence can still open us out into real expressions of faith.)

Third, a recognition of God's wider revelatory Presence will help us recover a more holistic understanding of the Spirit of God, not just as the Spirit of Christ but also as the Spirit in and through creation. This will lead us to a reconsideration of the *filioque* clause, as we have seen. But it will also benefit from, and feed into, a more robust trinitarian theology. We are still in our infancy in exploring the full ramifications of the Spirit as concurrently person and power. Those such as Jürgen Moltmann, Elizabeth Johnson, Amos Yong, and Clark Pinnock are providing helpful perspective. We can also benefit from those like Nils Bohr, whose reflection on how best to describe creation can provide us helpful analogies. With the first two millennia of the church's life given over to better understanding the Father and Son, it has only been in the last one hundred years that the church has focused its energy toward understanding the role of the Spirit, the third person of the Trinity. Certainly, a consideration of the Spirit's wider revelatory Presence outside the walls of the church, including within the religious traditions of those who are not Christians, will play an important role in our ongoing reassessment of the Spirit.

Finally, the common and biblically based realization that there are divine, human, and demonic spirits calls for concerted work in the area of discernment if God's wider revelatory Presence is to fulfill its role in a Christian theology of religions. There are, as in the practice of theology more generally, a variety of suggestions as to what this will mean. Certainly John V. Taylor is correct, as we have observed, in calling for increased "attention" to life itself. Pinnock finds a complementary, overarching criterion for judging the presence of God's revelation in the Great Commandment—love of God and neighbor (Matt. 22:35–40; Mark 12:28–34; and Luke 10:25–28). Moltmann's overarching criterion is also compatible: all that affirms Life. Yong writes more operationally of the theologian's need methodologically to listen carefully to the religious experiences of others, to use reason, to do careful exegesis

---

43. John Wesley, "The Scripture Way of Salvation," Sermon 43, 1.2, in *The Works of John Wesley*, vol. 2, *Sermons II, 34–70*, ed. Albert Outler (Nashville: Abingdon, 1985), 2:157.

of the biblical texts, and to learn from the community/tradition, recognizing that such discernment must ultimately await the eschaton. My suggestion in the introductory chapter was that discerning the validity of others' religious experiences is simply a particular example of the ongoing theological dialogue that Christians are called to entertain—one in which Scripture, the theology of the church past and present, the insights of our culture(s), and our own experiences are interlaced in an ongoing conversation as we open ourselves to the Spirit's guidance as we together seek truth, beauty, and goodness.

One need not choose between these various suggestions as how best to exercise discernment. Love of God and neighbor, as well as the Spirit as Life-giver, are crucial themes around which to orient one's discernment process. So too the need to "attend" carefully, listening for the Spirit speaking in and through the religious experiences of others. And Yong is certainly correct as to the importance of Scripture as our norm, as well as the need for insight from the Christian community, past and present, for openness to the experiential witness of others, understood contextually, as well as for a humble spirit rooted in prayer. In short, discernment of God's wider revelatory Presence is a theological process making use of the same resources and perspectives that constructive Christian theology more generally uses. Again, this monograph is not the place for an exhaustive exploration of a hermeneutic of religions. That is for another day. But it is only to say that such a challenge is an important and necessary task as the theological discussion moves forward. And an understanding of God's wider revelatory Presence will prove crucial for this endeavor.

Gavin D'Costa, a Roman Catholic born of Indian parents, raised in Kenya, and educated in England, helpfully points out that the process of discernment among the world's religions will always carry with it a "no" as well as a "yes." Here perhaps is a note on which to end our deliberation. This "no" with regard to the world's religions is not a negative judgment on non-Christian religions per se, but rather a recognition of the once-and-for-all nature of God's revelation in Jesus Christ. "I am the way, and the truth, and the life" (John 14:6), spoke Jesus. That is, though a Christian theology of religions need not (and should not) begin christologically but should first perfect the art of listening, of "attending," it must surely find its ultimate center there. Though, as we have argued, one can move in their trinitarian theology from Spirit to Word and not just from Word to Spirit, the move to Word, a move from universality to particularity, necessarily means a sorting process in which not all will be included. In light of God's self-revelation as the Triune God, though Christian judgments are certainly fallible and ultimately must await the eschaton, any claim by another religion that contradicts God's Triune self-revelation will

need correction, contextualization, and/or questioning. As the father says in
Life of Pi, "Believing in everything equals nothing."

There is, for D'Costa, however, also a "yes" that must be spoken. Such a "yes"
derives not primarily from that human (not only Christian) magnanimity that
Christians are called to display toward others—hospitality is the only context
in which meaningful dialogue can take place—but chiefly from the realization
of the scope of God's own self-revelation. For God's wider revelatory Presence
is also present in the religions. We address those of other religions as corecipi-
ents of God's gracious Presence throughout the world. Christians are called to
witness to the fact that God has been and continues to be active throughout
creation and history, active apart from Jesus Christ through the Spirit who
remains also the Spirit of Christ. In this, D'Costa writes, "Christians should
surely rejoice."[44] Thus, when aspects of God's revelation are disclosed to or
lived out in other religions (e.g., God's transcendence in Islam or the theistic
Isvara of Sankara's Advaita Hinduism), we should be willing as Christians to
acknowledge the reality of God's self-revealing Presence within that tradition.
When those of other faith traditions live out "Gospel values," thinks D'Costa,
the Spirit may be at work in and through them, as John Paul II recognized.
Rather than prejudge such thought and action as godless, it is better to have
a hermeneutic of open generosity and possibility. As D'Costa rightly argues,
"It is only *a posteriori* that any specific judgments can be made."[45] A theology
of religions, as with all reflection on God's wider revelatory Presence, must
flow out of our actual experiences. God's self-revelation is its own defense.

---

44. Gavin D'Costa, "Revelation and Revelations: Discerning God in Other Religions. Beyond
a Static Valuation," *Modern Theology* 10, no. 2 (April 1994): 170.
   45. Ibid., 175.

Selected Bibliography

Anderson, Ray. "Barth and a New Direction in Natural Theology." In *Theology Beyond Christendom: Essays on the Centenary of the Birth of Karl Barth, May 10, 1986*, edited by John Thompson, 241–66. Pittsburgh: Pickwick, 1986.

———. *On Being Human*. Grand Rapids: Eerdmans, 1982.

Anker, Roy. *Catching Light: Looking for God in the Movies*. Grand Rapids: Eerdmans, 2004.

———. *Of Pilgrims and Fire: When God Shows Up at the Movies*. Grand Rapids: Eerdmans, 2010.

Avis, Paul. "Does Natural Theology Exist?" *Theology* 87 (November 1984): 431–37.

Barna, George. *Revolution*. Wheaton, IL: Tyndale, 2005.

Barth, Karl. *Church Dogmatics*. Vols. II/2, IV/1, IV/2, IV/3, IV/4. Peabody: Hendrickson, 2010.

———. "Concluding Unscientific Postscript on Schleiermacher." *Studies in Religion/Sciences Religieuse* 7, no. 2 (Spring 1978): 117–36.

———. *Wolfgang Amadeus Mozart*. Grand Rapids: Eerdmans, 1986.

Berger, Peter. *A Rumor of Angels*. Garden City, NY: Doubleday / Anchor Books, 1970.

Berkouwer, G. C. *General Revelation*. Studies in Dogmatics. Grand Rapids: Eerdmans, 1955.

Blake, Richard. "From Peepshow to Prayer: Toward a Spirituality of the Movies." *Journal of Religion and Film* 6, no. 2 (October 2002): n.p. www.unomaha.edu/jrf/peepshow.htm.

Brant, Jonathan. *Paul Tillich and the Possibility of Revelation through Film*. New York: Oxford University Press, 2012.

Brazier, P. H. "C. S. Lewis: A Doctrine of Transposition." *The Heythrop Journal* 50 (2009): 669–88.

Brown, Robert McAfee. "Assyrians in Modern Dress." In *The Pseudonyms of God*, 96–103. Philadelphia: Westminster, 1972.

Brown, William P. *The Seven Pillars of Creation: The Bible, Science, and the Ecology of Wonder*. New York: Oxford University Press, 2010.

Brueggemann, Walter. *Cadences of Home: Preaching among Exiles*. Louisville: Westminster John Knox, 1997.

Brunner, Emil, and Karl Barth. *Natural Theology: Comprising "Nature and Grace" by Dr. Emil Brunner and the Reply "No!" by Dr. Karl Barth*. Translated by Peter Fraenkel. Eugene, OR: Wipf & Stock, 2002.

Calvin, John. *Institutes of the Christian Religion*. 2 vols. Translated by F. L. Battles. Edited by J. T. McNeill. Philadelphia: Westminster, 1960.

Castro, Emilio. "Mission in a Pluralistic Age." *International Review of Mission* 75 (1986): 198–210.

Come, Arnold. *Human Spirit and Holy Spirit*. Philadelphia: Westminster, 1959.

Conniry, Charles J., Jr. *Soaring in the Spirit*. Colorado Springs: Paternoster, 2007.

Crouch, Andy. *Culture Making*. Downers Grove, IL: InterVarsity, 2008.

Crouter, Richard. Introduction to *On Religion*, by Friedrich Schleiermacher. Edited and translated by Richard Crouter. Cambridge: Cambridge University Press, 1996.

Dark, David. *Everyday Apocalypse: The Sacred Revealed in Radiohead, The Simpsons, and Other Pop Culture Icons*. Grand Rapids: Brazos, 2002.

D'Costa, Gavin. "Revelation and Revelations: Discerning God in Other Religions: Beyond a Static Valuation." *Modern Theology* 10, no. 2 (April 1994): 165–83.

Deacy, Christopher, and Gaye Williams Ortiz. *Theology and Film: Challenging the Sacred/Secular Divide*. Oxford: Blackwell, 2008.

DeCou, Jessica. *Playful, Glad, and Free: Karl Barth and a Theology of Popular Culture*. Minneapolis: Fortress, 2013.

Demarest, Bruce. *General Revelation*. Grand Rapids: Zondervan, 1982.

Detweiler, Craig. *Into the Dark: Seeing the Sacred in the Top Films of the 21st Century*. Grand Rapids: Baker Academic, 2008.

———. "*The Tree of Life*: Cinema in Conversation." http://www.patheos.com/blogs/dochollywood/2014/02/tree-of-life-from-genesis-to-revelation.

Detweiler, Craig, and Barry Taylor. *A Matrix of Meanings: Finding God in Popular Culture*. Grand Rapids: Baker Academic, 2003.

Dulles, Avery. *Models of Revelation*. Maryknoll, NY: Orbis, 1994.

———. *Revelational Theology*. New York: Herder & Herder, 1969.

———. *A Testimonial to Grace: And Reflections on a Theological Journey*. Kansas City: Sheed & Ward, 1996.

Dyrness, William. "How Does the Bible Function in the Christian Life?" In *The Use of the Bible in Theology: Evangelical Options*, edited by Robert K. Johnston, 159–74. Atlanta: John Knox, 1985.

Ebert, Roger. Preface to *God in the Movies*, by Albert J. Bergesen and Andrew M. Greeley. New Brunswick, NJ. Transaction, 2000.

Edwards, Jonathan. "Sermon on Psalm 48:10." In *The Works of Jonathan Edwards.* Vol. 2. Edited by Edward Hickman. Edinburgh: Banner of Truth, 1974.

Eliot, T. S. "Burnt Norton." *Four Quartets.* In T. S. Eliot, *The Complete Poems and Plays, 1909–1950,* 117–22. New York: Harcourt, Brace & World, 1971.

Erickson, Millard. *Christian Theology.* Grand Rapids: Baker, 1986.

"Evangelical Perspectives from Canberra." In *Signs of the Spirit,* edited by Michael Kinnamon, 282–86. Geneva: WCC, 1991.

Fernando, Ajith. *Sharing the Truth in Love: How to Relate to People of Other Faiths.* Grand Rapids: Discovery House, 2001.

Forte, Bruno. *The Portal of Beauty: Towards a Theology of Aesthetics.* Translated by David Glenday and Paul McPartlan. Grand Rapids: Eerdmans, 2008.

Fretheim, Terence E. "Conversation or Conversion? Hearing God from the Other." *Word & World* 22, no. 3 (Summer 2002): 304–6.

Fuller, Robert C. *Spiritual, but Not Religious: Understanding Unchurched America.* New York: Oxford University Press, 2001.

Garrett, Greg. *The Gospel according to Hollywood.* Louisville: Westminster John Knox, 2007.

Geertz, Clifford. "Thick Description: Toward an Interpretive Theory of Culture." In Clifford Geertz, *The Interpretations of Cultures.* London: Fontana, 1993.

Gill, Theodore A. "Barth and Mozart." *Theology Today* 43, no. 3 (October 1986): 403–11.

Gire, Ken. *Reflections on the Movies: Hearing God in the Unlikeliest of Places.* Colorado Springs: Cook Communications Ministries, 2000.

Gonzalez-Andrieu, Cecilia. *Bridge to Wonder: Art as a Gospel of Beauty.* Waco: Baylor University Press, 2012.

Gorringe, T. J. *Discerning Spirit: A Theology of Revelation.* Philadelphia: Trinity Press International, 1990.

Greeley, Andrew. *The Catholic Imagination.* Berkeley: University of California Press, 2000.

———. *God in Popular Culture.* Chicago: Thomas More, 1988.

Green, Michael. *Evangelism in the Early Church.* Rev. ed. Grand Rapids: Eerdmans, 2003.

Gunton, Colin. *A Brief Theology of Revelation.* Edinburgh: T&T Clark, 1995.

———. "Mozart the Theologian." *Theology* 94 (1991): 346–49.

Hamilton, Kenneth. *The System and the Gospel.* New York: Macmillan, 1963.

Hardy, Alister. *The Spiritual Nature of Man: A Study of Contemporary Religious Experience.* Oxford: Clarendon, 1979.

Hay, David. *Something There: The Biology of the Human Spirit.* Philadelphia: Templeton Foundation Press, 2006.

Hay, David, and Kate Hunt. "Is Britain's Soul Waking Up?" *The Tablet,* June 24, 2000, 846.

———. "Understanding the Spirituality of People Who Don't Go to Church." Research Report. Centre for the Study of Human Relations, University of Nottingham. August 2000. www.facingthechallenge.org/nottingham.php.

Heschel, Abraham Joshua. *God in Search of Man: A Philosophy of Judaism*. New York: Farrar, Straus & Giroux, 1955.

Higgins, Gareth. *How Movies Helped Save My Soul: Finding Spiritual Fingerprints in Culturally Significant Films*. Lake Mary, FL: Relevant Books, 2003.

Hildebrandt, Wilf. *An Old Testament Theology of the Spirit of God*. Peabody, MA: Hendrickson, 1995.

Hodge, Charles. *Systematic Theology*. Vol. 2. Grand Rapids: Eerdmans, 1940.

Hoffmeier, James K. "'The Heavens Declare the Glory of God': The Limits of General Revelation." *Trinity Journal* 21, no. 1 (Spring 2000): 17–24.

Horne, Brian. "Art: A Trinitarian Imperative?" In *Trinitarian Theology Today*, edited by Christoph Schwöbel, 87–91. Edinburgh: T&T Clark, 1995.

Hyun-Kyung, Chung. "Come Holy Spirit—Renew the Whole Creation." In *Signs of the Spirit*, edited by Michael Kinnamon, 231–38. Geneva: WCC, 1991.

Jenson, Robert W. *Systematic Theology*. Vol. 1, *The Triune God*. New York: Oxford University Press, 1997.

———. *Systematic Theology*. Vol. 2, *The Works of God*. New York: Oxford University Press, 1999.

Johnson, Elizabeth A. "Pneumatology Revisited: Creator Spirit in Ecological Theology." Presidential Address, American Theological Society. Princeton, NJ, April 13, 2007.

———. *Quest for the Living God: Mapping Frontiers in the Theology of God*. New York: Continuum, 2007.

———. *She Who Is: The Mystery of God in Feminist Theological Discourse*. New York: Crossroad / Herder & Herder, 1992.

———. *Women, Earth, and Creator Spirit*. Mahwah, NJ: Paulist Press, 1993.

Johnston, Robert K. *The Christian at Play*. Grand Rapids: Eerdmans, 1983.

———. "Image and Content: The Tension in C. S. Lewis' Chronicles of Narnia." *Journal of the Evangelical Theological Society* 20, no. 3 (September 1977): 253–64.

———. *Reel Spirituality: Theology and Film in Dialogue*. 2nd ed. Grand Rapids: Baker Academic, 2006.

Kärkkäinen, Veli-Matti. "Theologies of Religions." *Evangelical Interfaith Dialogue* 1, no. 2 (Spring 2010): 3–7.

Klitsner, Judy. *Subversive Sequels in the Bible*. Jerusalem: Maggid Books, 2011.

Knitter, Paul, and John Hick. *The Myth of Christian Uniqueness—Toward a Pluralistic Theology of Religions*. Maryknoll, NY: Orbis, 1987.

Lambert, Yves. "A Turning Point in Religious Evolution in Europe." *Journal of Contemporary Religion* 19, no. 1 (2004): 29–45.

Lamott, Anne. *All New People*. Washington, DC: Counterpoint, 1989.

Lewis, C. S. *The Abolition of Man*. New York: Macmillan, 1947.

———. *An Experiment in Criticism*. Cambridge: Cambridge University Press, 1961.

———. *God in the Dock: Essays on Theology and Ethics*. Edited by Walter Hooper. Grand Rapids: Eerdmans, 1970.

———. *Mere Christianity*. New York: Macmillan, 1960.

———. "On Stories." In *Essays Presented to Charles Williams*, edited by C. S. Lewis, 90–115. Grand Rapids: Eerdmans, 1966.

———. *The Silver Chair*. New York: Macmillan / Collier Books, 1953.

———. *Surprised by Joy*. New York: Harcourt, Brace & World / Harvest Books, 1955.

———. *Transposition and other Addresses*. London: Geoffrey Bles, 1949.

———. *The Voyage of the "Dawn Treader."* New York: Macmillan / Collier Books, 1952.

———. *The Weight of Glory and Other Addresses*. Grand Rapids: Eerdmans, 1949.

Lindsay, Vachel. *The Art of the Moving Picture*. 1915. Reprint, New York: Modern Library, 2000.

Maddox, Randy L. "Wesley and the Question of Truth or Salvation through Other Religions." *Wesleyan Theological Journal* 27, nos. 1–2 (Spring–Fall 1992): 7–29.

Marsh, Clive. "On Dealing with What Films Actually Do to People: The Practice and Theory of Film Watching in Theology/Religion and Film Discussion." In *Reframing Theology and Film: New Focus for an Emerging Discipline*, edited by Robert K. Johnston, 145–61. Grand Rapids: Baker Academic, 2007.

McDonald, H. D. *Theories of Revelation: An Historical Study, 1700–1960*. Grand Rapids: Baker, 1979.

McGrath, Alister. *Christian Theology: An Introduction*. 5th ed. Oxford: Wiley-Blackwell, 2011.

———. *A Scientific Theology*. Vol. 1, *Nature*. Grand Rapids: Eerdmans, 2001.

McNulty, Edward N. *Praying the Movies II: More Daily Meditations from Classical Films*. Louisville: Westminster John Knox, 2003.

Moltmann, Jürgen. *God in Creation: A New Theology of Creation and the Spirit of God*. New York: Harper & Row, 1985.

———. *The Source of Life: The Holy Spirit and the Theology of Life*. Minneapolis: Fortress, 1997.

———. *The Spirit of Life: A Universal Affirmation*. Philadelphia: Fortress, 1992.

———. *Theology of Hope: On the Ground and the Implications of a Christian Eschatology*. New York: Harper & Row, 1967.

———. "Theology of Mystical Experience." *Scottish Journal of Theology* 32, no. 6 (1979): 501–20.

———. *Theology of Play*. New York: Harper & Row, 1971.

———. *The Trinity and the Kingdom of God*. London: SCM, 1981.

Moore, T. M. *Consider the Lilies: A Plea for Creational Theology*. Phillipsburg, NJ: P&R, 2005.

Neve, Lloyd. *The Spirit of God in the Old Testament*. Tokyo: Seibunsha, 1972.

Niebuhr, H. Richard. *The Meaning of Revelation*. New York: Macmillan, 1941.

Norris, Kathleen. *Acedia and Me: A Marriage, Monks, and a Writer's Life*. New York: Riverhead, 2008.

———. *Quotidian Mysteries: Laundry, Liturgy, and "Women's Work."* Mahwah, NJ: Paulist Press, 1998.

Oden, Thomas C. "Without Excuse: Classic Christian Exegesis of General Revelation." *Journal of the Evangelical Theological Society* 41, no. 1 (March 1998): 55–68.

Otto, Rudolf. *The Idea of the Holy*. New York: Oxford University Press, 1971.

Overstreet, Jeffrey. *Through a Screen Darkly*. Ventura, CA: Regal, 2007.

Pinnock, Clark H. *Flame of Love: A Theology of the Holy Spirit*. Downers Grove, IL: InterVarsity, 1996.

———. "Religious Pluralism: A Turn to the Holy Spirit." *McMaster Journal of Theology and Ministry* 5 (2002). www.mcmaster.ca/mjtm/5-4.htm.

———. *A Wideness in God's Mercy: The Finality of Jesus Christ in a World of Religions*. Grand Rapids: Eerdmans, 1992.

Rahner, Karl. "Anonymous and Explicit Faith." *Theological Investigations*. Vol. 16, 52–59. London: Darton, Longmann & Todd, 1979.

———. "Anonymous Christians." In *Theological Investigations*. Vol. 6, 390–98. London: Darton, Longmann & Todd, 1966.

Ramm, Bernard. *Special Revelation and the Word of God*. Grand Rapids: Eerdmans, 1961.

Reeves, James, ed. *Selected Poems of Gerard Manley Hopkins*. London: Heinemann, 1953.

Rollins, Peter. *The Fidelity of Betrayal: Towards a Church beyond Belief*. Brewster, MA: Paraclete, 2008.

———. *How (Not) to Speak of God*. Brewster, MA: Paraclete, 2006.

Roszak, Theodore. *Where the Wasteland Ends: Politics and Transcendence in Postindustrial Society*. Garden City, NY: Doubleday, 1972.

Ryrie, Charles. *Basic Theology*. Chicago: Moody, 1986.

Schleiermacher, Friedrich. *On Religion: Speeches to Its Cultured Despisers*. Introduction by Rudolf Otto. Translated by John Oman. New York: Harper & Row / Harper Torchbooks, 1958.

Schrader, Paul. *Transcendental Style in Film: Ozu, Bresson, Dreyer*. New York: De Capo Press, 1988. A reprint of the University of California Press edition, 1972.

Schweizer, Eduard. *The Holy Spirit*. Philadelphia: Fortress, 1980.

Solzhenitsyn, Aleksandr I. *East and West*. New York: Harper & Row / Perennial Library, 1972.

Steiner, George. *Real Presences*. Chicago: University of Chicago Press, 1989.

Taylor, John V. *The Go-Between God: The Holy Spirit and the Christian Mission*. Philadelphia: Fortress, 1972.

————. *The Primal Vision: Christian Presence amid African Religion*. Philadelphia: Fortress, 1963.

Thomas, Robert L. "General Revelation and Biblical Hermeneutics." *The Masters Seminary Journal* 9, no. 1 (Spring 1998): 5–23.

Tillich, Paul. *On Art and Architecture*. Edited by John Dillenberger and Jane Dillenberger. New York: Crossroad, 1989.

————. *On the Boundary: An Autobiographical Sketch*. New York: Charles Scribner's Sons, 1966.

Updike, John. Foreword to *Wolfgang Amadeus Mozart*, by Karl Barth. Grand Rapids: Eerdmans, 1986.

————. *Marry Me, Marry Me*. New York: Knopf, 1976.

————. *Of the Farm*. New York: Knopf, 1965.

————. "Packed Dirt, Churchgoing, A Dying Cat, A Traded Car." In *Pigeon Feathers and Other Stories*, 168–88. New York: Random House / Fawcett Books, 1963.

————. *Rabbit, Run*. New York: Knopf, 1960.

————. *Roger's Version*. New York: Knopf, 1986.

Vanhoozer, Kevin J., Charles A. Anderson, and Michael J. Sleasman, eds. *Everyday Theology: How to Read Cultural Texts and Interpret Trends*. Grand Rapids: Baker Academic, 2007.

Viladesau, Richard. *Theological Aesthetics*. New York: Oxford University Press, 1999.

Walsh, John. *Are You Talking to Me? A Life Through the Movies*. London: HarperCollins, 2003.

Wesley, John. "The Scripture Way of Salvation." Sermon 43, 1.2. In *The Works of John Wesley*. Vol. 2, *Sermons II, 34–70*, edited by Albert Outler, 150–60. Nashville: Abingdon, 1985.

Wright, N. T. *Simply Christian: Why Christianity Makes Sense*. San Francisco: HarperSanFrancisco, 2006.

Wuthnow, Robert. *All in Sync: How Music and Art Are Revitalizing American Religion*. Berkeley: University of California Press, 2003.

Yong, Amos. *Beyond the Impasse: Toward a Pneumatological Theology of Religions*. Grand Rapids: Baker Academic, 2003.

————. "Significant Turns in Contemporary Theology of Religions." *Theology News & Notes* 52, no. 1 (Winter 2005): 22.

Index